D0571587

About the Author

FRANK STAGG is James Buchanan Harrison Professor of New Testament Interpretation at Southern Baptist Theological Seminary in Louisville, Kentucky. Former professor of New Testament and Greek at New Orleans Baptist Theological Seminary, he has been teaching the book of Acts to young preachers and other Christian workers since 1945.

Born near Eunice, Louisiana, Dr. Stagg attended grade and high school there. He received his A.B. degree from Louisiana College in Pineville, and his Th.M. and Ph.D. from Southern Seminary.

Author of *New Testament Theology,* Dr. Stagg is a member of the Society of Biblical Literature and Exegesis. He has also been a member of the Southern Baptist Commission on the American Baptist Theological Seminary.

He is married and has three children.

THE BOOK OF ACTS

THE BOOK OF
Acts

The Early Struggle for an Unhindered Gospel

FRANK STAGG

New Testament Interpretation
Southern
Baptist Theological Seminary

BROADMAN PRESS
Nashville, Tennessee

COPYRIGHT, 1955 • BROADMAN PRESS

Nashville, Tennessee

Eighth printing

ISBN: 0-8054-1311-1

4213-11

Printed in the United States of America

2.5AL7113

TO EVELYN
TED, BOBBY, and GINGER

Preface

THE FARMER does not try to cultivate the whole countryside; he marks off definite limits within which to work. So the writer, even in a commentary, must recognize definite limits within which his work is to be done. This book is concerned primarily with Luke's major purpose and the major message of Acts. Of necessity, and to avoid detraction from this major message, many important matters will be left to other works on Acts.

Many technical problems will be avoided. There are excellent commentaries available for such studies. The five volumes edited by F. J. Foakes-Jackson and Kirsopp Lake, *The Beginnings of Christianity,* are almost exhaustive in this respect and go far beyond the powers of this writer. A. C. Clark in *The Acts of the Apostles,* C. S. C. Williams in *Alterations to the Text of the Synoptic Gospels and Acts,* and M. Black in *An Aramaic Approach to the Gospels and Acts* deal with the problem of major textual differences in the manuscripts. Some excursions into technical problems are avoided, too, because they would detract from the major concern of this work. However, this is not to say that this work is indifferent to such studies. In truth, many technical problems are dealt with.

Verse-by-verse exegesis is not contemplated. Such detailed study is indispensable to the serious student of Acts; but it, too, can detract from the major message of the book. One can fail to see the woods because of the trees. Excellent commentaries are available for verse-by-verse study as, for example, the commentaries by Kirsopp Lake and Henry J. Cadbury in *The Beginnings of Christianity,* R. B. Rackham in the "Westminster Commentaries," R. J. Knowling in *The Expositor's Greek Testament,* and the recent book by F. F. Bruce, *The Acts of the Apostles.*

This commentary is written with the sincere belief that there is need for a book on Acts which seeks to focus attention on its major message. Whatever the merit of commentaries already in use, there is little evidence that the message that Luke was most concerned to develop has been adequately grasped by his readers. If that be true, then another attempt is justified. In recognizing a major purpose in Acts, the dangers of a one-factor analysis are not forgotten, and it is hoped that such error is avoided.

vii

It is further to be acknowledged that the *Zeitgeist*, the spirit of the age, may influence one in what he sees in Acts. This should temper what one has to say in criticism of the views advanced at other times when students were affected by a different *Zeitgeist*. It should be recognized that this spirit of the age may betray the student into eisegesis, or it may lead him to see something more of the richness of an ancient book. An age of geographical discoveries and extension of geographical frontiers naturally caused earlier exegetes to make more of that factor in Acts. Exegetes writing under the impact of the modern missionary movement naturally made more of the gospel's penetration into new geographical territories. So now, in an atomic age when international and racial concerns are upon us as never before, it is natural that the universalist emphasis should loom larger for the exegete. The *Zeitgeist* is thus an inevitable factor, guiding or misguiding the exegete of any generation.

The writer may be open to the charge of excessive use in the exegetical section of qualifying adverbs—"possibly," "probably," "seemingly," and the like—but he found no way to avoid them. Though it is more satisfying to be able to make an unqualified statement, it should be admitted that certainty is beyond us in many matters. Where this is true, pride should yield to honesty, and dogmatism should be avoided.

A further charge to which the writer is open is that of preaching. This is to be admitted. The writer has sought to be objective in the interpretation of Acts, but he would never have written this book had his interest not included the desire to see the message of Acts, as he understands it, impinge upon the contemporary scene.

This writer is indebted to many men and books for whatever understanding he has of Acts. R. B. Rackham's excellent volume in the "Westminster Commentaries" provided the best single guide to the purpose of Acts. Attention was called to this fine work by my friend and former professor, Doctor Edward A. McDowell. The most fruitful stimulation to the study has come from working through Acts each year with classes in the New Orleans Baptist Theological Seminary. Many specific debts will be acknowledged in the footnotes, but doubtless much that was gained from others will escape documentation.

Special debt is acknowledged to my colleagues in the Department of New Testament, Doctors Ray Frank Robbins, A. Jack Roddy, and V. Wayne Barton; and to my wife, Evelyn Owen Stagg, for the first typing of the manuscript and for helpful suggestions. Also, the careful work of Mrs. R. C. Berry, who did the final typing, is appreciated.

FRANK STAGG

Contents

Introduction

EPITOME IN AN ADVERB

AN ADVERB is a strange word with which to end a book, but Luke did just that.[1] In fact, the two-volume work, Luke-Acts, is brought to a dramatic close and epitomized in an adverb.[2] Throughout his two volumes, Luke never lost sight of his purpose, and he planned well the conclusion to it all, achieving the final effort by the last stroke of the pen. "Unhinderedly," Luke wrote, describing the hard-won liberty of the gospel. This liberty came only after many barriers had been crossed, and it was won because its first home was in the mind and intention of Jesus himself.

Not until after the prominence and apparent significance of the term for hindrance (appearing in various forms) had been studied did this writer observe Professor Oscar Cullmann's study of the same. Cullmann arrived at an entirely different significance for the term, seeing in its use traces of an old baptismal formula. His study appeared as an appendix to his book, *Die Tauflehre des Neuen Testaments,* 1948 (English version: *Baptism in the New Testament,* 1950). The appendix is entitled: "Traces of an Ancient Baptismal Formula in the New Testament." Whatever the significance of the term, the case for its having significance is strengthened by Cullmann's study.

From the passages cited (Acts 8: 36; 10: 47; 11: 17; Matt. 3: 14; the Gospel of the Ebionites as reflected in Epiphanius 30: 13; Mark 10: 13-14) an interesting case is made for this hypothetical baptismal formula according to which the candidate would ask, "What hinders me from being baptized?" or someone else would

---

[1] Some manuscripts have a longer ending, with the additional words: "For this is Jesus, the Son of God, through whom all the world is about to be judged." No Greek manuscript has this longer ending, though it may have originated in Greek.

[2] The Greek word *akōlutōs* is an adverb translated literally as "unhinderedly." Although awkward, it is used occasionally in the book to stress adverbial usage while the adjective "unhindered" appears in the subtitle.

1

ask, "What hinders this one from being baptized?" The case is
far from being established, however. The term in its various
forms is used about twenty-five times in the New Testament and
seven times in Acts. The basic idea is always the same, that of
hindrance. Sometimes it has reference to neither baptism nor the
gospel. The instances in Acts cited by Cullmann involve baptism,
but they also involve the question of admission of people from
outside Judaism. It is not simply a question of admission to
baptism, but of the admission of non-Jews. Two of the instances
outside Acts concern the relation of John the Baptist and Jesus
where a unique problem arose and where "hindrance" would
have been expected. The last reference, Mark 10:13-14, offers
little evidence for a baptismal formula since nothing indicates
that the coming of those little children to Jesus was for baptism.

It was only natural that baptism should be the point at which
the question of admission would have arisen for some, while
there are many instances of baptism in which the question was
not raised. The term for hindrance was employed in some instances apart from baptism. In no case in Acts where the person
in question was a Jew was this term employed in connection
with baptism. The thesis of a baptismal formula, though not to
be excluded, is not established. It seems that a stronger case can
be made in the instances cited, taken along with Acts 28: 31, for
the reference to a *particular* problem leading to hindrance or
its absence.

On the other hand, even if we assume the correctness of Cullmann's thesis that traces of a primitive baptismal formula are
to be seen in the frequent use of "hinder," the case still is not
weakened for the theory that Luke employed the term with
reference to the major problem of hindrances to an unfettered
gospel—hindrances from which the gospel had to fight free. If
it had already become a *terminus technicus,* as he suggests, it
could easily be given a further usage in being related to the
gospel's early struggle for liberty. This writer feels, however, that
the term is better understood apart from any reference to a
baptismal formula.

May it be further stressed that the thesis advanced in this book

is not dependent upon the evidence of the term "unhindered."
In truth, the observation of the term came near the end of the
study, not at the beginning. Again, it is not contended that Luke
deliberately played up the word itself throughout Acts. It is
insisted that the term, whether by plan of the author or not,
well epitomized the major message of the book. If the choice was
deliberate, it accounts for the seeming abruptness in the conclusion to the work.

Many have puzzled over the close of the book of Acts. Some
have thought it incomplete; some have argued that Luke contemplated a third volume. These, it seems to this writer, utterly
miss the point of Luke-Acts. The book is not incomplete and
does not end abruptly. The conclusion of Acts is unexcelled for
its dramatic power. The major issues are brought together in the
last paragraph, and the major message is reaffirmed in the very
last word of the book, in the adverb, "unhinderedly."

It is strange and unfortunate that influential scholars have
construed as weak an ending which Luke seemingly so carefully
planned. Sir William Ramsay, to whom all students of the New
Testament own a great debt, was as wrong as dogmatic in saying:
"No one can accept the ending of Acts as the conclusion of a
rationally conceived history." [3] He argued that Luke would
not have left unanswered the questions of how the gospel reached
Rome and what the outcome of Paul's trial was. This falsely
assumes that Luke purposed to trace the geographical expansion
of Christianity and the life of Paul. Luke did give much of the
story of Christianity's geographical expansion, but that apparently was not his major purpose. He gave much of the life of
Paul, but that surely was not his major purpose.

F. F. Bruce is much nearer the truth in his treatment of the
conclusion of Acts, but he, too, obscures the matter at this most
vital point by saying:

> Yet, artistic and powerful as the conclusion is, it is strange that
> Luke has not told us explicitly what the result of Paul's appeal was.
> It may be a sufficient answer to say that this formed no part of his

---

[3] Sir William Ramsay, *St. Paul the Traveller and the Roman Citizen* (New York:
G. P. Putnam's Sons, 1896), pp. 351–352.

project; it would be more satisfactory to suppose that he wrote no more because he knew no more.[4]

This assumes an almost impossibly early date for Acts, around A. D. 60, and obscures the purpose of Acts.[5] It forms a weak conclusion to an excellent commentary. Luke left many of our questions unanswered, but they are *our* questions, not *his*. Luke let the curtain fall on many men without tracing out what would have been for us interesting biography; he, apparently, was not writing biography.

THE PURPOSE OF ACTS

THE DISCOVERY of a writer's purpose affords the best possible clue to the understanding of his work. It is to be expected that any serious writing will be governed by purpose, though the purpose may prove illusive for the reader. The importance of purpose to Acts and to its understanding is here assumed to be so great that serious quest for it is imperative.

Not the Acts of the Apostles.—The Acts of the Apostles is the title by which the treatise is best known, and it has gone far in giving to readers their understanding of the purpose of the book. It is found in Codex Vaticanus, one of the older extant manuscripts, produced about A. D. 350. Codex Sinaiticus, also from the fourth century, has the simpler title, Acts, though the larger title appears at the end in the subscription of the book and in the original hand. The Muratorian Canon, probably drawn up between A. D. 170 and 200, states that "the Acts of all the apostles

---

[4] F. F. Bruce, *The Acts of the Apostles* (London: The Tyndale Press, 1951), p. 481.

[5] Martin Dibelius, concerned with this very problem of "strange omissions" in the stories of Acts 22–28, develops the point that Luke's concern was with presenting the heathen mission as of God rather than a thing of man and the Christian good news as the fulfilment of Jewish hopes. He holds that Luke was concerned with the issues confronting the church at the time of its separation from Judaism, summing it up pointedly: "Luke wishes therefore in these chapters above all to present not what has been (*das Gewesene*) but what is (*das Seiende*)." That is, Luke was more interested in the gospel as it was being preached than in past events in the lives of Christians. Cf. Martin Dibelius, *Aufsätze zur Apostelgeschichte* (Göttingen: Vandenhoeck & Ruprecht, 1953), p. 117.

were written in one book: Luke compiled them for the most excellent Theophilus because they severally took place in his presence." By a similar title, Acts or Acts of (the) Apostles, it was known to Tertullian of Carthage and Clement of Alexandria, both of whom wrote around A. D. 200. But this title was apparently the work of a copyist and not of the author.

Clearly the purpose of the book is not to record the acts of the apostles. The author lists the eleven and then tells of the addition of the twelfth apostle. Nine apostles are heard of no more. One short sentence is all that is given to James, the brother of John, who was martyred by Herod (12: 2). John barely comes in for subsequent mention. Peter, along with Stephen and Philip, is featured through chapter 12, but beyond that we hear little more of him. Barnabas and Paul are given much attention, but the curtain drops on Barnabas at the scene of a conflict and on Paul while he is in jail awaiting trial for his life. We are left with a thousand questions, and with the exception of Stephen, the story of each person featured is broken off at a point of keen interest to us. The curtain falls on them one by one at points of interest because, apparently, Luke was not writing about the apostles.

Furthermore, the beginning of the significant mission to the Gentiles with which Luke was so much concerned is not ascribed by him to the apostles—not to the twelve, not to Peter, not to Barnabas or Paul—but to Hellenistic Christians in Jerusalem and unnamed men of Cyprus and Cyrene.[6] He demonstrated how an idea mastered the apostles rather than merely what the apostles did.

Not the Gospel of the Holy Spirit.— More than half a century ago the suggestion was made that Luke's second work should be termed the "Gospel of the Holy Spirit." This has found and continues to find advocates. It is readily admitted that this strikes close to the significance of Acts, but it is not satisfactory to leave it so ambiguously stated. Certainly in Acts we have the

---

[6] Adolf Harnack, *The Acts of the Apostles* (London: Williams and Northgate, 1909), p. xxviii.

account of something effected by the Holy Spirit—something
which could not have been effected apart from the Holy Spirit.
But Luke's concern surely was with that which was accomplished
and not with the Spirit himself. Here are two important aspects
of one reality, but it is important to see the aspect which most
concerned the writer.

To designate the book the "Gospel of the Holy Spirit" would
imply that there was the need for such a book. One may search
in vain for a *Sitz im Leben* (life situation) which indicated that
there was a problem among first-century Jews or Christians about
the reality, character, or importance of the Holy Spirit. (This
is not to forget the strange little group at Ephesus; its members
required information, not argument.) The Spirit was accepted,
not argued. There is evidence on every hand, however, to indicate
a titanic struggle between the ideas of the particularists and those
championed by such men as Philip, Stephen, and Paul. Though
Luke gave great prominence to the Holy Spirit, there was no occasion for a book which had the problem of the Spirit as its point of
departure. Jesus was at the center of controversies from the beginning, and there were constant debates as to his identity,
character, actions, words, and intention. But Jews and Christians
contemporary with Luke did not require a book debating these
matters concerning the Holy Spirit any more than they needed
a book proving the existence of God.

Thus, there was no call for a book outlining the acts of the
Holy Spirit, but there was occasion to debate the origin and character of ideas and acts which found expression among early Christians. Luke traced back to God—in terms of Jesus, the risen Christ,
or the Holy Spirit—many of these very ideas over which men
fought. There is not the least disposition here to minimize the
importance of the Holy Spirit in Acts, but it is important to bring
into focus the point of departure. *Luke's problem was not to
outline what the Holy Spirit did, but to demonstrate the origin
and character of certain ideas and activities as they found expression and became centers of controversy in the Christian communities of his time.*

An easier approach to the problem, though not necessarily a

better one, may be made in pointing to the fact that the Holy Spirit was not the object of Luke's interest in Acts in the sense that Jesus was in the Gospel. Anything so obvious scarcely requires demonstration. The Holy Spirit is mentioned only once (28:25) after Acts 21:11, and there, in connection with Isaiah! It is inconceivable that Luke could have named Jesus but twice in the eight concluding chapters of his Gospel! One is never in doubt that the Gospel is about Jesus; surely Acts is not about the Holy Spirit in the same sense.

Furthermore, the scarcity of references to the Holy Spirit in the latter half of Acts is, for the view under discussion, a more serious fact than such scarcity in the earlier half of Acts would be. All scholars, except those denying Lukan authorship, recognize that the author of Acts was a participant in much that belongs to the latter half of the book but was not an eyewitness of that which belongs to the earlier half. Thus, information for the first half of the book was gathered by Luke from sources, whether written or oral, outside of his own experience. It is an elementary observation that where a writer employs a source involving multiple elements, a given element in the source may or may not reflect his special interest. If his special interest is to be isolated anywhere, that can best be done where the materials are his own. It is precisely where Luke had the freest hand with his materials that one finds fewest references to the Holy Spirit. This does not mean that the Spirit was of little importance to Luke, but it does mean that his problem or point of departure was elsewhere. In the Gospels everything centers about Jesus, and one can never be in doubt that only as he is related to an event does it have importance. But in Acts one finds *eleven chapters* in which the Holy Spirit is not mentioned. He is prominent, certainly, in many chapters, but so are references to God, the angel of the Lord, and the one termed "the Lord."

Every student is aware of the prominence of the Holy Spirit in such crucial experiences as Pentecost, the defiance of the Sadducees, the conversion of Cornelius, and the commissioning of Barnabas and Saul. But it could also be observed that in other crucial developments the Spirit is not singled out for emphasis.

Paul and Stephen made a forceful impact upon the Christian movement, and each is represented as having seen Jesus himself. Luke tells us that each was filled with the Spirit; but for Paul, at least, nothing short of the appearance of Jesus himself effected the revolutionary change in his life and work. One may observe the many times Jesus stood by Paul in dark hours of crisis. One could also recall the appearance of the angel of the Lord (e.g., 12: 7-17, 23), the angel of God (27: 23), and "the Lord" (18:9; 23: 11; 26: 15) at crucial points in the experiences of early Christians. In Peter's speech at the home of Cornelius, the apparently equal reference to "God," "Jesus," and "the Holy Spirit" should be a caution against extracting one "person" from the Trinity as would be done by a book on the Gospel of the Holy Spirit. Peter seems to have been conscious of the guidance and power of the Triune God, and Luke was certainly aware of the Triune God. It is hardly credible, however, that he should so isolate the Holy Spirit from Jesus that he would write a book about each. This he seems not to have done.

There is no disposition here to understate the importance of the Holy Spirit in Acts, but there is a concern to gain the right perspective for understanding the book. It would be difficult to exaggerate the prominence of the Holy Spirit, at least in some chapters, but it seems grossly misleading to term this the "Gospel of the Holy Spirit." Rather it was a particular act or major development with which Luke was concerned. Certainly it was indispensable to his purpose to insist that this development—this liberation of the gospel—was of God and not of man. Nevertheless Luke's approach was from the standpoint of what was taking place instead of from the standpoint of the Holy Spirit, even though the Spirit's agency was so prominent in what happened. This distinction is here held to be indispensable to a proper understanding of Acts.

From yet another standpoint the untenable nature of the suggestion that Acts is the Gospel of the Holy Spirit should be obvious, and those people most concerned with appreciating the Holy Spirit should be first to see it. Had Luke undertaken to write the Gospel of the Holy Spirit, he thereby would have undertaken a most ambitious task. At what arbitrary point would one begin his narrative of the work of the Spirit or where would he terminate the record? The book itself makes reference to the Spirit's activity in David and Isaiah; Stephen closed his interpretative review of Hebrew history with the charge that his hearers were resisting the Holy Spirit as their fathers always had done (7: 51). In the book of Acts are recorded many significant and far-reaching acts of the Holy Spirit, but these form only a small part of what the Spirit has done in history.

One may protest that neither do the gospels give all of the acts of Jesus. To this it would be replied that no scholar for fifty years has suggested that gospels are "lives" of Jesus—they are interpretations based on selections from what he did and said. Acts, however, is neither a "life" of the Holy Spirit nor a portrayal of selected activities, such as the gospels are for Jesus. Failure to recognize this led Rackham in his great commentary to make the following unfortunate statement (cf. xxxviii): "The Acts in fact is a history of the new dispensation [i.e., under the Holy Spirit]; *and that is why it lacks a definite conclusion.*" (Italics are not Rackham's.)

It seems untenable to speak of the dispensation of the Holy Spirit as succeeding that of Jesus. It will be urged in the commentary (Acts 1: 1) that Luke was concerned to show that what developed in the Christian community was under the direction of the very Jesus of whom he wrote in the first treatise. The work of the incarnate Jesus and of the risen Christ was *one*. This fact was indispensable to Luke's defense of what emerged in the Christian community and the mission to the Gentiles. In the writings of Paul and John, sometimes there is a virtual identification of the risen Christ with the Holy Spirit. Only if this identification is also true in Acts could the work be called the Gospel of the Holy Spirit. Even that seems to miss the problem in the mind of Luke.

Not the spread of the gospel from Jerusalem to Rome.—There are many who take Acts to be a record of the early geographical expansion of Christianity. This persists even in recent publications.

The commission, "and you shall be my witnesses in Jerusalem and in all Judea and Samaria and to the end of the earth" is taken as an outline of the book. It is true that much of the development is narrated on this framework, but nothing can be farther from the author's purpose than simply showing how Christianity moved out from Jerusalem to the distant parts of the world. If this were Luke's purpose, then he is thirty years behind the actual development.

Geographical expansion on a vast scale took place soon after Pentecost. The gospel probably reached Rome twenty years before Paul did. The much-publicized idea that Paul introduced the gospel to Europe through Macedonia on his second missionary journey, fails to take note of previous expansion or first-century geography.[7] The event's significance is to be found apart from geography, as will be shown later. We are not told who founded the churches at Rome, Colosse, Laodicea, Ephesus, Troas, or Puteoli. There were Christians in Damascus before Paul became a Christian. Luke mentions it in connection with the conversion of Saul but says nothing about the beginning of the work or its later development. We do not know how much farther Christianity had reached to the north and east. Turning south, we also see early development. The Ethiopian eunuch was converted, and he returned to his homeland. What happened to him? What development followed in Africa? Luke is silent about this except to mention incidentally a fact which suggests Christian development in Africa *prior to* the first missionary journey of Barnabas and Saul (11: 20).

Throughout Acts incidental reference is made to expansion prior to and apart from the work of Paul. The curtain falls on Barnabas and Mark as they embark on a new journey. After his miraculous release from prison we are told of Peter that "he departed, and went to another place" (12: 7). To this day we

---

[7] Speakers continue to say naïvely, "Had Paul gone into Asia as he desired rather than into Macedonia, the gospel would have entered the East rather than the West, and now India and China would be sending missionaries to Europe and America." The "Asia" Paul desired to enter was the Roman province of which Ephesus was the center. It, along with Macedonia and Achaia, was a part of the great Greco-Roman culture centering around the Aegean Sea. The "Asia" Paul desired to enter was a part of the "West," not the "East."

do not know where this "place" was. Even Luke's supposed hero is left stranded in Rome; the curtain falls on Paul with no hint as to what followed. Luke possibly closed his book at this point because events had developed no further; but such explanation cannot be established, nor is it necessary.

There seems to be but one satisfactory explanation of all this: Luke was not giving a record of the geographical expansion of Christianity. To narrate subsequent experiences of the Ethiopian, Barnabas, Mark, Peter, John, or Paul—or the development at Damascus or in Africa—was not essential to his purpose.

Not an irenicon.—The Tübingen (Baur) thesis that Acts is an irenicon written in the time of Trajan (A.D. 98-117) or Hadrian (A.D. 117-138) and seeking to reconcile the supposed rivalry between the followers of Peter and Paul becomes less and less convincing. This theory of a second century invention of history to neutralize or harmonize these supposed rival factions is vulnerable at many points, and it has been generally abandoned as too precarious for serious consideration.

In Acts the extreme positions are not held by Peter and Paul but by James and Paul. Between these two are Peter, Mark, and Barnabas, each feeling the influence of both James and Paul. Cullmann is probably correct in suggesting that Peter and the twelve appear to have taken a mediating position between the Judaizers and the Hellenists until the situation was changed when James replaced Peter in the dominant role in Jerusalem.[8]

Somewhat recently, the thesis has been advocated that Luke-Acts was developed about A.D. 150 as an apologetic against Marcionism.[9] Marcion rejected the Old Testament and the twelve apostles, and formed a canon composed of a short form of Luke and ten Pauline epistles. To him, Paul was the only accredited apostle; the twelve had corrupted much of the church with their "Jewish apostasy." Some argue that to offset Marcion's canon, the "orthodox" Christians developed Luke as we now

---

[8] Oscar Cullmann, *Peter: Disciple, Apostle, Martyr,* trans. Floyd V. Filson (London: SCM Press, 1953), p. 36.

[9] Cf. John Knox, *Marcion and the New Testament* (Chicago: The University of Chicago Press, 1942).

have it and that Acts was written with the double purpose of acknowledging Paul yet subordinating him to the twelve. Thus the "orthodox" would have all that Marcion had, and far more.

This thesis cannot be established with present data, yet it is not one to be lightly discredited. Doubtless Marcion did create a crisis for second-century Christians which hastened the formation of the New Testament canon, but to say that Luke was enlarged and Acts brought into being to meet this crisis can, with present data, be little stronger than speculation. The thesis has the difficulty of establishing the late date of Acts and of handling the whole issue of the forming of the canon, about which so little is known; and it is unduly skeptical about the character of these New Testament writings. Apart from this, it is unconvincing to this writer by virtue of the very nature of Acts. There is much in Acts which would discredit Marcion, and yet there is much in it which could be used to give him support. Hence it is unlikely that an apology to meet Marcionism would have been written as Acts stands. However, our more positive answer to this thesis is the one to be developed in the book.

Triumph and tragedy.—What, then, is the author's major purpose in Acts? He writes to show a victory of Christianity—to show the expansion of a concept, the liberation of the gospel as it breaks through barriers that are religious, racial, and national. The author shows how Christianity broke through the narrow limitations which men sought to impose upon it and how it emerged in the liberty which Jesus had given it. In the first chapter, he shows us something of the narrow conception of Christianity which was held by early followers, who viewed it as a sect of Judaism open only to Jews and proselytes. We finally see it looking out from Rome as a religion open to all who meet its terms, regardless of race, nationality, or external circumstance.

In the first chapter the author introduces us to the major internal problem of primitive Christianity, the problem to be dealt with in Acts. In their parting conversation, the Jewish Christians asked Jesus, "Lord, will you at this time restore the kingdom to Israel?" (1: 6). Mark it—they did not ask *if* the kingdom would be restored to Israel; that they assumed. The only problem for them was *when*. Possibly they had begun to see that the kingdom was not temporal and political, yet they still thought of it as belonging to Israel. Luke goes on to show the gradual breaking down of that understanding of the kingdom. Slowly the conception grew that Christianity is designed for all. The door into the kingdom is not circumcision, or the law, or the synogogue, or Judaism itself. Nevertheless, this narrow concept that the kingdom belonged to Israel gripped early Jewish Christians. For the majority, it proved to be the issue which finally made them turn away from Christianity.

At first we see only Jews embracing Christianity, and these thought that Christianity was for Jews only. One not born a Jew could enter the kingdom only by being inducted into Judaism. We next see Hellenistic Jews, Stephen and Philip, and proselytes active in the movement. Next Samaritans, half-Jews, were received, though reluctantly by many. Finally, Gentiles were received, but this came by gradual steps.

The first Gentiles to be received were already on the outer fringe of Judaism. The Ethiopian and Cornelius were by no means looked upon by the Jews as mere pagans. They were Gentiles who already had moved near to Judaism. Only later are Gentiles received who had no previous connection with Judaism. The issue arose as to the acceptability of Gentiles on an equality with Jews, and this became the topic of a great conference in Jerusalem, where a victory was won. It may appear that the book should close with chapter 15, but Luke had many developments yet to present. The victory had yet to be won in the churches, and the final reaction of the Jews to the new position had yet to be shown.

Luke developed one thing clearly: the problem of accepting uncircumcised Gentiles became increasingly difficult for Jewish Christians, leading eventually to the self-exclusion of the Jews from the Christian community. A further aspect of the problem was hinted at without being explored so fully in Acts as in some of Paul's letters, namely, the place of the Jewish ritual law for the Jewish Christians themselves. Did it finally become apparent

that Christianity freed Jew as well as Gentile from the law and
the ritual? Luke was not so much concerned with this side of the
question as with the Jewish Christian's attitude toward uncircumcised Gentiles, although he was not silent about it. He
shows that the fear already clutched Jewish hearts that the freeing
of Gentiles from the ritual law would eventually suggest the same
thing for Jews.

This fear is clearly reflected in the words to Paul upon his
last recorded visit to Jerusalem: "You see, brother, how many
thousands [myriads] there are among the Jews of those who have
believed; they are all zealous for the law, *and they have been told
about you that you teach all the Jews who are among the Gentiles
to forsake Moses, telling them not to circumcise their children or
observe the customs*" (Acts 21: 20f.). One "concession," freeing
the Gentile Christian from the Law, could easily lead to another,
freeing the Jewish Christian.

Furthermore, as the essential character of the gospel more
clearly emerged, it became more obvious that it was impossible
ultimately to reconcile exclusivist principles with Christian
brotherhood. Jews must have seen the inevitable: table fellowship itself would make it impossible to follow some of the customs. Hence they saw in this Christian equality of Gentile with
Jew the inevitable destruction of their politico-economic kingdom hopes. Judaism was a nation as well as a religion. Gentile
Christians would recognize Christianity's relation to Judaism as
a religion but would reject its claims upon them as a nation. Thus
the final issue was not simply the basis upon which Gentiles
would be received. Even after the conference voiced its approval
of the reception of uncircumcised Gentiles, there continued to
be myriads of Jewish Christians. That which finally proved unacceptable to the Jews was the fact that Christianity threatened
the release even of Jews from the ritual law and demanded the
equality of Gentiles and Jews in the kingdom. It was here that
Christianity ceased to be Jewish and became Gentile.

From the first there was latent in Judaism a universalism.
Monotheism must logically lead to universalism; if there is but
one God, he must be the creator of all men, and he must include

all in his purpose. From Amos on, the concept of universalism was proclaimed by many voices in Judaism, proselytism being the practical application of the concept. However, this universalism was in conflict with nationalism. The resultant position was that God may be the God of any people provided they become Jews through the ritual. This was a mere disguising of the idea that he is the God of the Jews only. Someone has described this proselytism as reaching out for the Gentiles with one hand and holding them off with the other. In its universalism and proselytism, Judaism never proclaimed that the Gentile as Gentile, without induction into Judaism, could share in the kingdom. This induction demanded was into Judaism as a nation as well as a religion.

A contemporary Jewish scholar, Joseph Klausner, is insistent at this point: "For one simple fact must not be forgotten, . . . this fact is that Judaism is *not only a religion, but a nation as well—* a nation and a religion at one and the same time." [10] The fear that gripped Jewish hearts was that voiced by Klausner:

> The abrogation of the ceremonial laws would necessarily have served to obliterate the distinction between Israel and the nations . . . and if Judaism had listened to the voice of Paul, it would have disappeared from the world both as a religion and as a nation, without leaving any influence whatever upon the great pagan world.[11]

But the Jewish Christians were wrong even as Klausner is wrong. Certainly, such a course may have destroyed Israel as a nation but not as a religion. In the willingness to die as a nation, Israel had the opportunity to lead all the nations into that death to self in which life is found and in which a larger brotherhood is made possible.

After earlier progress away from nationalism, the experience of exile and conflict with other nations brought on a recrudescence of this spirit. A Jewish source may be quoted to this effect:

> With the return to Palestine of Ezra in 458 B.C.E. and of Nehemiah in 444 B.C.E. . . . . the particularist and isolationist spirit became domi-

---

[10] Joseph Klausner, *From Jesus to Paul* (New York: The Macmillan Co., 1944), p. 593.
[11] *Loc. cit.*

nant in Judaism and shaped the course of Jewish thought and the evolution of Judaism throughout subsequent Jewish history.[12]

So extreme was this program of isolation and nationalism that proselytism ceased.

This extreme isolation, however, soon gave way to a modified one. But as Israel turned again to an expression of its universalism, its method was to achieve it through ritual procedures: circumcision, dietary laws, and sacrifices. To quote Klausner again: "Judaism in the days of the Second Temple, and after, made Gentile proselytes 'sons of the covenant' in such a manner that they were absorbed into *the Jewish national community*." [13] Christianity did not demand of Gentiles that they be absorbed into the Jewish national community. Instead, it formed a new community in which Jew and Gentile were equal, or rather in which the matter of being Jew or Gentile was irrelevant. To the Jew this ultimately proved unacceptable; the Gentile was later to resist this same Christian principle.

The Jews did not reject Jesus because of his claim to be the Christ, the Son of God; thousands of Jews found no insuperable difficulty in that claim. They did not break with Christianity because of this claim; Acts demonstrates that myriads of Jews at Jerusalem and elsewhere accepted Jesus as the Christ. Yet before the end of the first Christian century, a movement which was thoroughly Jewish at its beginning, and which attracted thousands of devout Jews for many decades, became predominantly Gentile. *Missions and not messiahship made the difference.* Had the spiritual and universal character of Christianity not asserted itself triumphantly over the nationalistic interests of Jewish Christians, the Christian movement would probably have continued to attract myriads of Jews. Christianity in an amazingly short time became tremendously popular among Jews and then was rejected by these very people among whom it had its rise.

In his two-volume work, Luke-Acts, Luke traced this development. When he wrote, Christianity was already moving into

---

[12] Julian Morgenstern, "Universalism and Particularism," *The Universal Jewish Encyclopedia*, X, 356.
[13] *Op. cit.*, pp. 534f.

the Gentile world, and Jews were already at grips with the very issues in Christianity which ultimately turned them from it. In the Gospel, Luke demonstrated that the character which the Christian movement bore was due to Jesus himself; it was no perversion effected by Paul or some other. Jesus never contemplated a movement which would simply expand within nationalistic Judaism, but he purposed a new humanity which would embrace Jew and Gentile. In Acts, Luke demonstrated the outworking of that intention of Jesus, presenting its glorious triumph in the inclusion of the Gentile and its sad tragedy in the self-exclusion of the Jew. In the Gospels it is shown that Jesus repudiated the unreal distinction between the "righteous" and "sinners," showing that all are sinners. His bold claim, "I have not come to call the righteous, but sinners to repentance" (Luke 5: 32), was far-reaching and revolutionary. Jesus naturally applied the principle to Judaism first of all; but once established, it undercut all unreal distinctions among men. In Acts the unreal distinction repudiated was that between Jew and non-Jew.

Subsidiary purposes.—It would be oversimplification to try to reduce the book of Acts to one issue. There are doubtless several purposes subsidiary to the chief one.[14] Whatever his purpose, Luke wrote history; whatever his specific purpose, he intended to inform his readers about the past.[15] Luke's visit to Palestine doubtless gave the initial impetus to writing. The visit to Jerusalem brought him under the spell of the mother church and of the special tradition which he found there.[16] The visit with Mnason, an early disciple (Acts 21:16), provided a source of information and stimulation to write. Sheer interest in the material for its own sake is not to be ruled out; Luke could pursue a story simply because it was intriguing.

---

[14] For a good discussion of this, see R. B. Rackham, *The Acts of the Apostles* ("Westminster Commentaries"; twelfth edition; London: Methuen and Co., 1939) pp. xxxix ff.

[15] Cf. Henry J. Cadbury, *The Making of Luke-Acts* (New York: Macmillan and Co., 1927), p. 300.

[16] Cf. Wm. Manson, *The Gospel of Luke* ("The Moffatt New Testament Commentary"; New York: Harper and Brothers, 1930), p. vii.

Many see in Acts a defense of Christianity before Rome.
Others would reduce it to a defense of Paul before official Rome.
This latter seems improbable. This would be a rather round-
about way to defend a man in chains, although as a defense for
Christianity before a Roman world it offers much. Jesus died
on a *Roman* cross under charge of sedition, and Paul wore a
Roman chain. These facts would call for explanation, and especially would this be true in the time of persecution and war.
It is obvious that Luke took pains to show that Paul and other
Christian leaders stood repeatedly in the presence of Roman
officials and that these never found them guilty of offense against
Rome. On the other hand, Luke presented Roman officials as
repeatedly declaring the Christian leaders innocent. A book so
designed could be highly influential in the empire yet would be
a rather indirect approach to official Rome itself. It is almost incredible that a non-Christian Roman official would read through
the long books of Luke and Acts. Had Luke written for a non-
Christian, he probably would have omitted much that is in his
work.[17]

Another theme which is evident is the stand Christianity took
with respect to heathen religion. There was no compromise here.
Christianity was presented as intolerant of any other religion.
Such also was its stand with respect to magic, sorcery, false
spiritualism, pagan philosophy, and idolatry.

These and other subsidiary purposes may be observed, but
we return to the conviction that the chief purpose was the portrayal of Christianity asserting its universalism over against the
effort to limit it to the narrow concepts of first century Judaism.
This bitter struggle led to the glorious triumph of Christian
liberty and the recognition of a new humanity rising above
nation and race. With this, however, came the sad tragedy of
self-exclusion by the Jew, who preferred national survival to
world brotherhood.

---

[17] Dibelius, however, suggests that both the Gospel and Acts were intended not
only for the Christian community but also for the "bookmarket" (*Büchermarkt*),
appealing especially to the fact and the nature of the dedication to Theophilus.
Cf. *op. cit.*, p. 118.

DATE AND OCCASION

IN SEEKING to date Acts, the *terminus a quo,* or earliest possible date, is fixed by the events recorded in chapter 28. Paul spent two years in Rome awaiting trial before the emperor; Acts, obviously, can be no earlier than those two years. But it is a mistake to conclude that these two years are also the *terminus ad quem,* or latest possible date, as many have done.[18] To conclude that Acts ended where it did, without giving the outcome of Paul's trial, because events had developed no further, is to assume that Luke was interested in Paul's life for its own sake. In breaking off the story without giving the outcome of the trial, Luke did exactly what he had done throughout the book in dealing with many of his characters. He was far more interested in issues than in personalities. There is no conclusive reason for holding that Acts must have been written before the trial of Paul took place. The conclusion of Acts is more meaningful when Luke's real purpose is remembered (see above).

Paul appealed to Caesar (Acts 25:11) after Festus succeeded Felix as procurator of Judea, and his two years in Rome followed shortly thereafter. This provides a definite datum for Pauline chronology, but a problem remains in dating Paul's Roman imprisonment because there is uncertainty about the date when Festus succeeded Felix. From Josephus (*Antiquities,* XX, 8, 9ff. and *Wars,* II, 14, 1) we learn that Festus was appointed under Nero to succeed Felix and that he was followed by Albinus. It was possibly A.D. 55 or 56 that Festus became procurator, but this is not conclusive.[19] Probably it was the winter of 56 or 57

---

[18] It is disconcerting to find in such excellent commentaries as those of R. B. Rackham and F. F. Bruce the argument that the conclusion of Acts is abrupt, incomplete, and that it must have been written before the outcome of the trial was known. Cf. Rackham, *op. cit.,* pp. 1–1v and Bruce, *op. cit.,* pp. 10–14.

[19] It is known from Josephus (Antiquities, XX, 8, 9) that when Felix was recalled to Rome he was saved from utter ruin by the influence of Pallas, his brother. Pallas was dismissed from office by Nero about A.D. 55. Felix, therefore, was presumably recalled before the fall of Pallas. Cf. Kirsopp Lake and Henry J. Cadbury, editors, *Additional Notes,* Vol. V, *The Beginnings of Christianity* (London: Macmillan and Co., 1933), p. 466. Also see below, pp. 242f.

which Paul spent at Malta, following the shipwreck, and the spring of 57 or 58 when he reached Rome. The two years' imprisonment in Rome would, then, probably have reached into 59 or 60. Conclusive evidence is lacking, but this dating seems to suit the available data best. Acts, then, was written no earlier than about A.D. 59 or 60. This, however, does not indicate the lastest possible date for Acts. The trial of Paul has no necessary bearing on the date of Acts; the lengthy arguments in that connection only obscure the matter of Luke's purpose.

Many different dates have been suggested for Acts, some as late as the middle of the second century. John Knox has offered the thesis that Acts was written and Luke expanded to meet the threat of Marcionism.[20] This has already been discussed in the section on purpose (see pp. 11f.). Few today would date Acts so late. It is almost inconceivable that a book written in the time of Marcion could have been so widely held within a few years as the work of Luke. Irenaeus (ca. A.D. 185) quoted and summarized extensively from Acts in his work *Against the Heresies*,[21] and explicitly mentioned Luke as the author of the Gospel and Acts.[22] The Muratorian Fragment (ca. 170) explicitly ascribed the authorship of Acts to Luke, giving the tradition of Roman Christians. Clement of Alexandria (ca. 200) and those of the following generations held Luke to be the author. This is incredible if the work itself belongs to the middle of the second century. There are possible allusions to Acts in 1 Clement (A.D. 95), the Epistle of Barnabas (ca. 100), the Shepherd of Hermas (ca. A.D. 100-110), Ignatius (ca. 115), Epistle of Polycarp (ca. 120), and others.[23] More important, however, as argued earlier, this thesis that Acts was an irenicon to bring about harmony between the followers of Peter and of Paul obscures the real purpose of Acts and should have passed with Baur and the Tübingen school.

D. W. Riddle[24] argued that the threat of persecution under

[20] John Knox, *op. cit., passim.*
[21] See Rackham, *op. cit.,* p. xiv.
[22] See Bruce, *op. cit.,* p. 1.
[23] *Ibid.,* p. 8.
[24] D. W. Riddle, "The Occasion of Luke-Acts," *Journal of Religion,* October, 1930.

Domitian was the occasion for Acts, hence the date would be some years after A.D. 90. Riddle's argument was based on three propositions: that Luke-Acts was dependent upon Josephus, that the publication of Acts was responsible for the collection of Paul's letters, and that Theophilus was an official of the empire to whom Acts was addressed as an apology. None of these theories can be established; they are very weak arguments, the kind critics delight to attack when such are used to support a traditional position.

Others, not holding Riddle's particular thesis, date Luke-Acts after A.D. 93 on the grounds of Luke's supposed dependence on Josephus. Three passages are cited as reflecting dependence upon Josephus: the Theudas reference in Acts 5: 36f, Lysanias as tetrarch of Abilene in Luke 3: 1, and the reference to the Egyptian in Acts 21:38. These passages have been debated endlessly, but it does not follow that Luke was dependent upon Josephus. The section of the *Antiquities* (XX. 5. 1, 2) which relates the matters with which Luke is dealing is near the end of the work; it seems strange that Luke should work through that massive writing for so little material and then misread his source! Luke and Josephus could have had the same sources; and, with respect to Theudas, they could have had different men in mind.

Some would insist that Acts was later than A.D. 70 because the Gospel of Luke, earlier than Acts, reflects a date after the fall of Jerusalem in 70. It is argued that Luke's description of the siege of Jerusalem (Luke 19: 43f.; 21: 10-24) is too precise to allow for a date earlier than the event. Why should this follow? That Jesus was the Son of God and could foresee the fall of Jerusalem satisfactorily accounts for the precision in the description of the siege of Jerusalem. Apart from this, anyone who was alert to the times could have foreseen an inevitable clash between the Jews and Rome—the Zealots were agitating for revolt, which was the one unpardonable sin in Rome's eyes. Then, too, Jerusalem was always taken by siege because of its topographical setting. There is in this no conclusive argument for dating Luke, hence Acts, after 70. On the other hand, this does not require a date for Luke or Acts before 70. Luke and Acts could have been written before 70, but they were not necessarily written that early.

The date of Mark enters the picture as a major factor in the dating of Luke and hence of Acts. For nearly a century it has been almost universally recognized that Luke used Mark as one of the sources to which he referred in his preface (Luke 1: 1-4). Mark was probably written around A.D. 65 when Christians were suffering persecution under Nero and were further imperiled by the Jewish-Roman war, then under way. Luke was probably written a few years later. Acts followed Luke; how soon afterward cannot be determined.

The Jewish-Roman War (A.D. 66-70) brought on a major crisis for Jews and Christians. The final break of the Christians from the synogogue and the turning of the Jews from Christianity no doubt were hastened by this war. For some years the presence of uncircumcised Gentiles in the churches was a problem to Jews who held to the traditions. Those who held that Judaism was a nation as well as a religion insisted that Gentile converts be inducted into the nation. Jewish Christians had been forced to recognize that Gentiles were actually converted and that the Holy Spirit actually came upon them. But patriotism is never so tested as in the time of war. Concessions in the time of peace may be overlooked, but in war they are construed as treason. So, when the Jews were locked in a death struggle with Rome, the lines were sharply drawn. The middle wall of partition between Jew and non-Jew was insisted upon more strongly than ever. The Christians stayed out of the Jewish-Roman War, seeing that the true destiny of neither Jew nor Christian was to be realized through physical warfare. Few Jewish converts to Christianity seem to have been made after the war. From that point on the movement became increasingly Gentile.

The book of Acts seemingly was written during or soon after the Jewish-Roman War, probably just after. Acts was probably written when it was already becoming clear that the Jews were turning from Christianity. Luke is not so much arguing that Christianity should embrace the Gentile as showing how a movement which initially was Jewish had become Gentile. The Gospel of Luke traces back to Jesus the impulses and principles which gradually were expressed in his followers. Acts shows the outcome of this and what it meant for the Gentile in his inclusion and for the Jew in his self-exclusion.

AUTHORSHIP AND SOURCES

IT WAS FIRMLY BELIEVED in the second century that Luke, the beloved physician (Col. 4: 14), wrote the Gospel of Luke and the book of Acts. This ancient tradition has been challenged many times in the past century, but it remains by far the most plausible position. Luke and Acts are anonymous, as are all the Gospels, thus making no claim for themselves as to authorship. Apparently Luke was not prominent in the early Christian community, so it is not likely that authorship of these important and extensive writings would have been arbitrarily ascribed to him. It is understandable that the anonymous letter to the Hebrews would be arbitrarily ascribed to so forceful and prolific a writer as Paul, but this would not account for ascribing this two-volume work to Luke. The most satisfactory explanation for the early belief is that Luke actually wrote the two volumes.

The anti-Marcionite Prologue to Luke (*ca.* A.D. 160-180) identifies the author of the Gospel as Luke, an Antiochian of Syria, a physician by profession; and then it adds that "the same Luke afterwards wrote the Acts of the Apostles." [25] The Canon of Muratori (*ca.* A.D. 170) states that "Luke compiled for 'most excellent Theophilus' what things were done in detail in his presence." [26] Irenaeus and Clement of Alexandria both explicitly ascribe Acts to Luke, and Tertullian and Origen do so by implication, since they hold Luke to be the author of the Gospel.[27] This tradition was unchallenged until modern times.

Some sections of Acts are written in the first person and are

---

[25] Cf. Bruce, *op. cit.*, pp. 1 and 6f.
[26] Tr. by Henry J. Cadbury, *The Beginnings of Christianity*, ed. by F. J. Foakes-Jackson and Kirsopp Lake (London: Macmillan and Co., 1922), II, 211.
[27] Cf. Bruce, *op. cit.*, p. 1.

known as the "we" sections (cf. Acts 16: 10-17; 20: 5-15; 21: 1-18; 27: 1 to 28: 16).[28] Though some have argued to the contrary, the author of the "we" sections was most likely the author of Acts. The author of Acts certainly used sources, written and oral, in the Gospel and Acts; but one of his sources was his own personal experience. He plainly states that he was not a personal witness to much about which he wrote, but he does claim to have been a witness to and participant in some of the events. A writer so careful to acknowledge his sources (cf. Luke 1: 1-4) would not have been so crude as to incorporate another's diary into his own work without even changing the narratives from first to third person. Whoever wrote "we" also wrote the book.

A strong case can be made for the tradition which links the Luke in Paul's letters (Col. 4: 14, Philemon 24, and 2 Tim. 4: 11) with the author of the "we" sections. The Pauline letters, such as Colossians and Philemon, which represent Luke as being with Paul were probably written in Rome, and the "we" sections of Acts represent Luke as being with Paul in Rome at that time. (2 Timothy, of course, was not written until after the period covered by Acts, so it is not a factor here.) The author of the "we" sections was not with Paul at Corinth or Ephesus, and the Pauline letters written from those cities make no mention of Luke. Though this evidence is not conclusive, it is certainly congenial with the traditional position that Luke, Paul's companion, was the author of Acts, including the "we" sections.

Martin Dibelius, whatever his conclusions otherwise, is positive in his conclusion not only that Luke wrote both the Gospel and Acts but that the same author wrote the "they" passages and the "we" passages of Acts: "The 'they-passages' [Sie-Stücke] and the 'we-passages' [Wir-Stücke] in word selection and style appear very similar—so similar, that we have no right to ascribe them to different authors." [29]

If, indeed, Luke wrote Acts, and only unwarranted scepticism refuses to consider that as probable, we have the witness of one

---

[28] Cf. Morton S. Enslin, *Christian Beginnings* (New York: Harper and Brothers, 1938), p. 416.
[29] *Op. cit.,* p. 119.

who was a participant in much about which he wrote and who had access to many who shared in the other events of which he wrote. In the author, whoever he was, we have one who sought always to be honest and accurate in his work. He set forth in his preface (Luke 1: 1-4) his purpose to rely upon firsthand accounts. In both Gospel and Acts he used primitive sources for those events to which he was not a personal witness. He used Mark and other sources, written and oral, in the Gospel. The first fifteen chapters of Acts were probably based on such sources. Whether these sources were written or oral, they certainly were primitive. Much of the material of the early chapters perhaps circulated first in Aramaic, the language of Palestinian Jews, and then in Greek. Many have claimed that actual documents in Aramaic stand behind the Greek of the early chapters of Acts.[30] This may or may not be true; at least it seems that some of the stories of those chapters were once told in Aramaic and the discourses spoken in Aramaic. In other words, this is not material newly created by Luke but old material from the life of the earliest Christians.

Luke had access to many trustworthy witnesses and likely received information from such persons as James, the half-brother of Jesus; Peter; Paul; Barnabas; Mark; Philip, one of the seven; Mnason, a disciple since the beginning (Acts 21: 16); and possibly from Mary, the mother of Jesus. Visits to Jerusalem and two years at Caesarea, along with other travels, would provide abundant information and stimulation to write. While in Palestine, Luke had opportunity to become thoroughly acquainted with the oral tradition[31] of early Christians. Long before the earliest Gospel was written, Christians were repeating again

[30] Matthew Black, *An Aramaic Approach to the Gospels and Acts* (second edition; Oxford: Clarendon Press, 1954), offers the most recent and probably the most careful work on this difficult subject upon which few are competent to write. In his survey of results, he includes the following: "The most likely places where Semitic sources were used by Luke, apart from the sayings of Jesus, are in the first two chapters of his Gospel and in the speeches of Peter and Stephen in the early chapters of Acts." (p. 207).

[31] "Tradition" is used in a technical sense, with no suggestion whatever that these materials were fictional. The tradition included all that was transmitted: the information, but also interpretation, spirit, and all else that characterized the Christian group. Cf. 2 Thess. 2: 15; 3: 6.

and again the stories and the discourses which meant so much to them. This does not mean that finished books came from Luke's pen immediately, but work was begun which ultimately resulted in the immeasurably great books, Luke and Acts.

Much has been written about the speeches in Acts, many concluding that they are strictly Luke's own productions. It is claimed that Greek historians like Thucydides invented speeches suited to the occasions with which they dealt. But Thucydides did not say that he invented speeches. He acknowledged that he did not pretend to recite them in all their exactness, but he sought to give what might have been pertinently said on each occasion. At least he was concerned with actual speeches heard by himself or repeated to him by others (cf. *History of the Peloponnesian War*, I, 22).

Luke's pattern in handling speeches can be tested in the Gospels. In his Gospel, Luke reproduced the speeches drawn from Mark with striking accuracy. He took less liberty in changing the wording of the speeches than in changing the narratives taken from Mark. It may reasonably be concluded that he was equally careful in reporting the speeches in Acts. How Luke had access to all the speeches he reports is not clear, though it is not difficult to suggest possible sources for many of them. Some of them he may have heard, some could have been secured from written notes or oral reports. Rackham rightly observes that the speeches "are all exactly suitable to the occasion and are distinctly coloured by the particular and local circumstances." [32]

This is not to suggest that the speeches are verbatim reports; that was not contemplated or thought necessary. We, today, are insistent upon exact reproduction in direct quotations, but the first century did not have that concern. It is an easy observation in the study of the Synoptic Gospels, as any harmony will show, to see that no attempt was made at verbatim accuracy. Matthew, Mark, and Luke reproduce many of the discourses of Jesus, and each takes the liberty to make word changes. The same pattern can be demonstrated in Acts, in the stories of Paul's conversion. The story of Paul's conversion is given three times in Acts, in

[32] Rackham. *ob. cit.*. p. xliii.

chapters 9, 22, and 26, with minor variations in each. To cite no more, one may compare the statement in 9: 5-6 with the one in 22: 10. In 9: 5-6 we read, "I am Jesus whom you persecute, but stand up and enter into the city, and it will be spoken to you, that which it is necessary for you to do." In 22: 10 we read, "And the Lord said to me, standing up, go into Damascus, and there to you it will be spoken concerning all of which it has been ordained for you to do." [33] What Paul heard was in Aramaic, so the Greek accounts are translations, which in part explains the differences. But, apart from this, it is clear that the New Testament writers were not slaves to verbatim reporting of speeches. They were concerned to reproduce correctly the substance of a speech, or even to interpret a speech, but they were not concerned to satisfy modern standards of writing.

---

[33] Translations are the author's, and attempt is made to bring out the word order in the Greek, showing differences.

The Acts of the Apostles

LUKE'S PREFACE [1: 1-5]

1 In the first book, O Theophilus, I have dealt with all that Jesus began to do and teach, 2 until the day when he was taken up, after he had given commandment through the Holy Spirit to the apostles whom he had chosen. 3 To them he presented himself alive after his passion by many proofs, appearing to them during forty days, and speaking of the kingdom of God. 4 And while staying with them he charged them not to depart from Jerusalem, but to wait for the promise of the Father, which he said, "you heard from me, 5 for John baptized with water, but before many days you shall be baptized with the Holy Spirit." [1]

IN BOTH the preface to Luke (which may actually be the preface to Luke-Acts) and the preface to Acts, the author gives an informal description of his work as having to do with the things accomplished among the early Christians through what Jesus did and taught (Luke 1: 1 and Acts 1: 1).[2] When Luke wrote, already the issues with which he was concerned had emerged with force, and in an important respect the course of Christianity had been determined; Christianity had already asserted its inherent universalism,[3] having broken out of the narrow limitations in which

---

[1] Unless otherwise indicated, the English translation used will be that of the *Revised Standard Version* (New York: Thomas Nelson and Sons, 1952), and the Greek text used will be that of D. Eberhard Nestle (revised by his son, D. Erwin Nestle, twentieth edition; New York: American Bible Society, 1950). These texts will repeatedly be but points of departure as direct appeal will be made to textual evidence, and fresh translation will be made necessary.

[2] Cf. Kirsopp Lake and Henry J. Cadbury, *The Acts of the Apostles*, Vol. IV, *The Beginnings of Christianity* (London: Macmillan and Co., Ltd., 1933), p. 2.

[3] A friendly critic suggested that the word "universalism" be avoided because of the odium attached to "isms" and its theological abuse. The word is a good one, however, and must be retained. Many "isms" are excellent, e.g. "evangelism" and "baptism." By "universalism" this writer means the recognition of humanity above nationality and race; he does not use the term, as do some, to claim that eventually all people will be saved. By "particularism" he means the narrow concern for one's own nation or race above the claims of humanity.

28

many would have confined it. When Luke wrote, the Christian movement had largely dissociated itself from the nationalistic coloring of much messianic hope and had already embraced great numbers of uncircumcised Gentiles. A movement which seemed to be completely Jewish at its birth had in the amazingly brief span of a few decades become predominantly Gentile.

Luke does not need so much to plead for world missions as to tell how Christianity became a world movement and to justify that fact. This universalism was to be traced back to the intention of Jesus himself as reflected in what he did and said. Luke, then, is interpreting history, "the things accomplished among us." His special purpose is to demonstrate that in transcending considerations of nationality, race, and the legalism which supported the narrow particularism of many Jews and Jewish Christians, Christianity was true to the intention of Jesus. In Acts he shows that it was the risen Lord himself who, through the Holy Spirit, was guiding his followers through painful steps to the recognition that the kingdom was spiritual and universal in nature.

Luke is careful to stress that the work through the Spirit is the continuing work of Jesus. He shows that Jesus, after his resurrection, appeared to his disciples over a period of forty days and was clearly the dominant force in the movement. He was the one who commanded his followers to await the baptism in the Holy Spirit which had been promised by the Father. Jesus, then, was as vitally related to the postresurrection movement as to the movement before his death. The movement that became world-wide, throwing off national limitations, was the very movement which Jesus initiated and sustained.

During the forty days of his appearances to the disciples, he spoke the things concerning the "kingdom of God." He did not simply speak about the kingdom of God, but he spoke the things pertaining to it; that is, he declared its nature and its scope; he stamped his character upon it. The kingdom of God is primarily the reign of God. In Jesus, God is asserting uniquely and finally his sovereign claims upon man. Men everywhere are called upon to recognize and yield to the kingship of God, becoming his willing subjects. For all he had spoken of the "kingdom," his followers yet had much to learn about its nature. They still thought that the kingdom of God would be expressed through the Jewish nation.

To summarize, in verse 1, Luke reminds the reader that in his first [4] book, he had presented Jesus and what he initiated in terms of what he did and said. (What he did and said are inseparable. What he did is to be interpreted by what he said, and what he said is to be interpreted by what he did.) That with which Luke is to deal in Acts is rooted in the historical Jesus, and what developed in the Christian movement did so because of what Jesus had done and said. Many commentaries virtually explain away as meaningless the word "began," but this probably loses a vital point. The one who initiated the movement is yet directing it. In verse 2, Luke stresses the pre-ascension command of Jesus to the apostles (Luke 24: 49). The expression "through the Holy Spirit" may be connected with the commanding or the choosing of the apostles; the Greek allows either. Although the former is more natural to the Greek sentence, the latter is more natural otherwise. The apostles were of his selection, and he commissioned them. For all this, however, these very apostles on many points struggled against his plain teaching and against the leading of the Spirit. Verse 3 stresses the fact that for forty days Jesus made himself visible to them and gave demonstrating proofs that he was alive and in their midst.[5] During these days he spoke the things that pertain to the kingdom, shaping it and declaring its character and object. Jesus, then, was vitally linked with and personally responsible for the movement both before and after his death. Luke asserts that Jesus was the one who

---

[4] Luke's use of the term "first" does not necessarily imply that a third volume was contemplated. The Greek superlative was often used for the comparative, as is true in English. One speaks of the "first" floor of a house with only two stories; grammarians do not like the practice, but the people do.

[5] Verse 4 presents a translation problem in the word rendered in the RSV "while staying with them" and in other versions "while eating with them." The Greek is uncertain as to derivation. It may have the meaning of "assembling," "eating salt with," or simply "eating with." The problem is yet more complicated if all manuscript readings are considered. Cullmann insists, possibly with unwarranted certainty, that the reading should be "took salt with," i.e., ate with them, citing in support Latin, Syriac, and Coptic renderings of the term. Cf. *Urchristentum und Gottesdienst* (Zurich: Zwingli-Verlag, 1950), p. 19.

gave the command that the disciples remain in Jerusalem and await the Father's promise of the Spirit. Jesus, then, was the directing force in these things accomplished among them. Jesus, not Paul or any other, was responsible for the movement which became world-wide.

Some time after the above lines were written, the conclusion of Dibelius concerning the significance that Luke sees in the conversion of Cornelius was observed: "The idea that the heathen without legal obligation are made fellow members in [einzugliedern] the church springs not from Paul and not from Peter, but from God." [6] Again, arguing that Luke shows himself to be a historian in his concern for the "directional significance" (Richtungssinn) of an event, Dibelius says: "But Luke wants to show [i.e., through the Spirit's overriding of both Peter's prejudices relating to Cornelius and Paul's desire to go to Bithynia] that the destiny of Christianity in the final analysis was not determined by the apostle Paul, or by men at all, but by a superhuman power." [7]

The promise of the Father which they had heard from him and for which they were to wait was apparently the one presented in Luke 24: 49. It is not a passive waiting that is pictured but a positive one. Probably the verse in Luke, to which Acts 1: 4 seems to point, should be translated: "And behold, I will send the promise of my Father upon you; but remain in the city until you get yourselves clothed with power from on high." The work before them would be so heavy in its demands that nothing short of this power could equip them for it. It was not a task for weakness and fear, but for those living in the presence and power of the Holy Spirit.

The baptism in the Holy Spirit which Jesus' disciples were to anticipate, a baptism which was contrasted with John's baptism in water (1: 5), is to be understood in terms of the obvious reference to John's witness found in Luke 3: 16–17: "I baptize you with water; but he who is mightier than I is coming, the thong of whose sandals I am not worthy to untie; he will baptize

---

[6] Martin Dibelius, op. cit., p. 107.
[7] Ibid., pp. 115f.

you with the Holy Spirit and with fire." John's baptism was characterized by repentance (Luke 3: 3), and he clearly did not think of it as having any efficacy in itself, else he would not have refused it to so many (Luke 3: 7). This water baptism was offered only to those who gave evidence that they had already repented (Luke 3: 8).

However, John looked beyond this to a "baptism" in the Holy Spirit and in fire (Luke 3: 16). Acts 1: 5 apparently refers to this. Baptism in the Holy Spirit on the day of Pentecost thus meant a fuller release of power in and through those who already were Christians. This is not to be understood as their first encounter with the Spirit. They were Christians already, and it is inconceivable that they could have been brought to repentance and faith apart from the Spirit. They were ones already born not only of water but of the Spirit (cf. John 3: 5). Paul described Christian conversion—not some subsequent blessing—in saying: "For by one Spirit we were all baptized into one body—Jews or Greeks, slaves or free—and all were made to drink of one Spirit" (1 Cor. 12: 13).

This baptism in the Spirit as it related to the disciples on Pentecost, then, is a further experience in which the Spirit gained a fuller possession of them. The coming of the Spirit, of course, would not be a physical movement of the Spirit; he was already there. The change would be one effected in the disciples. They would become fully awakened to his presence and more receptive to his presence and power. In Caesarea, the Spirit came upon God-fearing Greeks as they heard the gospel, and Peter recognized this as another fulfilment of Jesus' promise (Acts 11: 16). There the conversion and the mighty release of power, paralleling that of Pentecost, came together.

The New Testament is far from clear concerning the gift of the Holy Spirit, but the pattern can be somewhat discerned. The water baptism of John is clearly distinguished from the baptism of the Spirit. Later, it seems that the gift of the Spirit is associated with Christian baptism (cf. Acts 19: 3 and 1 Cor. 12: 13); yet even here it is not made dependent upon water baptism. In Samaria (Acts 8: 15ff.), the Spirit came with the laying on of hands by the apostles *after* the Samaritans had been baptized by Philip. Apparently, there was no repetition of water baptism. In Caesarea (Acts 10: 44–48) the Spirit came upon Cornelius and his companions *before* they were baptized and apart from the laying on of hands. In Ephesus (Acts 19: 1–7) the Spirit came upon a group of about twelve men *after* they were baptized in the name of Jesus and after Paul laid hands upon them; they previously had been baptized "into John's baptism." (See further on pages 120f. and 195ff.)

The baptism in fire (Luke 3: 16 and Matt. 3: 11 but not in Mark 1: 8 or Acts 1: 5; 11: 16) is probably to be understood in terms of the verse following, as the separating of the wheat from the chaff. John's water baptism, within limits, marked off the true from the false in that he was discriminating in this baptism, offering it only to those who brought forth fruits indicating repentance. However, as careful as John or any baptizer might be, there would still be some false ones who would secure water baptism. This baptism was not final in its marking off the saved from the lost. Nevertheless, there was a baptism beyond that, a baptism "in the Holy Spirit and fire," that could not be misapplied; such baptism would invariably separate wheat from chaff. The great event of which John spoke would involve the pouring out of the Holy Spirit upon the faithful (the "wheat" of Matt. 3: 12 and Luke 3: 17) and the judgment of the ungodly (the "chaff" of the same verses).[8]

A brief word may be in order about Theophilus, to whom the two volumes were addressed. This was not an uncommon name, used by Greeks, Romans, Egyptians, and Jews,[9] and meaning something like "friend of God." Although debatable, it is here probably a proper name for a real person known to Luke rather than merely an ideal "friend of God." The title "most excellent" is found in Luke 1: 4 but not here. It is generally held that Theophilus was not a disciple when addressed as "most excellent Theophilus," for early Christians did not use such titles for one

---

[8] C. K. Barrett, *The Holy Spirit and the Gospel Tradition* (New York: The Macmillan Co., 1947), p. 126.
[9] Lake and Cadbury, *Commentary*, p. 2.

another. Its presence in the Gospel and absence in Acts has led
some to the conclusion that Theophilus was not a Christian when
the Gospel was written but was one when Acts was written.[10]
This may be true, but it is probably too much to assume that it
is established. More important than any of this is the evidence,
in the mention of Theophilus at the outset of both the Gospel
and Acts, for a close relation between the two volumes. They are
not only two volumes by one author; they constitute two parts
of one work.

---

[10] Cf. R. C. H. Lenski, *Interpretation of the Acts of the Apostles* (Columbus, Ohio: The Wartburg Press, 1944), p. 21.

PART ONE

The Hebrew Church: Christian Judaism

[1: 6 to 6: 7]

THEME: NARROW NATIONALISM OR A SPIRITUAL AND UNIVERSAL KINGDOM [1: 6-8]

6 So when they had come together they asked him, "Lord, will you at this time restore the kingdom to Israel ?" 7 He said to them, "It is not for you to know times or seasons which the Father has fixed by his own authority. 8 But you shall receive power when the Holy Spirit has come upon you; and you shall be my witnesses in Jerusalem and in all Judea and Samaria and to the end of the earth."

IMMEDIATELY we are introduced to the narrow conception of the disciples from which Christianity had to free itself: "Lord, will you at this time restore the kingdom to Israel?" It was assumed that the kingdom belonged to Israel; the question had to do with the time of its realization. No doubt the disciples had been freed by this time from the earlier idea of a temporal and political kingdom—the crucifixion forced them to abandon cruder kingdom ideas—but they still placed a national interpretation upon the kingdom. Somehow, they felt, the kingdom would expand within Judaism, and Judaism was to them a nation as well as a religion.

Jesus replied, in substance, that the kingdom will be the disciples' when they, under the power of the Holy Spirit, witness to the ends of the earth. "It is not for you to know the times or seasons which the Father has fixed by his own authority," he said to them (1: 7). That is, the kingdom will not come by rules of the calendar, but through witnessing to the ends of the earth by men empowered by the Holy Spirit. This is set over against the selfish expectation that God would deliver the kingdom to the disciples because of their being Israel according to the flesh. Jesus sought to turn them from national ambition to world missions. Acts presents the struggle between these two ideas and interests. Sadly enough, as Professor John Macmurray has said, "The Hebrew community to whom Jesus appealed to undertake the task was not prepared to sink its individual identity in a universal fellowship." [1]

The statement in verse 8, "and you shall be my witnesses in Jerusalem and in all Judea and Samaria and to the end of the earth," has been popularly accepted as the outline for Acts and the indication of Luke's purpose. Certainly this provides some framework against which Luke wrote, but it by no means indicates his major point of interest. Contrary to commentaries old and new, Luke did not show how the gospel traveled from Jerusalem to Rome. We do not know until this day how the gospel reached Rome, Damascus, Cyprus, Cyrene, Antioch of Syria, Ephesus, Troas, Corinth, Crete, or innumerable other places. Luke did not give this information because, apparently, his purpose was in another direction.

This is not to say that in Acts great attention was not given to geographical expansion; to the contrary, Christians were presented as on the move constantly. Travels and campaigns were described throughout the book. That is obvious. It is urged here, however, that to be preoccupied with this factor is to miss a greater one—the very one which Luke seemed most concerned to present. The boundaries most difficult to cross—then as now— were religious, national, and racial, not geographical. *It is easier today to send missionaries to Africa than to have fellowship across racial lines at home.* From Acts it is obvious that Christianity easily moved from Jerusalem, Judea and Samaria, and to the end of the earth, but in so doing it precipitated the issue which led to the ultimate break between synagogue and church, and to the self-exclusion of the very people of whom Christianity was born.

---

[1] John Macmurray, *Conditions of Freedom* (London: Faber and Faber Ltd., 1950). p. 97.

RAPID GROWTH OF CHRISTIAN JUDAISM
[1: 9 to 6: 7]

The Ascension of Jesus [1: 9-11]

9 And when he had said this, as they were looking on, he was lifted up, and a cloud took him out of their sight. 10 And while they were gazing into heaven as he went, behold, two men stood by them in white robes, 11 and said, "Men of Galilee, why do you stand looking into heaven? This Jesus, who was taken up from you into heaven, will come in the same way as you saw him go into heaven."

LUKE'S DESCRIPTION of the ascension is a touching though reserved one. The disciples gazed longingly as though their eyes and hearts were carried away into heaven with Jesus.[2] The Revised Standard Version follows the most generally accepted manuscripts, but a strong case could be made for the text preserved in Codex Bezae (a fifth century manuscript). Verse 9 in this ancient manuscript reads: "And these things saying, a cloud received him and he was taken up from their eyes." This would imply that a cloud enveloped him as he stood on earth, rather than as he was ascending, and he thus was removed from their sight.[3] In either case the disciples remained gazing into heaven until their attention was redirected by the two men in white robes (presumably angels). Personal privilege in a great experience carries with it a stewardship responsibility, and the disciples were turned from that scene to the work at hand. Blessings are to be shared or lost.

The promise of the return of Jesus in the manner of his ascension obviously referred to his coming at the end of the age. It also proved true, however, that the disciples realized most his abiding presence precisely when they shared him with others in their daily witnessing. Even as they awaited his return they learned the truth of the promises: "Where two or three are gathered in my name, there am I in the midst of them" and "Lo, I

---

[2] R. J. Knowling, "The Acts of the Apostles," W. Robertson Nicoll, editor, *The Expositor's Greek Testament* (Grand Rapids, Michigan: Wm. B. Eerdmans Publishing Co., n.d.) II, 57.

[3] C. S. C. Williams, *Alterations to the Text of the Synoptic Gospels and Acts* (Oxford: Basil Blackwell, 1951), p. 75.

am with you always, to the close of the age." In the New Testament are found both a futurist and a realized eschatology: Jesus is to come and yet he is here. His reign is realized and yet awaits its consummation at his return at the end of the age.

Only Acts in the New Testament tells of the forty days between the resurrection and the ascension. From Paul it would appear that Jesus was raised in a spiritual body (as contrasted with a flesh and blood body) and that his appearances were those of a heavenly being, for he argued that flesh and blood cannot inherit the kingdom of God.[4] Resurrection and ascension are apparently not distinguished in Paul. From John one would get the impression that the ascension to the Father followed his appearance to Mary Magdalene, to whom he said: "Do not hold me, for I have not yet ascended to the Father" (John 20: 17). Jesus had given the promise (John 16: 7): "If I do not go away, the Comforter will not come to you, but if I go, I will send him to you." This promise was apparently fulfilled when he appeared later to the disciples (cf. John 20: 22f.). John, then, seems to imply that the ascension took place between the appearances to Mary and the disciples.[5] Luke and John emphasize that Jesus was raised in the same body in which he was buried (cf. Luke 24: 39 and John 20: 27ff.). Even here, however, the picture is not clear. John 20: 26 gives the impression that Jesus entered the room through closed doors, but the next verse points to the wounds in his hands and side. One reference suggests a spiritual body and the other a material one. It should be admitted that we lack answers to many questions.

According to Luke the purpose of the forty days and the appearances of the risen Lord apparently was to demonstrate the fact of the resurrection (Acts 1: 2) and to give further instruction to the disciples (Acts 1: 3). The ascension was declared necessary in order that his followers might receive the Holy Spirit (Acts 2: 33; John 16: 7; 20: 22f.). The visible, tangible, risen Jesus withdrew that they might realize more fully his presence and power as the returning Lord, recognized as the

---

[4] Lake and Cadbury, *Additional Notes*, p. 17.
[5] *Ibid.*, p. 19.

Holy Spirit. Paul and John virtually equate the risen Lord and the Spirit. Although the easy interchange between the reference to the risen Lord Jesus and the Holy Spirit is most apparent in John and Paul, the same may be found elsewhere. In Mark 13: 11, the promise is given that in persecution and trial they need not be anxious beforehand about what to say: "For it is not you who speak, but the Holy Spirit." In the parallel passage in Luke 21: 15, Jesus himself is represented as saying, "For I will give you a mouth and wisdom." The Great Commission in Matthew 28: 18-20 is accompanied with the promise, "And lo, I am with you always, to the close of the age." Surely this presence of the risen Christ is to be thought of in terms of the Spirit.

Christians worship one God, not three. The very God who revealed Himself in Jesus of Nazareth is the God whose presence is known in the Holy Spirit. The risen Christ is one with the Spirit. In Romans 8: 9-11, for example, Paul speaks of the Spirit, the Spirit of God, the Spirit of Christ, and Christ with no apparent distinction. This is not to say that the New Testament does not distinguish between the risen Christ and the Holy Spirit, but it is to insist that whatever distinction is made is one that it can set aside at any moment in recognizing their oneness. Paul could even write: "The Lord is the Spirit" (2 Cor. 3: 17).

A minor problem arises in connection with the place of the ascension. Luke 24: 50-51 indicates Bethany as the place where Jesus departed from the disciples and was carried up into heaven. Acts 1: 12 seems to imply that the ascension took place on the mount called Olivet. To Luke the two may have been virtually identified as in Luke 19: 29 (following Mark 11: 1) where they are mentioned together. This may follow in Luke 21: 37 where Jesus is said to have spent the nights on Olivet, whereas Mark (11: 11f.; 14: 3) indicates that it was at Bethany.[6]

Early Christians were firm in the conviction that Jesus arose from the dead, that he was in communication with his disciples after his resurrection, and that he would visibly return to them. Primitive Christianity cannot be understood apart from these

---

[6] Lake and Cadbury, *Additional Notes*, p. 21.

convictions. Early Christians expected Jesus to return in their time, and in each generation since, many have looked for his immediate return. Though Christians in each age have been mistaken about the time of his return, the expectation of an early return has done much good as well as harm. Christians, so it would seem, should feel Jesus to be so near that he could make himself visible at any time, but this should not lead to unfortunate attitudes and deportment such as obtained at Thessalonica. Christians are to expect his return, but they disobey his command when they try to predict the time of his return. It is unfortunate when preoccupation with his return renders secondary the sense of his presence.

Waiting in Jerusalem [1: 12-14]

12 Then they returned to Jerusalem from the mount called Olivet, which is near Jerusalem, a sabbath day's journey away; 13 and when they had entered, they went up to the upper room, where they were staying, Peter and John and James and Andrew, Philip and Thomas, Bartholomew and Matthew, James the son of Alphaeus and Simon the Zealot and Judas the son of James. 14 All these with one accord devoted themselves to prayer, together with the women and Mary the mother of Jesus, and with his brothers.

The atmosphere of this paragraph is Jewish and takes the reader back to primitive Christianity; Luke is surely following a primitive source, whether written or oral. The "sabbath day's journey" is a Jewish description, referring to the restriction of Jewish travel on the sabbath to two thousand cubits (about half a mile) measured from the city walls.

The "upper room" may have been in the home of John Mark; if so, that would in part account for Mark's acquaintance with Christian history. Possibly this room was the scene of the Last Supper. It is clear from Acts 12: 12 that the house of Mary, the mother of John Mark, was later a meeting place for Christians in Jerusalem, so it is at least possible that these early meetings were there, too.

The eleven, with others, are listed here. There are three other lists of the apostles (Mark 3: 16-19; Matt. 10: 2-4; Luke 6: 13-16). There is some difficulty in correlating some of the names in the four lists,[7] and most of the twelve apostles are little more than names to us. It is strange that almost nothing is known of most of the twelve; the elaborate second century apocryphal stories about the twelve are unconvincing and reflect the fact that almost nothing was known of them shortly after the first age of Christianity. The most plausible answer to this almost incredible puzzle is implied by the book of Acts—most of the twelve seem never to have gotten beyond a national outlook. Particularists perish with the little world in which they imprison themselves. At least, it must be said, there is no evidence that most of the twelve ever entered with any enthusiasm into world missions.

The family of Jesus is mentioned at this point. Mary, the mother of Jesus, is not again mentioned in Acts, and only John mentions her in connection with the death and resurrection of Jesus. She was perhaps highly esteemed as the mother of Jesus, but there is no evidence that she was a dominant figure. The brothers are unnamed here, but are named in Mark 6: 3 (James, Joses, Judas, and Simon). Paul tells of the appearance of Jesus to James (1 Cor. 15: 7), and it was probably then that he was converted. It is assumed that the James of whom Paul wrote is also the James so prominent in Acts, but there is no explicit statement to that effect. It is further assumed that the James so prominent in Acts is also the brother of Jesus, but that also is not explicit.

The "brothers of the Lord" were surely the sons of Mary, though other theories have been argued. Epiphanius, in the fourth century, argued that these were the sons of Joseph by a former marriage. This theory may have arisen as early as the second century, when apocryphal legends were growing up around the family of Jesus. The view is championed by some who want to believe in the perpetual virginity of Mary. Jerome, also of the fourth century, contended that these were not brothers, but cousins. Helvidius, a contemporary to Jerome, accepted the term "brothers" in a literal sense; certainly the New Testament

---

[7] Cf. A. T. Robertson, *A Harmony of the Gospels for Students of the Life of Christ* (New York: Harper and Brothers, 1922), pp. 271-273, for a careful comparative study of the four lists. Also see Lake and Cadbury, *Additional Notes*, pp. 41ff.

has not the faintest suggestion that the term is to be taken otherwise. There is no evidence that Joseph was previously married, and the New Testament has no sympathy with the ideas of the perpetual virginity of Mary or of celibacy as a virtue above marriage.

Verse 15 gives the number of disciples as about one hundred and twenty. This is apparently the number of Christians, mostly Galileans, who had come together at Jerusalem. Paul states that Jesus appeared to over five hundred brethren at one time (1 Cor. 15: 6), so evidently there was a larger following outside Jerusalem. Acts implies that there were other Christians in Palestine.[8] This is another evidence that Luke's concern is not to trace the geographical expansion of Christianity; he passes over the stories of many Christian communities with which he doubtless was acquainted.

Election of Matthias, Witness to the Resurrection [1: 15-26]

15 In those days Peter stood up among the brethren (the company of persons was in all about a hundred and twenty), and said, 16 "Brethren, the scripture had to be fulfilled, which the Holy Spirit spoke beforehand by the mouth of David, concerning Judas who was guide to those who arrested Jesus. 17 For he was numbered among us, and was allotted his share in this ministry. 18 (Now this man bought a field with the reward of his wickedness; and falling headlong he burst open in the middle and all his bowels gushed out. 19 And it became known to all the inhabitants of Jerusalem, so that the field was called in their language Akeldama, that is, Field of Blood.) 20 For it is written in the book of Psalms,

'Let his habitation become desolate,
and let there be no one to live in it';

and

'His office let another take.'

21 So one of the men who have accompanied us during all the time that the Lord Jesus went in and out among us, 22 beginning from the baptism of John until the day when he was taken up from us—one of these men must become with us a witness to his resurrection." 23 And they put forward two, Joseph called Barsabbas, who was surnamed Justus, and Matthias. 24 And they prayed and said, "Lord, who knowest the hearts of all men, show which one of these two thou hast chosen 25 to take the place in this ministry and

---

[8] Cf. Acts 9: 31.

apostleship from which Judas turned aside, to go to his own place."
26 And they cast lots for them, and the lot fell on Matthias; and he
was enrolled with the eleven apostles.

Peter.—Symeon or Simon is best known in the New Testament
and to us as Peter. Symeon was his Hebrew name, used only in
Acts 15: 14 and in some manuscripts of 2 Peter 1: 1. Simon, the
Greek name, appears frequently in the Gospels and several times
in Acts. Cullmann suggests that Peter may have been given the
Hebrew name Symeon and the Greek name Simon from the outset (cf. Saul-Paul).[9] Simon was given the descriptive title,[10]
Cephas, an Aramaic word meaning "stone" or "rock" and translated into Greek as "Petros," hence into English as "Peter."

The prominence of Peter in the earliest Christian community
is a fact to be recognized; the sad truth that his name has been
exploited and his role distorted by a major church body should
not be permitted to obscure the true role of this great apostle.
It is an uncontested fact that Paul had such respect for Peter
that after his conversion he made a trip to Jerusalem to get
acquainted with him (Gal. 1: 18).

Peter's leadership in the Jerusalem church soon gave way to
that of another. Cullmann makes the important observation that
though Peter is commonly thought of in terms of church administration, he really exercised that function for only a short
time and then exchanged it for missionary work. He sums it up
clearly in saying, "Peter is not the archetype of the church official
but of the missionary."[11]

There are no grounds for holding that Peter was at any time
the bishop of Jerusalem in the later monarchical sense. He had
a recognized leadership role for a brief time until it was transferred to James, the brother of Jesus. The twelve throughout this
period exercised a distinctive role which in itself would have
ruled out any idea of a "monarchical episcopate." Beyond that,
the whole congregation exercised an authority which prohibited

[9] *Peter*, pp. 17f.
[10] *Ibid.*, p. 18.
[11] *Ibid.*, p. 41.

any such rule by one man as gradually emerged in succeeding centuries. It is equally clear that no episcopal authority was transferred from Jerusalem to Rome. We do not know when Christianity reached Rome; probably it reached there at a very early date, but without the presence of any apostle. Paul wrote to the Roman Christians several years before he first reached Rome. If Peter ever saw Rome, it was only after the church was well established. Cullmann [12] aptly points out the fact that Peter had assumed a missionary role and James had succeeded to the administrative role in Jerusalem before Paul wrote his letter to the Galatians. Whatever administrative role Peter had in Jerusalem fell to James and was not transferred to Rome. For some time Peter served as leader of the Jewish Christian mission under the direction of Christians at Jerusalem who looked to James as their leader. At Antioch of Syria, Peter was rebuked by Paul and feared those who came from James (cf. Gal. 2: 11f.). Clearly, Peter the missionary had no episcopal office to transfer from Jerusalem to Rome or elsewhere.

The twelve.—The selection of Matthias to serve with the eleven apostles points to the uniqueness of the twelve. Judas was replaced by Matthias, but there is no suggestion that this apostolate was to be perpetuated through successors. Bruce aptly observes:

It was his apostasy, not his death, that necessitated the filling of the vacancy; there is no suggestion of filling the vacancy left by the martyrdom of James the son of Zebedee (xii. 2).[13]

Hierarchical systems of later days are not to be read back into this simple situation. Foakes-Jackson suggests:

The word "bishopric" in the A.V., which Moffatt renders by *charge,* is perhaps an echo of the controversies as to church government in the sixteenth century, and is intended to emphasize the view that each Apostle had his own episcopate." [14]

The term thus translated by the Authorized Version (King

    [12] *Ibid.,* pp. 40ff.
    [13] Bruce, *op. cit.,* p. 76.
    [14] F. J. Foakes-Jackson, *The Acts of the Apostles* ("The Moffatt New Testament Commentary." New York: Harper and Brothers, 1931), p. 8.

James) literally means "overseership," but is not to be taken in a technical sense; it is used interchangeably with "ministry" (vs. 17 and 25) and "apostleship" (v. 25).[15]

The apostolate was not transferable; this is clear from its Hebrew origin as well as from New Testament history. Professor T. W. Manson, to whom this paragraph is owed, clearly demonstrates this important point.[16] The Hebrew equivalent of the Greek *apostolos* is *shaliach* from the verb *shalach* to send. The emphasis is on the sender rather than the one sent. The one who was sent was viewed as an extension of the personality of the sender. The *shaliach* (= *apostolos*) apparently could not transfer his commission to another. Manson cites an instance from the Mishnah (*Gittin* iii.6) where a *shaliach* became ill and was unable to complete his mission; the court appointed a new *shaliach* but made it clear that the new *shaliach* was the *shaliach* of the court and not *shaliach* of the original *shaliach*. In the same context, this author[17] cites the parallel maxim in English law: *Delegatus non potest delegare* (i.e., A delegate is not able to delegate.). *The shaliach* received a specific commission in the nature of a function rather than a status, and he could return the commission only to the one from whom he received it; he could not delegate it to another. The apostolate in the New Testament seems to follow this pattern. The idea of apostolic succession is foreign to the Hebrew background and to New Testament practice.

One is compelled to recognize a varied use of the term apostle in the New Testament. The twelve were apostles, and they had no successors (Judas being the apparent exception). Beyond the twelve were others recognized as apostles of the Lord. Paul claimed to be an apostle, commissioned directly by the Lord. James, the brother of Jesus, is alluded to as an apostle (Gal. 1: 19). Paul and Barnabas (Acts 14: 4, 14) and apparently Andronicus and Junias (Rom. 16: 7) are termed apostles. Yet a third usage appears in connection with apostles of churches. Addressing the Philippians (2: 25), Paul speaks of "your apostle."

---

[15] Cf. Bruce, *op. cit.*, p. 79.
[16] T. W. Manson, *The Church's Ministry* (London: Hodder and Stoughton Ltd., 1948), pp. 31–52.
[17] *Ibid.*, pp. 36f.

In 2 Corinthians 8: 23 he refers to the "apostles of the churches." These seemingly are distinguished from apostles of the Lord; that is, no claim is made for them that they were commissioned by the Lord himself. The rise of false prophets has been cited as evidence that the number of apostles was not fixed. This larger group was never confused with the twelve. None of these claimed to be of the twelve. When James was martyred there is no indication that his place was filled.

From our passage in Acts (1: 15-26) it is clear that there were three basic requirements for this "ministry and apostleship": one must have been of the men who had been in the following of Jesus from the baptism of John until the ascension (1: 21f.), he must have been a witness to the resurrection (1: 22), and he must have had the appointment of the Lord himself (1: 24f.). The eleven were appointed personally and immediately by Jesus, while the replacement for Judas was to be the Lord's own selection. Paul claimed that he was an apostle—"not from men nor through man, but through Jesus Christ and God the Father, who raised him from the dead" (Gal. 1: 1). Cullmann observes that on this issue Paul and his Judaizing opponents were of one opinion: "An apostle is one who is called through Christ *without mediation* [*ohne Vermittlung*], in other words: outside a chain of succession [*Traditionskette*]." [18] An apostle of the Lord received his commission directly from the incarnate Jesus or the risen Christ; it was therefore immediate, unique, and non-transferable.

In his book *Die Tradition* (as yet untranslated into English), Cullmann develops a strong argument for the normative force of the apostolic tradition, indicating at the same time the importance and function of these apostles of the Lord. Building upon the thesis advanced earlier in his *Christ and Time*, he argues that the period from the birth of Jesus until the death of the last apostles, that is, to the death of the last eyewitnesses who had seen the risen Jesus and who had received from the incarnate or the risen Jesus Christ an immediate and specific

---

[18] Oscar Cullmann, *Die Tradition als exegetisches, historisches und theologisches Problem* (Zurich: Zwingli-Verlag, 1954), p. 31. Tr. here from the German, which in turn was tr. from the French by Pierre Schönenberger.

commission, is the middle point of all redemption history (*Heilsgeschichte*). That middle period is the orientation point or norm by which each subsequent period is to be measured. Subsequent revelation is to be measured by the witness of that center with its immediate revelation (cf. especially p. 29). It is correct to recognize the continuing revelation through the Holy Spirit but false to think that it is independent of the normative period— the period of the eyewitnesses chosen and commissioned to witness to the life, death, and resurrection of Jesus.

Cullmann correctly points out that this apostolic witness is met in the New Testament.[19] Second-century Christians recognized that a unique period had terminated with the death of the last apostolic eyewitnesses, and they expressed their recognition of this fact by their efforts to form a New Testament canon. Only those writings which were thought to have come directly or indirectly from an apostle were recognized as cononical. (E.g., Mark and Luke, although not apostles, were thought to have been closely associated with Peter and Paul.) Every student knows something of the long struggle and debate over the canonical status of many writings (there has never been complete agreement in Christendom as to what writings are canonical), but, as Cullmann observes, the point remains that these second-century Christians recognized a difference between the apostolic witness and subsequent witness. However well or poorly Christians of the second century or since have distinguished between this apostolic witness and all later tradition, the significant point holds that *early Christians realized that the difference was there and that it was important.* The church itself recognized that this apostolic witness was the norm. The living Christ is thus encountered in this apostolic witness.[20]

Later church tradition can never have the value of this apostolic norm; it cannot become the norm. Cullmann states it succinctly: "One must not confuse *inspiration* [*Eingebung*] and the criterion of inspiration [*Kriterium der Eingebung*]." [21] For some years this writer, with less success, has sought to make this

[19] *Ibid.*, p. 34.
[20] *Ibid.*, pp. 34 f.
[21] *Ibid.*, p. 38.

very distinction, pointing to a two-fold danger: either a virtual
denial of the unique place of the Bible or a virtual denial of the
continuing inspiration of the Holy Spirit. One error leads one
to pay lip service only to continuing inspiration and to worship,
let us say, the King James Version of the Bible. The other error
leads one to pay lip service to the Bible and to come, for example,
to worship the virgin Mary on the basis of gradually emerging
dogmas which refuse to recognize the normative value of the
apostolic witness.

Selecting Matthias.—One cannot exaggerate the importance of
the requirement that the successor to Judas was to be a witness
to the resurrection of Jesus, one who had shared with the disciples
from the baptism of John until the ascension of Jesus. As already stated, the Christian movement is not to be understood
apart from the resurrection of Jesus; it was the most significant
fact in the experience of the Christian group. Without the resurrection, the movement would have died. The fact of the resurrection rallied the disciples and made them a dynamic group.
Everything stood or fell with the resurrection. But the resurrection did not lessen the importance of the life and death of
Jesus; it provided the light in which his life and death could be
seen and interpreted.

Extremists in form criticism[22] have erred in holding that
primitive Christians were so utterly lost in the expectancy of
the return of Jesus that they had no interest in his earthly life.
This story of the election of Matthias is explicit in its indication
of the importance of the earthly life of Jesus to the earliest
Christians. The account has every evidence of being primitive; it
reflects Jewish Christianity, not the rewriting of history at a
later date. These early Christians were watching the skies for a

---

[22] Form criticism is a method by which an attempt is made to recover the accounts
of the life and teaching of Jesus as they existed when transmitted orally. Its exponents, differing widely among themselves, have made major contributions in
calling attention to the importance of the years between the crucifixion and the
writing of the gospels, and in stressing the importance of thousands of eyewitnesses
in preserving these accounts. Some of them, however, have done a disservice even
to form criticism in their skepticism and radical conclusions.

returning Lord, but they were also repeating the stories of one whose life in the flesh could not be forgotten.

In selecting a successor to Judas, lots were cast. This was an ancient and familiar device, practiced by Jews and Gentiles alike. It was viewed as a means for finding God's will. Though there is no evidence that Christians used this method after Pentecost, there is no reason for explaining it away at this point. Lake and Cadbury[23] hold out the possibility that the meaning may be "gave their votes," which possibility is strengthened by the term translated "enrolled" or "numbered." This latter term may picture the casting of stones as ballots or votes. The idea of democratic voting is very appealing, but no conclusive case can be made for it here. The Roman soldiers at Golgotha cast lots for the robe of Jesus, and the identical term is used (Luke 23: 34); that was hardly a democratic election. Clearly, however, their dependence was not upon the lot itself, but upon God for whose guidance they prayed. When the lot fell on Matthias he was "enrolled" with the eleven apostles.

Judas.—There is an apparent disagreement between stories relating to the death of Judas. Acts represents Judas as having fallen headlong whereas Matthew says that he hanged himself. Both could be true, each being but a partial account of what happened. Possibly he hanged himself and later was cut loose or fell from the place of hanging. The point is a minor one and has no value in itself. A further apparent contradiction seems to be found between Matthew's account that the priests bought a field with the betrayal money and the statement in Acts that Judas "obtained a field from the reward of iniquity"; the Greek is better translated "obtained" than "bought." In a real sense Judas "obtained" it, even if the actual purchasing was done by the priests. The real value of Acts is neither diminished nor enhanced by the study of these peripheral questions; such questions can, however, serve as an escape, turning the censorious critic or die-hard

---

[23] *Commentary,* p. 15.

defender from the real issues by which he should be confronted and disciplined.

The Day of Pentecost [2: 1-47]

Filled with the Holy Spirit [2: 1-4]

> 1 When the day of Pentecost had come, they were all together in one place. 2 And suddenly a sound came from heaven like the rush of a mighty wind, and it filled all the house where they were sitting. 3 And there appeared to them tongues as of fire, distributed and resting on each one of them. 4 And they were all filled with the Holy Spirit and began to speak in other tongues, as the Spirit gave them utterance.

Pentecost came fifty days after the Passover, climaxing the week of weeks following the offering of the sheaf of the wave offering during the feast of unleavened bread (cf. Lev. 23: 15ff.). The day marked the close of the harvest, and it seems also to have commemorated the giving of the Law on Sinai. Some see in this the giving of the new law written by the Spirit on the hearts of men. The suggestion is attractive but cannot be established.

To Luke this presence of God in power in the Christian community is a turning point in the life of the community, taking its place among the most significant events of the sacred story. This coming of the Holy Spirit upon the Christian community on the day of Pentecost parallels the coming of the Holy Spirit upon Jesus at his baptism (Luke 3: 22). Divine guidance in terms of the Holy Spirit is a recurring emphasis in Acts, especially in the first half of the book. The Spirit's presence and power is stressed in connection with such occurrences as Pentecost (2: 4, 17, 33, 38), the defense before the Sanhedrin (4: 8), the assembly following the release of Peter (4: 31), the exposure of the sin of Ananias (5: 3), the choice of the seven (6: 3, 5), the defense of Stephen (7: 55f.), the consummation of the work in Samaria (8: 17), the directing of Philip to the eunuch (8: 29), the sending of Peter to Cornelius (10: 19), the conversion of Cornelius and his companions (10: 44), Peter's defense of his entering the home of uncircumcised men and eating with them (11: 12, 15f.), the setting apart of Barnabas and Saul (13: 2, 4), the decision of the apostolic council in Jerusalem (15: 8, 28), the selection of a mission field (16: 6), the fuller experience of the followers of John the Baptist (19: 2, 6), Paul's journey to Jerusalem (20: 23), the care of the church at Ephesus (20: 28), the warning of Agabus (21: 11), and the Holy Spirit's speaking through Isaiah (28: 25).

This divine intervention is not always presented as the presence of the Holy Spirit. For example, in the story of Philip and the eunuch, there is an interchange between the "angel of the Lord" (8: 26) who sent Philip to the Jerusalem-Gaza road and the Spirit (8: 29) who directed Philip to "join this chariot." Apparently it was the same Spirit (the Spirit of the Lord) who caught up Philip after the eunuch was baptized (8: 39). In Paul's conversion it is Jesus who spoke directly to Paul (9: 4, 5) and the Lord (Jesus) who spoke to Ananias (9:10, 15, 17); the Holy Spirit is mentioned only indirectly (9: 17). In the latter part of Acts the references to the Holy Spirit are less frequent. He is mentioned only once (28: 25) after 21: 11 and there in connection with the preaching of Isaiah.

The major importance of the Holy Spirit (especially in the first half of Acts) parallels the same emphasis in the Gospel of Luke. In the Gospel it is shown that John the Baptist was to be "filled with the Holy Spirit, even from his mother's womb" (1: 15). The Holy Spirit was to come upon Mary and the power of the Most High was to overshadow her (1: 35). Elizabeth was "filled with the Holy Spirit" (1: 41). Zacharias was "filled with the Holy Spirit" (1: 67). The Spirit was upon Simeon, and he saw in Jesus, God's salvation for all people (2: 25). At his baptism, the "Holy Spirit descended in bodily form" upon Jesus (3: 22). It was as he was "full of the Holy Spirit" and as he was "led by the Spirit" that Jesus settled the major problem of the character of the kingdom which he would effect and the method by which he would do so (4: 1). So, in the Gospel and Acts alike, emphasis falls upon the presence and power of the Holy Spirit.[24]

The Holy Spirit came with great power upon the waiting

[24] R. R. Williams, *The Acts of the Apostles* (London: SCM Press Ltd., 1953), p. 39.

disciples on the day of Pentecost, but this is not to be understood
as the first coming of the Spirit. The Old Testament is witness
to the Spirit's activity in all the history of man; and, in the New
Testament, the Spirit's activity is represented as relating to the
earliest events with which it is concerned. Rackham gives expression to an erroneous view in saying:

> Previously the Holy Spirit had acted on men from without, like
> an external force; as the prophet Ezekiel describes it, "the hand of
> the Lord was upon me." But now the Holy Spirit acts from within.
> He is in man (John 14: 17). Before Pentecost his manifestations had
> been transient and exceptional: now his presence in man's heart is
> an "abiding" one and regular.[25]

This widely-held view breaks down at many points. If appeal
be made to grammar, the reverse position could be established.
The passage from Joel to which Peter appealed to explain the
experience of the disciples preserved the promise that God would
pour out his Spirit *"upon* all flesh" (Acts 2: 17). On the other
hand, "Elizabeth was *filled* with the Holy Spirit" (Luke 1: 41),
as was Zechariah (Luke 1: 67). This "proof text" method proves
nothing. The supposed distinction between the Spirit acting
"in" and "on" a person is utterly misleading. It not only will
not stand the test of the Scriptures but also assumes a spatial,
physical, and mechanical relationship of the Spirit to a person
which is altogether out of keeping with his nature and ours.
How can the Spirit ever deal with a human being except in terms
of such personal and interrelated factors as one's intelligence,
emotions, and will? The Holy Spirit never works in mechanical
fashion "on" an individual, manipulating him like a puppet.
He worked with Moses, the prophets, David, and Elizabeth just
as he has worked with all since Pentecost, by his impact upon
man's interrelated faculties of mind, emotions, and will.

The great release of power on the day of Pentecost is not
in the least to be minimized, but it evidently did not stand out
so uniquely for first century Christians as for some of us. This day
is not mentioned in extant first-century writings outside the
second chapter of Acts. The resurrection, not Pentecost, was the

---

[25] Rackham, *op. cit.,* p. 14.

day that stood out. Without the resurrection of Jesus there would have been no Christian Pentecost. Then, too, it must be observed that there are other occurrences recorded in Acts comparable to this one. When the gospel reached Cornelius (Acts 10) and some followers of John the Baptist (Acts 19), there were outpourings of the Spirit similar to that in Jerusalem. These major stages in the progress of the gospel into new groups were authenticated by the Spirit in forceful demonstrations.

It requires but mention that the presence of the Holy Spirit is not to be confused with the outward signs. The coming of the Spirit was attended by a sound similar to that of a violent gust of wind. Early exegetes recognized that Luke is not describing the sound of wind, but of something like the rush of a mighty wind. Neither does Luke say that tongues *of* fire appeared to the disciples but that tongues *similar to* fire appeared to them.[26] The tongues were not "cloven"; they were distributed and rested upon each. These audible and visible signs were but passing phenomena; the presence and power of the Holy Spirit was the permanent and important reality.

The belief in the presence of the Spirit was based upon experience. It was not a mere doctrine which the disciples sought to perpetuate but an existential experience which they could not help declaring. They found themselves conscious of a Presence, saying and doing things which seemed to them and to others "to be due to an irresistible power which made them do or say things which they had never previously contemplated."[27]

Speaking with tongues [2: 5-13]

5 Now there were dwelling in Jerusalem Jews, devout men from every nation under heaven. 6 And at this sound the multitude came together, and they were bewildered, because each one heard them speaking in his own language. 7 And they were amazed and wondered, saying, "Are not all these who are speaking Galileans? 8 And how is it that we hear, each of us in his own native language? 9 Parthians and Medes and Elamites and residents of Mesopotamia, Judea and Cappadocia, Pontus and Asia, 10 Phrygia and Pamphylia, Egypt and the parts of Libya belonging to Cyrene, and

---

[26] Knowling, *op. cit.*, p. 72.
[27] Lake and Cadbury, *Additional Notes*, p. 110.

visitors from Rome, both Jews and proselytes, [11] Cretans and
Arabians, we hear them telling in our own tongues the mighty
works of God." [12] And all were amazed and perplexed, saying to
one another, "What does this mean?" [13] But others mocking said,
"They are filled with new wine."

That we have more questions than answers in this chapter we
should frankly admit. Did the twelve alone speak in other
tongues, or were the one hundred and twenty included? That
depends upon the group to which "all" in 2:1 and 2:4 refers,
and there seems to be no way of determining the matter. Were the
hearers made up of Jews and proselytes only, or were Gentiles included? Manuscripts disagree in 2:5, but the weight of evidence
probably favors the retention of "Jews." Verses 22 and 36 apparently rule out Gentiles. Did the disciples speak in various foreign
languages, or was it in the hearing only that the language differences took place? To restate the question: was it a miracle of
speech or hearing or both? If final answers were possible, there
is little likelihood that competent scholars would continue to
differ so widely.

In 2:4, it is said that "they" all began to speak "in other
tongues." The Greek word for "other" (*heterais*) may mean
"other of a different kind," suggesting here a different kind of
utterance, but this need not follow. Some exegetes maintain
that "other tongues" refers to the various foreign languages or
native languages of the groups present. If so, it is not clear why
the charge of drunkenness was made; surely these pilgrims had
heard foreign languages before. Others insist that *glossolalia*,
ecstatic and unintelligible speech, is to be pictured. Luke, however, twice (vs. 6 and 8) asserts that each heard in his own language. The term used in these verses (*dialektō*) may actually
mean language or dialect; possibly both are intended here, seeing that both different languages and dialectical differences of
the same language were spoken by the multitude. If the utterance
was that of *glossolalia,* or if these Galileans merely spoke their
own language, then Luke implies a miracle in hearing. The one
certain datum, according to Luke, is that the speakers were
understood by various ones, each in his own language.

Whatever the character of the "tongues" at Pentecost, the gift was not a permanent endowment. Some Christians have sought at various times to revive the phenomenon. The purpose served at Pentecost, to give external evidence of the Spirit's presence and to make the witness understandable to various language groups, is not achieved by the usual endeavors of those who would repeat the practice. The pride which usually characterizes the modern efforts stands opposed to the "more excellent way" (1 Cor. 12: 31) to which Paul sought to turn the Corinthians. The church is not edified, and "outsiders or unbelievers" are neither enlightened as to the gospel nor persuaded by these tongues that the Holy Spirit is present (cf. 1 Cor. 14).

A major problem arises in the comparison or contrast of the "tongues" at Pentecost with "tongues" as at Corinth. The problem is complex and not of easy solution. In Corinth it is clear that the speaking in tongues was unintelligible, ecstatic speech, which may have meant much to the one who uttered it but did not edify the church and could bring scorn from outsiders. Paul did not forbid it but viewed it as the least valuable of all Christian gifts (1 Cor. 12-14). Paul urged the Corinthians to speak in tongues only if there were one to interpret (1 Cor. 14: 27). This does not suggest that the "tongues" would be intelligible to the interpreter. Rather the interpreter probably was one who could relate something of the background and experience out of which came the ecstatic utterance of his friend. It is possible that one would enjoy some great blessing and would give expression to it in an emotional overflow and ecstatic utterance. To the congregation it would convey no meaning unless someone present could supply the information about the background experience producing the otherwise meaningless utterance.

At Pentecost the situation is not clear. Verses 8 and 11 declare beyond all doubt that the words spoken were understood by each in his own language. The miracle implied would be one of hearing, and possibly speech also. On the other hand, some concluded that the disciples were "filled with new wine," implying that the speech was unintelligible. This need not mean, however, that the speech was unintelligible to all because unintelligible

to some. Those who made the charge of drunkenness may have
been unable to understand the speech because they were un-
sympathetic. If the miracle was in the hearing, this would mean
that not all experienced it. Or, it may be that they did understand and being disturbed by what they heard, tried to dismiss
it lightly by terming it drunkenness. Ridicule is always a handy
tool for those who are unwilling to face reality.

The speaking in "tongues" at Caesarea, and elsewhere, probably is to be understood as ecstatic speech similar to that at
Corinth. At least, there would not be there the language problem
which would make necessary a miracle of speech or hearing.

Luke states significantly that on this day of Pentecost "there
were dwelling in Jerusalem Jews, devout men from every nation
under heaven" (2: 5). Foakes-Jackson is probably correct in
suggesting that "the miracle was symbolical of the coming uni-
versality of the gospel." [28] This was certainly the intention of
God, but at this point the gospel has reached the Jews only. It
is true that the term "Jews" is absent from one of our old oldest
manuscripts,[29] but the support for it is too strong for rejection.
Then, too, the whole narrative contemplates a Jewish audience
(cf. 2: 14, 22, 36). This chapter affords the best clue to the rapid
and widespread extension of the gospel to all parts of the Greco-
Roman world. At an early date there were Christians in many
places over the empire, but they were Jewish Christians. Geographical lines were crossed soon after Pentecost, but racial lines
were harder to cross.

The preaching of Peter [2: 14-36]

14 But Peter, standing with the eleven, lifted up his voice and addressed them, "Men of Judea and all who dwell in Jerusalem, let
this be known to you, and give ear to my words. 15 For these men
are not drunk, as you suppose, since it is only the third hour of the
day; 16 but this is what was spoken by the prophet Joel:
17 'And in the last days it shall be, God declares
    that I will pour out my Spirit upon all flesh,
    and your sons and your daughters shall prophesy,
    and your young men shall see visions,
    and your old men shall dreams dreams;

---

[28] F. J. Foakes-Jackson, *The Acts of the Apostles,* p. 11.
[29] Codex Sinaiticus of the fourth century.

18 yea, and on my menservants and my maidservants in
   those days
I will pour out my Spirit; and they shall prophesy.
19 And I will show wonders in the heaven above
   and signs on the earth beneath,
   blood, and fire, and vapor of smoke;
20 the sun shall be turned into darkness
   and the moon into blood,
   before the day of the Lord comes,
   the great and manifest day.
21 And it shall be that whoever calls on the name of the
   Lord shall be saved.'

22 "Men of Israel, hear these words: Jesus of Nazareth, a man at-
tested to you by God with mighty works and wonders and signs
which God did through him in your midst, as you yourselves
know 23 this Jesus, delivered up according to the definite plan and
foreknowledge of God, you crucified and killed by the hands of
lawless men. 24 But God raised him up, having loosed the pangs
of death, because it was not possible for him to be held by it. 25 For
David says concerning him,
   'I saw the Lord always before me,
   for he is at my right hand that I may not be shaken;
26 therefore my heart was glad, and my tongue rejoiced;
   moreover my flesh will dwell in hope.
27 For thou wilt not abandon my soul to Hades,
   nor let thy Holy One see corruption.
28 Thou hast made known to me the ways of life;
   thou wilt make me full of gladness with thy presence.'
29 "Brethren, I may say to you confidently of the patriarch David
that he both died and was buried, and his tomb is with us to this
day. 30 Being therefore a prophet, and knowing that God had
sworn with an oath to him that he would set one of his descendants
upon his throne, 31 he foresaw and spoke of the resurrection of the
Christ, that he was not abandoned to Hades, nor did his flesh see
corruption. 32 This Jesus God raised up, and of that we all are
witnesses. 33 Being therefore exalted at the right hand of God,
and having received from the Father the promise of the Holy
Spirit, he has poured out this which you see and hear. 34 For David
did not ascend into the heavens; but he himself says,
   'The Lord said to my Lord, Sit at my right hand,
35 till I make thy enemies a stool for thy feet.'
36 Let all the house of Israel therefore know assuredly that God
has made him both Lord and Christ, this Jesus whom you crucified."

This great message was addressed to Jews; to this point the movement is strictly Jewish. The listeners were first called "Men, Jews,
and all those inhabiting Jerusalem" (v. 14), and then, "Men,

Israelites" (v. 22), and, "house of Israel" (v. 36).[30] The term
"Jew" designates one as a member of the nation or as an
inhabitant of Judea. The term "Israelite" designates him religiously as of the "chosen people." So the message is directed
to those who are Jews nationally and religiously. The burden
of this message is to indicate that what had taken place, including
the death of Jesus, was something for which Israelites should
have been prepared. The crucified and risen Jesus is the very
Lord and Christ for whom Israel should have been waiting. The
God of Israel is to be recognized in the person of Jesus.

The first major task of apostolic preaching was to deal with
the "scandal of the cross." The word "scandal" is of Greek origin;
it was the word for the trigger on a trap, and then for anything
over which one might trip or stumble. The crucifixion of Jesus
was a scandal to the Jews; until understood, it stood between
them and the acceptance of Jesus as the Christ. The Jews had
suffered much under foreign people: Assyrians, Babylonians,
Persians (though this was a lenient rule), Egyptians, Syrians, and
Romans. Some of their own leaders had added to their suffering.
They longed for a Messiah to deliver them and re-establish the
Davidic kingdom. They had had more than enough of suffering
and humiliation; now they yearned for vindication and reward.
A suffering Messiah was at this time inconceivable and unwanted.
The cross was indeed "a stumbling-block [scandal] to Jews and
folly to Gentiles" (1 Cor. 1: 23).

In a real sense, the scandal cannot be removed from the cross,
certainly not for the world with its wisdom. Paul refused to make
the gospel acceptable by the arts of wisdom. The word of the
cross has "foolishness" at its heart, and to remove this by making
the cross reasonable is to deny its meaning. Against world wisdom
with its self-assertion, the cross with its self-denial must ever seem
foolish. The cross must contradict world wisdom or it ceases to
be the cross.*

It is clear from the Gospels that the crucifixion of Jesus was

---

[30] The author's translations.
* For the classic exposition of Paul's thought in First Corinthians, see Johannes
Weiss, *Der erste Korintherbrief* (Göttingen: Vandenhoeck & Ruprecht, 1910), pp.
23 ff.

a major problem for even the closest disciples. They were unwilling to listen to Jesus as he foretold his death (cf. Matt. 16: 21-23), and the crucifixion stunned them and utterly demoralized them. They had been prepared to hail him as the Son of God and God's Anointed (Messiah) King (cf. Psalm 2), but they were not prepared to combine with that the role of the Suffering Servant (cf. Isa. 52-53 and Zech. 9). A still harder role for them to recognize was that of Son of man (cf. Dan. 7), in which the kinship of this heavenly man is seen to be a kinship to humanity and not merely to national Israel. (See comment on Acts 7: 56.)

Peter dismissed the charge of drunkenness as untrue. The Jews did not eat until the fourth hour, reckoned from sunrise, so about 10 A.M.; on the sabbath they did not eat until noon. Instead of being filled with new wine, they were filled with the Spirit.

Peter thought of that day as belonging to the "last days," as spoken of by the prophet Joel. This view is that which prevails in the New Testament (cf. 1 Tim. 4: 1, 2 Tim. 3: 1, Jude 18, 2 Peter 3: 3). The age which climaxes all the ages has come in Jesus! The *eschaton* (last age) has broken into history. The powers of the "age to come" have actually come and are operative within history. This does not mean that this age will be exhausted in history, but that it is actual here and now. Its climax will come when Jesus returns at the end of this stream of life which we call "history." In Jesus, God is asserting his sovereign claims upon men and is releasing his sovereign power for the triumph of his kingdom. Satan's kingdom is now being broken by the kingdom of God (cf. Matt. 12: 28, Luke 11: 20, etc.), and the major instrument of this victory is the cross. Satan rules wherever the principle of self-assertion is followed; Satan's kingdom gives way to God's wherever the principle of the cross, self-sacrifice and self-giving, is followed.

Many of the expressions in the passage from Joel are certainly to be understood as the dramatic imagery of apocalyptic and are not to be taken in a literal sense. Surely it is not meant that on the day of Pentecost "blood, fire, and vapor of smoke" (2: 19) were poured out in a literal sense or that the sun was actually turned into darkness and the moon into blood. For anyone familiar with the dramatic method of apocalyptic, there is no problem here. Unfortunately, many of the would-be interpreters of "last things" have a crudely literal approach to the poetic and dramatic thought of apocalyptic which would astound those who wrote it. Peter's treatment of the apocalyptic passage could well be a pattern for all.

The evangelistic note is clearly sounded in verse 21, "And it shall be that whoever calls on the name of the Lord shall be saved." In the Hebrew text of Joel the term for "Lord" is "Jehovah." As is frequently done, the New Testament here refers to Jesus a statement which in the Hebrew Old Testament refers to Jehovah. In Jesus one encounters God directly and personally, and in committing oneself by faith to him is salvation. The heart of salvation is a life shared with God. This vital union is based on mutual faith as God commits himself to man and man commits himself to God. Certainly God trusts man; he places himself in such a position before man that man can love him or hate him, accept him or reject him, rejoice his heart or break it. When man, in turn, so loves and trusts God, whom he encounters directly and personally in Jesus, that he yields himself to God, a creative relationship with God is formed. Then men share in the very life of God—thinking, feeling, choosing, and working with him. That is salvation!

In dealing with the death of Jesus, Peter gave an amazingly full treatment in a few words. The death was not divorced from the life (v. 22)—the life which preceded and the resurrection which followed were indispensable to the meaning of the cross. The death was not that of a helpless martyr who was simply overpowered by circumstances which he did not anticipate; Jesus foreknew it. When the eternal Word entered into the redemptive work, he foresaw the cost, yet did he give himself to it. This does not mean that Jesus sought to be killed or that the Father wanted men to crucify him, but it does mean that when the choice to redeem was made, the cost was foreseen. However, men are not freed of the guilt of crucifying Jesus: Peter placed the major guilt upon the Jews, but the lawless Gentiles [31] also came in for their share of guilt.[32] But Peter's climactic point is the fact of the resurrection. God raised up the very one whom men crucified as a sinner. The resurrection provided the light in which the death of Jesus could be reinterpreted not as defeat but as triumph.

Hades (the realm beyond death) was in birth pangs and gave up Jesus, so the way was now open for others (2: 24-28). The resurrection of Jesus is the assurance of the Christian's life eternal.

Peter closed his message with the declaration that the crucified, now risen, Jesus is Lord and Christ (2: 36). The promise to David that one of his descendants would be set upon his throne (2: 30) has been accomplished! Christ is already King by virtue of the resurrection (2: 31). The Davidic or Messianic kingdom has already been realized; its consummation is yet ahead, but it is already an accomplished fact. Millennial systems which place the kingdom in the future alone, need to reckon with this passage. His kingdom—his rule—is being accomplished through his death-resurrection, not through carnal weapons.

The call to repentance [2: 37-40]

37 Now when they heard this they were cut to the heart, and said to Peter and the rest of the apostles, "Brethren, what shall we do?" 38 And Peter said to them, "Repent, and be baptized every one

---

[31] "Lawless men" probably refers to the Romans; if so, it is strong evidence that Luke did not compose the speech. He would not have so designated the Romans. Cf. Bruce, *op. cit.*, pp. 91f.

[32] It is fashionable today in many circles to say that the Jews did not crucify Jesus, that the Romans did that. The claim is made that the Gospels, written after Christianity had ceased to be Jewish, transferred the guilt from the Romans to the Jews. The motive of these present-day writers, reacting to the terrible anti-Semitism of our day, is good, but the judgment is poor. To charge the Gospels with whitewashing the guilty and incriminating the innocent is a most serious—and false—charge. These modern writers are also naïve in overlooking conclusive evidence that the Jews did initiate the killing of Jesus. Paul, a man who dearly loved his own people and who cannot be charged with anti-Semitism, in what is probably his earliest extant letter, wrote bluntly that the Jews "killed both the Lord Jesus and the prophets" (1 Thess. 2: 15). Jewish writers in the early centuries are in agreement with the Gospels, Acts, and Paul at this point. It is well to protest as ungodly and inhuman any semblance of anti-Semitism, but no service is done any cause by ignoring or misrepresenting the facts of history.

of you in the name of Jesus Christ for the forgiveness of your
sins; and you shall receive the gift of the Holy Spirit. 39 For the
promise is to you and to your children and to all that are far off,
every one whom the Lord our God calls to him." 40 And he testified with many other words and exhorted them, saying, "Save
yourselves from this crooked generation."

A much disputed verse (38) appears in this paragraph. Is baptism
represented as a condition for forgiveness of sins? This is a
favorite "proof text" for those who believe in baptismal regeneration. Before one builds his theology on the text, however,
he should consider a number of things. In the first place, the
"proof text" method is a poor device, whoever may use it. One
can just about "prove" what he sets out to prove; at least he
proves it to his own satisfaction. A proof text is one which stands
alone, having no clear support of the scriptures as a whole or even
being contradicted by the scriptures as a whole. A climactic text
is one which gathers up into one classic statement a great teaching
or number of teachings. John 3: 16 is a climactic text, not a "proof
text," for the truths it embodies are clearly established in the
New Testament apart from this great verse. The clear teaching
of the New Testament as a whole would rule out baptismal
regeneration. Then, too, common sense rules it out; the desired
spiritual result is not achieved through a physical means. This
is not to overlook the important fact that any physical function
takes on moral and spiritual significance in terms of the attitudes
and motives out of which it arises. It is to say that forgiveness of
sins and the gift of the Holy Spirit are not bound to an arbitrary
physical rite. God is never arbitrary.

A possible translation, permitted by the Greek, is as follows:
"Repent, and let each of you be baptized in the name of Jesus
Christ *on the basis of* the forgiveness of your sins, and you shall
receive the free gift of the Holy Spirit." This translation depends
upon the possibility of the causal use of the Greek preposition
eis followed by the accusative case. Though this construction in
the Greek New Testament usually denotes result, there can be
no doubt that it is used for grounds or reason (causal) a few

times in the New Testament.[33] This construction may be found, for example, in Matthew 12:41: "The men of Nineveh will arise at the judgment with this generation and condemn it; for they repented *at the preaching of Jonah.*" They did not repent *with the result* that Jonah preached, but *because* Jonah preached. This does not prove that the causal force of *eis* and the accusative is to be found in Acts 2:38, but it proves that it is possible.

Probably the phrase in question, "for the forgiveness of your sins," is to be taken primarily with "repent" rather than with "be baptized."[34] Forgiveness followed repentance, not baptism. Baptism was a means of portraying the repentance, a public confession of faith in Jesus.[35] Acts 3:19, where baptism is not mentioned, would strongly support this.

"Cut to the heart" by Peter's message, the people were thus brought under conviction. They were compelled to look back upon their deed, and now they began to see it in its true character. In rejecting Jesus they had been on the side of wrong rather than right. They had served neither God nor country in crucifying Jesus. God had raised to a throne the very one whom they had hanged on a cross as though he were accursed. In the Holy Spirit they now sensed the presence of this risen Christ.

As something of the awful reality of their sinful state and their recent sinful deed bore down upon these people, they felt completely undone. In despair they cried out, "What shall we do?" This very despair was their only hope. Only as men see that they are nothing can they possibly become anything. Only when they see their helplessness are they able to accept God's help. Karl Barth forcefully states the truth:

When men, as men, have scaled the world's highest peaks, and there discover that *all the world is guilty before God*—then it is that their

[33] A running debate on "causal *eis*" between J. R. Mantey and Ralph Marcus in the *Journal of Biblical Literature;* March, 1951; June, 1951; December, 1951; and March, 1952; is rewarding for the student of grammar, but is of little help here. Whether "causal *eis*" is found in non-biblical Greek or not, it is clearly found a few times in the New Testament.
[34] Cf. Lake and Cadbury, *Commentary,* p. 26; Bruce, *op. cit.,* p. 98.
[35] Cf. Rackham, *op. cit.,* p. 30.

peculiar advantage is established, maintained, and confirmed; . . .
then it is that God asserts His faithfulness, and reveals that it has not
been deflected by the unfaithfulness of men.[36]

Again Barth cuts to the heart of the matter in saying: "The
arrogance with which we set ourselves by the side of God, with
the intention of doing something for Him, deprives us of the
only possible ground of salvation, which is to cast ourselves upon
His favour or disfavour." [37]

Verse 39 gives assurance of the availability of the promise—
the forgiveness of sins and the gift of the Holy Spirit—to everyone
whom God calls. The teaching that the Christian life is a calling
is fundamental to the Bible. In the Hebrew-Christian religion,
God is always known as the one who takes the initiative in
revelation and redemption. The first step is always taken by
God, not by man. God awakens man in and to his own presence
and draws man to himself. This is the Bible doctrine of election,
not the choice of one man instead of another man but God's
choice of man rather than man's choice of God.

The universal character of the gospel is proclaimed in Peter's
message, but Luke will show that the apostles were slow to
recognize this universalism in actual practice.

Growth in Christian Judaism [2: 41-47]

> 41 So those who received his word were baptized, and there were
> added that day about three thousand souls. 42 And they devoted
> themselves to the apostles' teaching and fellowship, to the breaking
> of bread and the prayers.
> 43 And fear came upon every soul; and many wonders and signs were
> done through the apostles. 44 And all who believed were together
> and had all things in common; 45 and they sold their possessions
> and goods and distributed them to all, as any had need. 46 And
> day by day, attending the temple together and breaking bread in
> their homes, they partook of food with glad and generous hearts,
> 47 praising God and having favor with all the people. And the
> Lord added to their number day by day those who were being
> saved.

Here is presented a vigorous Christian movement, Jewish in

[36] Karl Barth, *The Epistle to the Romans*, trans. Edwyn C. Hoskyns (Oxford:
University Press, 1933), pp. 88f.
[37] *Ibid.*, p. 84.

constituency and popular with the Jewish people. Three thousand people were baptized in one day. Evidently these were all Jews or proselytes (Gentiles who had been inducted into Judaism as a nation and a religion). These converts were made while Jerusalem was filled with Jews "from every nation under heaven" (2: 5). Extreme parts of the Roman Empire were represented, from Mesopotamia in the east to Rome in the west and down into Africa. It is not said that converts were made from all these sections, but subsequent references to Christians in Damascus, Cyrene, Cyprus, Rome, and other places would so indicate.

It is important to note that to this point, and for some time afterward, the Christian movement was popular among the Jews. To this point the major barrier for the Jew was the "scandal of the cross," but that was satisfactorily explained in the light of the resurrection. As this barrier was crossed, thousands of Jews accepted Jesus as Messiah. Soon the number became five thousand (4: 4); later, Acts simply says that multitudes of both men and women were added (5: 14). So rapid was the spread of Christianity among the Jews that the Sadducees became alarmed, for they feared that a movement of such vigor and numerical strength might cause Rome to fear an uprising.

The movement soon became so strong at Jerusalem that the apostles could openly defy the Sanhedrin (4: 18-20), and the rulers were afraid to use violence against the apostles lest the Jewish people stone the rulers (5: 26). The movement spread rapidly outside Jerusalem (5: 16), even many of the priests being obedient to the faith (6: 7). All of this indicates something of the magnitude of the Christian movement among the Jews. Nothing is clearer than that to this point Christianity was acceptable to multitudes of Jews. Why, then, is it that by the end of the first century Christianity became Gentile and lost all appeal to the Jew? Something developed which caused a movement to which multitudes of Jews were rallying finally to lose its Jewish following. Whatever it was had not emerged at this point. *It was not the requirement that Jesus be recognized as the Christ, the Son of God, which caused the Jews finally to reject him.*

Here is a picture of a joyous and congenial group of Jewish Christians, sharing in the teaching, fellowship, breaking of bread,

66 THE BOOK OF ACTS

and prayers. Though a distinct group, as disciples of Jesus, they still were Jews, and as exemplary Jews they attended the temple (2: 46). As Christian Jews they had the favor of the people (2: 47) and were growing day by day.

The "breaking of bread" may refer to the Lord's Supper, to the love feast (fellowship meal), or to both; it normally describes a regular meal. Probably these early disciples met each evening in the homes and shared a common meal. This meal, the *agape* (love feast), served a double purpose, fellowship and the care of the poor. Probably the Lord's Supper (Eucharist) was observed at each of those meetings. Cullmann is probably correct in saying: "It may be taken for granted that the oldest celebration of the meal [the Lord's Supper] took place in the framework of a real meal." [38] After remarking that according to Acts 2: 46 the essential characteristic (*Wesensmerkmal*) of this meal was its expression of joy, he suggests that this joy was not caused primarily by the remembrance of the Last Supper but is best understood as being from the remembrance of those other meals when Jesus after the resurrection appeared with his disciples "at the table" (cf. Emmaus, Luke 24: 30; the eleven, Luke 24:36; at the sea, John 21: 12ff.).[39] Of course, the Lord's Supper observance was directly connected with the Last Supper (1 Cor. 11: 23ff.), and the resurrection enabled the disciples to remember with joy the Last Supper itself for all the sadness with which it was otherwise surrounded. If correct, Cullmann's thesis that the disciples also looked back to those post-resurrection appearances during which they ate with Jesus does make more understandable the great joy characterizing these Christian meals.

Markus Barth* has argued convincingly that the Last Supper was a Passover meal and that as such, its mood was one of joy. The paschal lamb, slain in the afternoon, was eaten at night in celebration of a triumph in Egypt (cf. Exodus 12); it was celebrated in the joy of a crisis passed! If this be true, then two

[38] *Urchristentum und Gottesdienst,* p. 18.
[39] *Loc. cit.*
* Markus Barth, *Das Abendmahl: Passamahl, Bundesmahl und Messiasmahl* (Evangelischer Verlag A. G. Zollikon-Zürich, 1945), 67pp.

factors point to a joyous celebration of the Lord's Supper: the joy of deliverance in Egypt as finding its higher realization in the deliverance in Christ and the joy of the post-resurrection meals shared with the risen Christ. The Lord's Supper thus looks back to a crucified Saviour and forward to a returning Lord, but it also affirms the joyous fact of a present and living Christ, now incarnate in his church, the body of Christ.

The Revised Standard Version is correct in the translation, "And the Lord added to their number day by day those who were being saved" (2:47). The Authorized Version unfortunately has a mistranslation, "such as should be saved." The idea of predestination is completely foreign to the text, appearing only in the inexcusable mistranslation.

The common life.—Luke, at the risk of redundancy, almost repeats himself (2:42-47), in the attempt to describe what apparently was the indescribably happy fellowship (*koinōnia*) of these early Christians. They were devoted to *fellowship* (v. 42). All who believed were *together* and had all things in *common* (v. 44). They sold their possessions and goods and distributed them to all, as they had need (v. 45). Day by day, they were attending the temple *together*. Breaking bread in their homes, they partook of food with *glad* and *generous hearts* (v. 46).

It is impossible to exaggerate the importance of *koinōnia*—community or fellowship—as it appears here in Acts. There is no more vital concept in the New Testament than that of the oneness of those who are in Christ. This unity is variously described in the New Testament; probably the most forceful description is Paul's analogy of the church as the body of Christ—not construed as an organization on a local or denominational level, but as the aggregate of those who are in Christ (cf. Rom. 12:4f.; 1 Cor. 12:12f., 12:27; Eph. 1:22f., 4:4-6, 4:12, 5:22-30; Col. 1:18).

These early Christians were not a mere society of co-operating people but a community in the deepest sense. Macmurray has demonstrated the important fact of an essential difference between two types of association: "There is a type of association which is constituted by a common purpose. There is another which consists in sharing a common life." [40] These he distinguishes by the terms "society" and "community," respectively. (The distinction holds, whether these two particular widely used terms are the best or not.) He points out that a society is an organization of functions, one being a member by virtue of the function he performs in the group, each co-operating member contributing to the pursuit of the common end.[41] In this type of association, the members are not associated *as persons,* but only in respect to functions performed in relation to the purpose which constitutes the group. This then is not a personal unity but merely an organic one. In contrast, a community has a deeper constitutive principle: "It is not organic. Its principle of unity is personal. It is constituted by the sharing of a common life." [42]

A society may be formed out of people who neither know nor care for one another, but who find themselves with a common purpose. A burial society, for example, is constituted by people who have a common purpose, to provide for their own burials. But the constitutive principle of a community is its common life—its kinship, its fellowship, its brotherhood. Common objectives serve to express the common life and provide for further cultivation of that common life, but the community is not constituted by these common goals. These Christians at Jerusalem were no mere society—they were a community, even the church, the body of Christ. In him they shared a common life. All of their shared activities had meaning only in that they expressed this common life which they had in Christ.

It is important to distinguish the fellowship of these Jerusalem Christians from mere co-operation. Almost daily, co-operation is eulogized as an ideal. In truth, co-operation in itself is not good and it is not bad; it is a colorless neutral. Gangsters band themselves together because of a common goal, possibly to rob a bank, and they achieve co-operation in their crime. Co-operation is an easy, and in itself meaningless, goal, achieved daily by depraved men who happen to have desires that are shared by others. These

[40] John Macmurray, *op. cit.,* p. 54.
[41] Cf. *ibid.,* pp. 54ff. for his excellent discussion upon which the whole of this paragraph is based.
[42] *Ibid.,* p. 56.

Christians at Jerusalem were living a common life; they were not merely co-operating. A slave may be included in a society providing for masters and slaves, and in that system he is able to co-operate with his master. But this is a society, not a community. Jesus said, "No longer do I call you slaves, for a slave does not know what his master is doing; but I have called you friends" (John 15: 15—"Slave" is the marginal reading). Jesus calls us into a fellowship in which we are privileged to live a common and creative life with him and with his people.

Even being in "accord" or "together" is of itself a colorless neutral. Luke uses the word *homothumadon* ("one accord," "agreement," "together") ten times in Acts (eleven times, if authentic in 2: 1). It describes the united prayer of the disciples (1: 14), waiting together for the day of Pentecost (2: 1), attending the temple together (2: 46), praying together for courage following the release of Peter and John (4: 24), banding together of the Christians in Solomon's porch (5: 12), listening together by the Samaritans as Philip preached (8: 6), and the agreement of the apostolic council (15: 25). All of this is beautiful.

But the identical word also describes the murderous assault on Stephen (7: 57), the hypocritical flattering of Herod Agrippa by the people of Tyre and Sidon (12: 20), the united attack of the Jews upon Paul (18: 12), and the rushing together into the theatre by the mad mob at Ephesus (19: 29). Obviously, men may be "in accord," "together," or "in agreement" for evil or for good. Accord is not enough. It is only that fellowship among men which is derived from a fellowship with God that is necessarily good. The church, the body of Christ, is such a fellowship. To be "in Christ" is to be at the same time in the body of which he is the Head. That fellowship alone is the distinctively Christian one. Luke seems here to be describing such a fellowship.

Conviction and confession of sin opened the way to this common life. Karl Barth may be cited as pointing to this indispensable principle of Christian community:

There is no positive possession of men which is sufficient to provide a foundation for human solidarity; for every positive possession—religious temperament, moral consciousness, humanitarianism—already

contains within itself the seed of the disruption of society. These positive factors are productive of difference, since they distinguish men
from one another. Genuine fellowship is grounded upon a negative:
it is grounded upon what men lack. Precisely when we recognize that
we are sinners do we perceive that we are brothers.[43]

The insight is certainly sound. When we think in terms of our
supposed "virtues," "rights," and "works," we are jealous com-
petitors; when we think of our sin, we are brothers. This is
precisely the "negative" to which these in Jerusalem had come
on the day of Pentecost—they were "cut to the heart" and in
despair stood before God and before their sin. The beautiful
fellowship in Christ that Luke describes had its beginning at
the point of recognition of their nothingness and in their casting
themselves upon God for "his favor or disfavor."

Luke significantly presents together this *koinōnia* and salvation. It is precisely in this Christian *koinōnia*, Christian community or fellowship, that personal salvation is consummated.
Personality was once thought to be closed and exclusive, but
it is now recognized to be open and inclusive. Macmurray sums
it up neatly: "In fact, it is the sharing of a common life which
constitutes individual personality. We become persons in community, in virtue of our relations to others." [44] The Greek idea
of a soul as some separate entity is foreign to the Bible. In the
Bible man is thought of as a whole; he is not viewed as *having*
a soul, but as *being* a soul. It is only as man, a complex of interrelated factors, is drawn into a faith-love relationship in Christ
that he is saved. But a man in Christ is by that very fact also a
part of the body of Christ. The kinship with Christ involves
the kinship with all who are in Christ. It is in this relationship
that one becomes truly a person and truly saved. Christ saves
individuals but in saving them he makes them more than individuals; they become persons, living in this relationship.

Later, when the necessary implication of *koinōnia* was seen
in terms of the equality, freedom, and brotherhood of Gentiles
and Jews in Christ, many found themselves unwilling to acknowledge that implication. In denying this brotherhood to uncir-

---

[43] *Op. cit.,* pp. 100f.
[44] *Op. cit.,* p. 56.

cumcised Gentiles, they denied the body of Christ, choosing thereby to be a torso. A torso not only has no limbs; it has no head. One may pretend to acknowledge the Head while denying the members of the body of Christ, but he is thereby self-deceived. Luke's closing scene in Acts is precisely this: an unhindered gospel and the self-exclusion of those who denied this *koinōnia*.

The Healing of a Lame Beggar at the Temple [3: 1-10]

1 Now Peter and John were going up to the temple at the hour of prayer, the ninth hour. 2 And a man lame from birth was being carried, whom they laid daily at that gate of the temple which is called Beautiful to ask alms of those who entered the temple. 3 Seeing Peter and John about to go into the temple, he asked for alms. 4 And Peter directed his gaze at him, with John, and said, "Look at us." 5 And he fixed his attention upon them, expecting to receive something from them. 6 But Peter said, "I have no silver and gold, but I give you what I have; in the name of Jesus Christ of Nazareth, walk." 7 And he took him by the right hand and raised him up; and immediately his feet and ankles were made strong. 8 And leaping up he stood and walked and entered the temple with them, walking and leaping and praising God. 9 And all the people saw him walking and praising God, 10 and recognized him as the one who sat for alms at the Beautiful Gate of the temple; and they were filled with wonder and amazement at what had happened to him.

This miracle provided further evidence that the gift of the Spirit was real; it filled the people with wonder and amazement (3: 10). It was more than a miracle (wonder); it was a sign (4: 22) in which a picture was given in the physical of what could be done in the spiritual; just as a man made whole physically (4: 9-12) so could one be made whole spiritually.

This scene again is a portrayal of Christian Judaism. Peter and John went naturally to the temple at the hour of prayer. The following address contemplates a strictly Jewish situation.

Peter's Sermon to the Jews [3: 11-26]

11 While he clung to Peter and John, all the people ran together to them in the portico called Solomon's, astounded. 12 And when Peter saw it he addressed the people, "Men of Israel, why do you wonder at this, or why do you stare at us, as though by our own power or piety we had made him walk? 13 The God of Abraham

and of Isaac and of Jacob, the God of our fathers, glorified his servant Jesus, whom you delivered up and denied in the presence of Pilate when he had decided to release him. 14 But you denied the Holy and Righteous One, and asked for a murderer to be granted to you, 15 and killed the Author of life, whom God raised from the dead. To this we are witnesses. 16 And his name, by faith in his name, has made this man strong whom you see and know; and the faith which is through Jesus has given the man this perfect health in the presence of you all.

17 "And now, brethren, I know that you acted in ignorance, as did also your rulers. 18 But what God foretold by the mouth of all the prophets, that his Christ should suffer, he thus fulfilled. 19 Repent therefore, and turn again, that your sins may be blotted out, that times of refreshing may come from the presence of the Lord, 20 and that he may send the Christ appointed for you, Jesus, 21 whom heaven must receive until the time for establishing all that God spoke by the mouth of his holy prophets from of old. 22 Moses said, 'The Lord God will raise up for you a prophet from your brethren as he raised me up. You shall listen to him in whatever he tells you. 23 And it shall be that every soul that does not listen to that prophet shall be destroyed from the people.' 24 And all the prophets who have spoken, from Samuel and those who came afterwards, also proclaimed these days. 25 You are the sons of the prophets and of the covenant which God gave to your fathers, saying to Abraham, 'And in your posterity shall all the families of the earth be blessed.' 26 God, having raised up his servant, sent him to you first, to bless you in turning every one of you from your wickedness."

Peter first accounts for the power which made the lame man whole: it was due to no power or piety of the apostles themselves but to the God of Israel who thus glorified his servant Jesus, the very one whom they delivered up and denied. This Jesus is now a living power in their midst. The basic points stressed here seem to have characterized the earliest preaching: the Jews killed the one whom the God of their fathers sent; in so doing they were guilty; the innocency of Jesus was recognized by Pilate; the suffering proved to be the way to glory and triumph; the suffering was foretold by the prophets; and the fact of the resurrection called for a completely new evaluation of the death of Jesus.

But Peter's aim was to win these Jews, not simply to condemn them. He acknowledged an element of ignorance on the part of the people and their rulers. This may seem to contradict the implications of verses 13-16, but Peter probably was not relieving them of all guilt. Of course they were responsible for a willful rejection of one whose innocence was recognized by Pilate; but for all this sin against light, they did not really know what they were doing. Along with the deliberate closing of their eyes, there was an actual blindness to the real person and intention of Jesus. Jesus himself said, "they know not what they do" (Luke 23: 34); that is, they did not really understand what they were doing.

Then came the clarion call to "repent" and "turn." The repentance would involve a change of mind and contrition of heart. The turning would refer to conversion, or a change of direction. Change of mind (attitude or disposition) is closely related to the change of life's direction. The results of this change of mind would be twofold: the forgiveness of their sins and the establishing of the kingdom (rule) of God.

In the closing part of the sermon, Peter deals with Jewish questions about the establishing of the kingdom (3: 21). The apparent delay does not reflect a negligence on the part of God; rather it reflects their slowness to repent. The kingdom has primary reference to the reign of God; their repentance is an acknowledgement of that reign.

The highest Christology is reached in this sermon. The miracle of healing seems first to be ascribed to "the God of Abraham and of Isaac and of Jacob" (3: 13), and then it seems to be ascribed to Jesus (3: 16). Verse 16 is difficult; but it seems that Peter, in the reference to the "name," is placing Jesus in the position of the Lord of the Jews.[45] This virtual identifying of Jesus with God is borne out by Acts 3: 6 and 4: 10.

Sadducees, Alarmed by Growing Movement and Resurrection Theme, Arrest, Then Release, Peter and John [4: 1-31]

Sadducees annoyed [4: 1-4]

1 And as they were speaking to the people, the priests and the captain of the temple and the Sadducees came upon them, 2 annoyed because they were teaching the people and proclaiming in Jesus the resurrection from the dead. 3 And they arrested them and put

---

[45] Cf. Rackham, *op. cit.*, p. 49.

them in custody until the morrow, for it was already evening. 4 But
many of those who heard the word believed; and the number of
the men came to about five thousand.

The first persecution of the disciples was initiated by the
Sadducees. The reasons are clear: they resented the fact that the
disciples were teaching as though rabbis, and they were annoyed
by the proclamation of the resurrection. Probably they were
alarmed at the emphasis upon the kingdom, easily construed
as inflamatory propaganda. "Resurrection" meant more to the
Jew then than it does to Christians today. As Foakes-Jackson
sums it up, "To the Jew at this time it meant imminent world-
catastrophe, in which the powers of the earth would be destroyed
and a new order miraculously set up." [46] Thus it suggested revolution to those who favored the *status quo*.[47]

There are several persecutions of Christians presented in Acts,
and it is important to see that each persecuting group had its
own reasons for resisting the gospel. The Sadducees, Pharisees,
Herodians, and various pagan groups opposed the Christian
movement, but each for different reasons. These must be observed in turn as they appear in the unfolding story.

The Sadducees were a minority; but as a wealthy aristocracy,
they controlled the temple and were powerful in the government.
Much of their wealth was in lands, property that could easily
be confiscated by a conquering nation. This in part accounts for
the fact that they were willing to collaborate with foreign rulers.
The Pharisees opposed, and at times bitterly resisted, foreign
rulers; it may be that their economic or sociological situation
was a factor of importance. Louis Finkelstein, a contemporary
Jewish scholar, suggests that the Sadducees emerged from the
landed gentry and the Pharisees from tradesmen, and that these
origins account for many of their traits and interests.[48] Whether
this thesis be true or not, it is clear that the Sadducees in the

---

[46] Foakes-Jackson, *The Acts of the Apostles*, p. 32.
[47] See Louis Finkelstein, *The Pharisees, the Sociological Background of Their
Faith* (Philadelphia: The Jewish Publication Society of America, 1946). I, 145-159,
for a Jewish treatment of the opposition of Sadducees and Pharisees in this matter.
[48] *Ibid., passim.*

first century retained their wealth and power by collaborating with the Romans, who since 63 B.C. had dominated Palestine.

Since the major concern of the Sadducees was to maintain their power in the nation and over the Temple, they cultivated the good will of the Romans. They determined at all costs to maintain order among the Jews, for the one unpardonable sin in the eyes of official Rome was the insubordination of any of her subject nations. The high priesthood was by Roman appointment. Even the high priest's robes were kept by a Roman official and issued to him only when needed for the ritual services. All this aristocratic group was daily dependent upon Rome. Any semblance of sedition or revolt could bring down the wrath of Rome, and the Sadducees could be held accountable for the trouble.

The magnitude of the growing group of disciples and their unbounding enthusiasm would be a cause for Sadducean alarm. The excitement over miracles and the emphasis upon Christ, an anointed King, and his kingdom would frighten the Jewish rulers. They were annoyed by the preaching of the resurrection, chiefly because of its political implications to the Jews. By these issues the Pharisees, in contrast, were not disturbed. They believed in the resurrection, so welcomed support from the disciples on that issue; and they opposed Roman rule, though they did not usually favor physical revolt.

In the Gospels and Acts the same pattern can be detected with reference to the opposition of Pharisees and Sadducees. The Pharisees opposed Jesus because of his conflict with them on points of the law, but the Sadducees were not disturbed until the following of Jesus was strong enough to threaten the peace. The new alarm, over the followers of Jesus, came first to the Sadducees and only later to the Pharisees, when the latter saw that inherent in the Christian gospel were those principles which conflicted with their legalism and narrow nationalism.

When, then, the people became excited over the miracles done in the name of Jesus and when the numbers of disciples increased so rapidly, the Sadducees, in alarm, determined to crush the movement. It is highly significant that the full force of Sadducean resistance could not check the movement. At this point Christianity was popular with the Jewish people and unopposed by the Pharisees.

Peter and John challenged by the Sanhedrin [4: 5-22]

5 On the morrow their rulers and elders and scribes were gathered together in Jerusalem, 6 with Annas the high priest and Caiaphas and John and Alexander, and all who were of the high-priestly family. 7 And when they had set them in the midst, they inquired, "By what power or by what name did you do this?" 8 Then Peter, filled with the Holy Spirit, said to them, "Rulers of the people and elders, 9 if we are being examined today concerning a good deed done to a cripple, by what means this man has been healed, 10 be it known to you all, and to all the people of Israel, that by the name of Jesus Christ of Nazareth, whom you crucified, whom God raised from the dead, by him this man is standing before you well. 11 This is the stone which was rejected by you builders, but which has become the head of the corner. 12 And there is salvation in no one else, for there is no other name under heaven given among men by which we must be saved."

13 Now when they saw the boldness of Peter and John, and perceived that they were uneducated, common men, they wondered; and they recognized that they had been with Jesus. 14 But seeing the man that had been healed standing beside them, they had nothing to say in opposition. 15 But when they had commanded them to go aside out of the council, they conferred with one another, 16 saying, "What shall we do with these men? For that a notable sign has been performed through them is manifest to all the inhabitants of Jerusalem, and we cannot deny it. 17 But in order that it may spread no further among the people, let us warn them to speak no more to any one in this name." 18 So they called them and charged them not to speak or teach at all in the name of Jesus. 19 But Peter and John answered them, "Whether it is right in the sight of God to listen to you rather than to God, you must judge; 20 for we cannot but speak of what we have seen and heard." 21 And when they had further threatened them, they let them go, finding no way to punish them, because of the people; for all men praised God for what had happened. 22 For the man on whom this sign of healing was performed was more than forty years old.

The Sanhedrin was the highest ruling body among the Jews, receiving considerable authority over internal affairs from the Romans, under whom it served. It was a council of about seventy members, made up of the groups listed here: rulers, elders, and scribes. The high-priestly families were the "rulers," the elders were leading citizens, and the scribes were students of the law, chiefly Pharisees.

At this time Caiaphas was the high priest, though his father-in-law, Annas, exerted major influence. Annas had served as high priest from A.D. 6 to 15, and one son served as high priest soon after his term of office. Following Caiaphas, four other sons of Annas held the high priesthood. The chief rival to the family of Annas was that of Boethus, an Alexandrian Jew into whose family Herod the Great had married. When the Herods were in power, a member of the family of Boethus usually held the high priesthood. There were other high-priestly families, but they were of less influence than those of Annas and Boethus. The high priesthood had formerly been for life and by succession in the family of Aaron. In the time of Ptolemy IV (182-146 B.C.), however, the last high priest of the Aaronic line went to Leontopolis, in Egypt, and subsequently the high priests were appointed by whoever ruled the Jews: Seleucid kings, the Maccabees, Herods, or Romans.[49]

The Sanhedrin challenged the disciples in terms of authority, "By what power or by what name did you do this?" (4: 7). English translations can hardly preserve the scorn which the Greek achieves by ending the question with "you." A valid paraphrase would be, "By what authority or by what name did you do this, *such as you!*" Their contempt for the disciples is due partly to the fact that they were "uneducated, common men" (4: 13). That is, these disciples had not received rabbinical training or appointment to any official position in the nation. The familiar translation, "unlearned and ignorant men" is misleading. It is not implied that they were illiterate but that they lacked formal training and appointment.

Peter was fearless before the Sanhedrin; he was sure of his ground. None could shake him for the faith that Jesus was risen and present in this powerful work. His authority was the exalted Christ, not the Sanhedrin. Not only did Peter stand firmly for this, but he summoned rulers and all to recognize this rejected

---

[49] Lake and Cadbury, *Commentary*, p. 42.

one as the "head of the corner" and the one in whom alone was salvation. This boldness of Peter, undaunted before the Sanhedrin, faltered when a new issue arose later—the question of the Gentiles.

The Sanhedrin "recognized that they had been with Jesus" (4: 13), and this was for them further reason for annoyance. The popular idea that the Christlikeness of the men was apparent is not the point. However true that may be, all that is meant is that these rulers recognized them to be a part of the very movement which they had tried to destroy in crucifying Jesus. Jesus, too, had taught with an authority which they challenged; and he, too, had knowledge and wisdom which had not been derived from the rabbinical schools.

The most embarrassing fact to the rulers was the presence of the healed man (4: 14). Their inexcuseable crime was their unwillingness to face the implications of facts which could not be denied (4: 16). Their only concern was to check a movement which threatened the *status quo*. They resorted to threats, but this was to no avail because of the disciples' deathless compulsion to speak what had been seen and heard (4: 20), and because of the popularity of the disciples with the people (4: 21).

Allegiance to the sovereign Lord [4: 23-31]

23 When they were released they went to their friends and reported what the chief priests and the elders had said to them. 24 And when they heard it, they lifted their voices together to God and said, "Sovereign Lord, who didst make the heaven and the earth and the sea and everything in them, 25 who by the mouth of our father David, thy servant, didst say by the Holy Spirit,
'Why did the Gentiles rage, and the peoples imagine vain things?
26 The kings of the earth set themselves in array, and the rulers were gathered together, against the Lord and against his Anointed'—
27 for truly in this city there were gathered together against thy holy servant Jesus, whom thou didst anoint, both Herod and Pontius Pilate, with the Gentiles and the peoples of Israel, 28 to do whatever thy hand and thy plan had predestined to take place. 29 And now, Lord, look upon their threats, and grant to thy servants to speak thy word with all boldness, 30 while thou stretchest out thy hand to heal, and signs and wonders are performed

through the name of thy holy servant Jesus." [31] And when they had prayed, the place in which they were gathered together was shaken; and they were all filled with the Holy Spirit and spoke the word of God with boldness.

The issue had been clearly drawn for Peter and John by the Sanhedrin, and they had declared themselves determined to be true to their experience (4: 19f.). Now the larger group acknowledged the authority of God, whom they address as "sovereign Lord" (4: 24). The Greek term used corresponds to the English word *despot*, but without the modern connotation of "tyrant"; it acknowledges absolute rule.

The disciples were prepared to obey God as sovereign Lord by continuing to witness to the resurrection of Jesus and to do works in his name. They were prepared to face the forces within their nation and from the Gentiles which opposed Jesus (4: 27). They had freed themselves from the Sanhedrin, but they were to have a harder fight in the struggle for liberty from the narrow ideas of Christian Jews within their own ranks.

When they prayed, the place was shaken, and all were filled with the Holy Spirit (4: 31). The Spirit vindicated these disciples who had freed themselves from the Sanhedrin. The Sanhedrin condemned them; the Spirit authenticated them.

Fellowship, Fraud, and Fear [4: 32 to 5: 16]

32 Now the company of those who believed were of one heart and soul, and no one said that any of the things which he possessed was his own, but they had everything in common. 33 And with great power the apostles gave their testimony to the resurrection of the Lord Jesus, and great grace was upon them all. 34 There was not a needy person among them, for as many as were possessors of lands or houses sold them, and brought the proceeds of what was sold 35 and laid it at the apostles' feet; and distribution was made to each as any had need. 36 Thus Joseph who was surnamed by the apostles Barnabas (which means, Son of encouragement), a Levite, a native of Cyprus, 37 sold a field which belonged to him, and brought the money and laid it at the apostles' feet.

5: 1 But a man named Ananias with his wife Sapphira sold a piece of property, 2 and with his wife's knowledge he kept back some of the proceeds, and brought only a part and laid it at the apostles' feet. 3 But Peter said, "Ananias, why has Satan filled your heart to lie to the Holy Spirit and to keep back part of the proceeds of the land? 4 While it remained unsold, did it not remain your own? And after it was sold, was it not at your disposal? How is it that you have contrived this deed in your heart? You have not lied to men but to God." 5 When Ananias heard these words, he fell down and died. And great fear came upon all who heard of it. 6 The young men rose and wrapped him up and carried him out and buried him.

7 After an interval of about three hours his wife came in, not knowing what had happened. 8 And Peter said to her, "Tell me whether you sold the land for so much." And she said, "Yes, for so much." 9 But Peter said to her, "How is it that you have agreed together to tempt the Spirit of the Lord? Hark, the feet of those that have buried your husband are at the door, and they will carry you out." 10 Immediately she fell down at his feet and died. When the young men came in they found her dead, and they carried her out and buried her beside her husband. 11 And great fear came upon the whole church, and upon all who heard of these things.

12 Now many signs and wonders were done among the people by the hands of the apostles. And they were all together in Solomon's Portico. 13 None of the rest dared join them, but the people held them in high honor. 14 And more than ever believers were added to the Lord, multitudes both of men and women, 15 so that they even carried out the sick into the streets, and laid them on beds and pallets, that as Peter came by at least his shadow might fall on some of them. 16 The people also gathered from the towns around Jerusalem, bringing the sick and those afflicted with unclean spirits, and they were all healed.

Fellowship in the church.—This is an expansion of a theme already introduced (2: 44-45), as the believers are pictured in a unity in which they "had everything in common" (4: 32). From the two passages several facts can be gleaned: (1) these early Christians recognized that all believers are one people; (2) they recognized that a believer has no "rights"; (3) they recognized that each should give the other access to what he possessed as it was needed; (4) they actually practiced this sharing; (5) the needy were actually cared for; (6) the sharing was strictly voluntary; (7) property was made available to the believers only as needed; (8) the movement was not "communistic," for private ownership of property continued and the sharing was designed only to meet community needs, not to equalize the believers economically; (9) it was not a communism of production or of possession.

Two errors should be avoided in the study of these two passages (2: 44f. and 4: 32ff.): (1) this early Christian sharing should not be confused with modern communism; (2) in differentiating it from communism, its great principles should not be lost. This Christian sharing had little in common with present day communism, as is shown above, but it had much which should characterize Christians of every age.

This "noble experiment" may seem to have failed at many points. It is true that poverty soon overtook this whole group and Christians elsewhere were called upon to relieve the poor in Jerusalem. It is doubtless true that the expectation of an early return of Jesus made it easier for one to be generous with property which he would soon not need, anyway. Probably others than Ananias and Sapphira were "proud of their humility" and gave to be seen of men. Perhaps, as at Thessalonica later, some were encouraged to "sponge" on their fellows. But granting to the fullest the faults of this practice, there were in it Christian principles of tremendous importance. *Pagans insist upon their "rights," but the real Christian prefers to think of his debts.* The disposition to deny self and to relate oneself to another for his good is the basic message of the Cross.

Barnabas: fellowship at its best.—Joseph, called Barnabas, was one of the truly great men in early Christianity. His action in selling a field and placing the proceeds at the disposal of the apostles is cited as fellowship at its best. A native of Cyprus (featured in 11:20 in the extension of the gospel to the Greeks), he was a man of some wealth, as was the mother of John Mark, to whom he was related (Col. 4: 10). The appellation, "Barnabas (which means, Son of encouragement)," was vindicated as he stood by Paul in Jerusalem when few were willing to trust the newcomer. He also stood by John Mark, and it is an open question as to whether Paul or Barnabas took the better stand (see later). Whatever his judgment on any given occasion, his disposition was to help, and that won for him the name "Son of encouragement." The Greek word with which Luke interprets the name

"Barnabas" [50] is a cognate of Paraclete, and it literally means "a calling alongside." The resultant idea may be that of "exhortation" or "consolation," both of which are included in the word "encouragement." [51]

Ananias and Sapphira: the big lie.—For one concerned to find evidences that Acts is trustworthy, it is reassuring to see that Luke is writing history, not fiction; he is painting a picture that is real, not ideal. This sin within the Christian community is more painful than the persecution from without. Luke draws back the veil to show hypocrisy, murmuring (chap. 6), dissension and sharp contention (chap. 15) among the believers. Many times he shows the narrow nationalism of some. [52]

The basic sin of Ananias and Sapphira was that of hypocrisy or unreality; [53] they were living a lie. Their attempt to win praise through deception was by deliberate plan, for they had "agreed together" (5: 9). In the New Testament no sin is considered more serious than that of willful blindness to or rejection of the truth. Those who crucified Jesus did so with eyes deliberately closed to truth and right, and it is in connection with this disposition that the unpardonable sin is declared. Some defense may be made for sins of ignorance or weakness, but none can be made for willful blindness to truth or willful rejection of light. If the consequences to Ananias and Sapphira seem unduly severe, it must be recognized that the view taken here toward dishonesty at the foundation of one's character is no more serious than that reflected in the Gospels. Sin against the Holy Spirit—deliberate rejection of truth and right—is inexcusable. The sinner, if he turns from it, may be forgiven, but the sin itself is inexcusable.

A sin yet more serious may be suggested in 5: 3, depending upon what is the correct translation. The accusative case, not

---

[50] Barnabas is a Semitic name of uncertain origin; *Bar* means "son," but no conclusion is now possible as to the meaning of *Nabas,* which may be Hebrew or Aramaic. Luke's Greek interpretation is true to the man, whatever the origin of the Semitic name.
[51] Cf. Rackham, *op. cit.,* p. 63.
[52] *Ibid.,* p. 64.
[53] *Loc. cit.*

the usual dative, follows the infinitive commonly translated "to lie." Possibly the translation should be: "Ananias, how is it that Satan filled your heart *to falsify* the Holy Spirit . . .?" The charge would not be simply that he lied *to* the Holy Spirit, but that he falsified the Spirit as he sought to represent his fraudulent deed as something inspired by the Spirit. Thus he tried to make the Spirit a party to his own crime.

The burial of Ananias without his wife's knowledge (5: 7) is past our understanding. It was customary to bury on the day of one's death, but was it lawful or right to bury the husband without the wife's knowledge? This is one of the many questions left unanswered in Acts; we simply have no satisfactory answer.[54] It may serve to remind us, however, that Luke was concerned with his questions and not ours. Our curiosity is aroused at many points only to be left uninformed, because Luke's purpose in writing did not contemplate many of our interests. When Acts closes with no word about the outcome of Paul's trial, Luke was again dealing with issues vital to his purpose, but he was not concerned with answering all our questions.

A serious moral consideration grows out of the story of the sudden deaths of Ananias and Sapphira. Were these deaths punitive measures effected by an arbitrary act of Peter, divinely empowered, or by God himself? Such an interpretation—other New Testament passages give possible support to this view (cf. 1 Cor. 5: 5, 11: 30; 1 Tim. 1: 20; James 5: 20; 1 John 5: 16f.)—poses a serious problem about God's method of dealing with evil. The prevailing New Testament view seems to be that wrath is operative as a natural, not arbitrary, law; sin is serious enough to carry its own consequences. Many have concluded that Ananias and Sapphira died of shock, not by the arbitrary decree of God. This view, if true, is more readily harmonized with the larger New Testament teaching. These deaths can be accounted for psychologically. The many signs accomplished in those days gave all the believers an awareness of divine power operative in their midst and struck awe and fear in their hearts. The sudden ex-

---

[54] My colleague, Professor Ray Frank Robbins, states that while in China he observed a custom which may be parallel to the one reflected in Acts. He saw the bodies of the dead taken from the streets to temporary places for burial. This was done without consulting the family.

posure of Ananias' sin against God could easily have produced the shock resulting in his death. Sapphira experienced that shock and also the shock that came with the news of her husband's death.

Fear and growth.—The next little paragraph (5: 12-16), though at first glance very simple, contains some difficult, if not insoluble, problems. The persons referred to in verse 13 cannot be identified with any certainty. Who are "the rest"? Who are those referred to as "them"? Possibly "the rest" are Christians who dared not claim a place with the apostles, who would thus be the ones referred to as "them." Again, "the rest" may be non-Christians who were afraid to join the disciples, lest they become liable to the fate of Ananias and Sapphira. Verse 14, however, seems to rule out the latter possibility. These problems cannot be solved by grammatical study, and there are no conclusive data otherwise. Possibly the major message of the paragraph is clear, whatever the answer to many of its problems.

Clearly there was a new release of power through signs and wonders with two results: even greater numbers were drawn into the movement, and all had a greater respect—or fear—for the movement, and especially for the apostles. It is understandable that both these reactions should be so. The paragraph undoubtedly points up the power and influence of the apostles, which evidently reached its height at this time. Strange indeed that these men who now towered over all should fade so completely out of the picture, not only in Acts but in all Christian history. Almost nothing is known about most of them today. Was it because they did not keep pace with the larger ideas that were to emerge in the Christian movement? For it was not these, but men yet unmentioned, who were the ones that dared to cross national and racial lines and deliver the movement from narrow nationalism into its true liberty.

The signs and wonders call for comment.—It is not said explicitly that any were actually healed as Peter's shadow fell upon them, but evidently that is the implication (5: 15). Paralleling this, it is explicitly said later that the sick were cured by handkerchiefs and aprons carried away from Paul's body (19: 12). Whatever the problem posed for the modern reader, Luke represented some of these early Christians as trusting such miracles, and Luke himself accepted their validity. Though one's faith is taxed to a greater degree than usual by such stories, it is still a matter of degree for one who accepts miracle at all. Though the stories of some miracles may seem less plausible than others, if miracles are possible, they are possible in any extreme. Miracles in the physical realm were at best but elementary devices for beginners. Jesus performed many miracles but repeatedly protested against the necessity for them. His greater works would be miracles in terms of moral and spiritual change. If, then, miracles as such represented an elementary method for beginners, it is understandable that the almost superstitious faith of simple people in the time of Peter and Paul was honored. This stage for the majority gave way to greater works; for some it yet survives in its kindergarten stage and in a perverted expression, in the worship of the dubious relics of departed "saints."

Sadducees Frustrated; Pharisees Undecided [5: 17-42]

17 But the high priest rose up and all who were with him, that is, the party of the Sadducees, and filled with jealousy 18 they arrested the apostles and put them in the common prison. 19 But at night an angel of the Lord opened the prison doors and brought them out and said, 20 "Go and stand in the temple and speak to the people all the words of this Life." 21 And when they heard this, they entered the temple at daybreak and taught.

Now the high priest came and those who were with him and called together the council and all the senate of Israel, and sent to the prison to have them brought. 22 But when the officers came, they did not find them in the prison, and they returned and reported, 23 "We found the prison securely locked and the sentries standing at the doors, but when we opened it we found no one inside." 24 Now when the captain of the temple and the chief priests heard these words, they were much perplexed about them, wondering what this would come to. 25 And some one came and told them, "The men whom you put in prison are standing in the temple and teaching the people." 26 Then the captain with the officers went and brought them, but without violence, for they were afraid of being stoned by the people.

27 And when they had brought them, they set them before the coun-

cil. And the high priest questioned them, 28 saying, "We strictly charged you not to teach in this name, yet here you have filled Jerusalem with your teaching and you intend to bring this man's blood upon us." 29 But Peter and the apostles answered, "We must obey God rather than men. 30 The God of our fathers raised Jesus whom you killed by hanging him on a tree. 31 God exalted him at his right hand as Leader and Savior, to give repentance to Israel and forgiveness of sins. 32 And we are witnesses to these things, and so is the Holy Spirit whom God has given to those who obey him."

33 When they heard this they were enraged and wanted to kill them. 34 But a Pharisee in the council named Gamaliel, a teacher of the law, held in honor by all the people, stood up and ordered the men to be put outside for a while. 35 And he said to them, "Men of Israel, take care what you do with these men. 36 For before these days Theudas arose, giving himself out to be somebody, and a number of men, about four hundred, joined him; but he was slain and all who followed him were dispersed and came to nothing. 37 After him Judas the Galilean arose in the days of the census and drew away some of the people after him; he also perished, and all who followed him were scattered. 38 So in the present case I tell you, keep away from these men and let them alone; for if this plan or this undertaking is of men, it will fail; 39 but if it is of God, you will not be able to overthrow them. You might even be found opposing God!"

40 So they took his advice, and when they had called in the apostles, they beat them and charged them not to speak in the name of Jesus, and let them go. 41 Then they left the presence of the council, rejoicing that they were counted worthy to suffer dishonor for the name. 42 And every day in the temple and at home they did not cease teaching and preaching Jesus as the Christ.

The disciples did not cease *preaching Jesus as the Christ in the temple* (5: 42)! This is almost inconceivable to the modern mind. For about nineteen centuries Judaism and Christianity have lived as two distinct religions, sometimes at war with each other, but usually ignoring each other. It is commonly thought that the issue of Christology provided the cleavage—that the Jews rejected Jesus as the Christ, the Son of God. This is not so. For some time, Jesus was preached as the Christ in the temple, in the synagogues, on the streets of Jerusalem, and in the homes. Thousands of Jews actually joined the movement; the multitudes were favorable enough to it that they utterly frustrated the determined purpose of the Sadducees to destroy it. The disciples

openly defied the positive command of the high priest and the
Sadducees, and for all their rage, these leaders were helpless to
stop them (5: 17, 28f., 33).

The Pharisees adopted a "hands-off" policy for some time;
they would wait and see. Gamaliel suggested that the Sanhedrin
let the movement stand or fall on its own merits (5: 38-39). He
even held out the possibility that this work—preaching Jesus as
the Christ—might be of God! It was at least an open question.
The Sanhedrin accepted his advice to wait and see, although
they did beat them and charge them to be silent (5: 40).

The Jews as a people did not reject Jesus as the Christ, the
Son of God; they rejected him as the Son of Man, the Savior of
the world! The point of cleavage was the middle wall of partition
between Jew and non-Jew, not Christology. The proposition
of a new humanity in which Jew and uncircumcised Gentile
were to live together as brothers was the decisive issue and is to
this day.

Luke's accuracy has been widely debated in connection with
the reference to Theudas (5: 36). The charge is made that he
confused the relative dates of Judas and Theudas. To say that
if there was an error, it was that of Gamaliel, not of Luke, misses
the point. Josephus (*Antiquities* XX, 5, 1) mentions a Theudas
in the time of the Roman procurator Cuspius Fadus, who was not
appointed to office until after the death of Herod Agrippa, A.D. 44,
some years after Gamaliel's speech. Judas (of Gamala), mentioned by both Josephus and Luke, led a revolt, A.D. 6, to protest
the census in the time of Quirinius, the governor of Syria; Josephus held this to be the origin of the Zealots, who finally precipitated the wars with Rome. Thus, it appears to many that Luke
misread Josephus, making the mistake of placing "Theudas" before "Judas." There are several possible solutions: (1) Josephus
could be in error; (2) Josephus and Luke could refer to different
men bearing the familiar name "Theudas"; (3) the name "Theudas," as Blass has suggested, could be a Christian interpolation
into the text of Josephus. At best, the problem is unsolved, and
Luke is too trustworthy a writer to be arbitrarily condemned in
a case still awaiting further light.

Hellenists, Hebrews, and the Seven [6: 1-6]

1 Now in these days when the disciples were increasing in number, the Hellenists murmured against the Hebrews because their widows were neglected in the daily distribution. 2 And the twelve summoned the body of the disciples and said, "It is not right that we should give up preaching the word of God to serve tables. 3 Therefore, brethren, pick out from among you seven men of good repute, full of the Spirit and of widsom, whom we may appoint to this duty. 4 But we will devote ourselves to prayer and to the ministry of the word." 5 And what they said pleased the whole multitude, and they chose Stephen, a man full of faith and of the Holy Spirit, and Philip, and Prochorus, and Nicanor, and Timon and Parmenas, and Nicolaus, a proselyte of Antioch. 6 These they set before the apostles, and they prayed and laid their hands upon them.

Hellenists and Hebrews.—There is no certain clue as to the amount of time covered by the first five chapters of Acts, but evidently there is a considerable lapse of time between chapters 5 and 6. A new atmosphere is felt in chapter 6 as a Hellenistic (Grecian) element is distinguished from the Hebrews. Though the point may be debated, the "Hellenists" were probably Greek-speaking Jews residing temporarily or permanently at Jerusalem, and the "Hebrews" were Aramaic-speaking Jews. Hebrew was still the language of the scholars, but Aramaic was the spoken language of most Palestinian Jews. Greek had become the language of many Jews outside of Palestine.

The Hellenists supplied the keenest students of the gospel; they also supplied some of its bitterest opponents, men who were alert in seeing its far-reaching implications for Jewish institutions. Men like Stephen and Philip found it easier to see the spiritual character and universal outreach of the gospel than did the twelve, who had been brought up in a nationalistic atmosphere and tradition. But men like Saul of Tarsus and unnamed Hellenists were quickest to see that these emphases would undermine some of their cherished institutions and break down the middle wall of partition between Jew and Gentile. It is normal and understandable that these two conflicting attitudes should develop from the identical background. Fellowship with the

larger world liberalized some of the Jews, and their particularism
gave way to universalism, as they saw the importance of humanity
beyond the nation. Other Jews, in the same situation, reacted
violently to the nations about them and determined to maintain
the wall of separation, whatever the cost.

Philip and Stephen.—It is ironical that those who were too busy
with "spiritual" matters to "serve tables" failed to provide the
deeper insights into the gospel. The twelve, who insisted that
they must devote all their time to "prayer and the ministry of
the word," were slow to see that with God there is "no respect
of persons." Stephen, Philip, and five others were mundane
enough to be assigned this table-serving job, but somehow they—
at least Stephen and Philip—developed the keenest insights into
the gospel and provided the leadership for a Christianity truly
spiritual rather than legal, embracing humanity rather than just
a nation.

Peter and the other apostles purposed to be "spiritual" and
students of the word, but they were bound by tradition. They
were building Christian Judaism instead of a church that was
spiritual in character and universal in outlook. Stephen and
Philip experienced a real freedom under the Spirit. Were Peter
and the twelve too much concerned with institutions really to
see people? Peter, by his own later confession (10: 14 and 28),
had placed the institutions of nationality and ritual ahead of
humanity. There are some indications that he had a natural love
for people, whoever they were, but he had been religiously con-
ditioned to view the Gentiles as unclean and unfit for fellowship.
He was not comfortable in this prejudice and particularism and
was a not-too-stubborn convert from it. However, he had great
difficulty in freeing himself from the fear of fellow Jews who
made racial prejudice a mark of piety and orthodoxy. Stephen
and Philip were primarily concerned with humanity instead of
institutions.

This brings to mind the cry of Jesus over the people who
appeared to him as sheep, tattered and scattered, not having a
shepherd—a field ripe for harvest, not having harvesters (Matt.

9: 36 ff.). The point is missed unless it is remembered that when
Jesus uttered this cry over the neglected people, Palestine was
crowded with religious workers, both clerical and lay. There
were twenty thousand priests, and several thousands among the
Pharisees, Sadducees, Essenes, and many other sects. There were
thousands of religious leaders concerned for the Sabbath, circumcision, washing hands, separation from Gentiles, keeping the
altar fires burning, and so forth, but few who cared for the
people as people.

The seven.—The seven may or may not have been deacons; there
has been much debate, but the data are lacking for a conclusion.
It is not satisfactory to acknowledge that a problem is insoluble,
but pride should yield to honesty. It should be admitted that
we do not know. These men are called "the seven" (21: 8), but
are never called "deacons." It may be that the seven, as the
twelve, were unique and had no successors. Certainly, deacons
at a later time had similar responsibilities, but no actual connection can be traced.

The seven were elected by the congregation (6: 3, 5); this is
the first clear evidence that the authority was in the church
as a whole. It is implied, but is not explicit, in the selection of
Matthias (1: 23-26). The laying on of hands is commonly viewed
as the ordination of the seven. In the Old Testament the laying
on of hands was practiced in several connections which include
blessing another, setting one apart for service, and the sending
away of the scape goat. In each case it symbolized the transfer
of something from one to another. The Mishna (*Sanh.* iv, 4)
indicates that members were admitted to the Sanhedrin by the
laying on of hands.[55] The practice of the early Christians without
doubt was patterned on the Jewish custom, but exactly what
the meaning of the Christian practice was, is not clear. Possibly
it symbolized the transmission of authority; if so, the apostles
only acted in behalf of the congregation whose authority they
recognized. The congregation in turn was acting in terms of its
understanding of God's will, which was the ultimate authority

---

[55] Cf. Bruce, *op. cit.*, p. 154.

behind the appointment of the seven, whatever the part of the congregation or the twelve.

If the grammatical antecedent is strictly observed, it follows that "the whole multitude," not merely the apostles, "laid their hands upon them" (6: 5-6). Finding this contrary to their presuppositions, writers of commentaries usually ignore the point of grammar, or conclude that there is a "change of subject." [56] But is it Luke or the commentators by whom the subject is changed? There is little room for dogmatic statement about who laid on the hands. (See further the discussion of 13: 1-3.)

The seven all had Greek names, but this does not force the conclusion that all were Hellenists; two of the twelve, Philip and Andrew, had Greek names but were not Hellenists. The likelihood is, however, that the seven were Hellenists. Tradition has woven stories around them, as around the twelve, but these are not very convincing. Nicolaus has been identified as the founder of the Nicolaitans mentioned in Revelation 2: 16, but evidence is entirely lacking for this. Luke's real interest is not in the seven as such or even in the incident which occasioned their election. His interest is in Stephen and Philip, and their impact upon the Christian movement.

Summary Statement: The Magnitude of Christian Judaism [6: 7]

> 7 And the word of God increased; and the number of the disciples multiplied greatly in Jerusalem, and a great many of the priests were obedient to the faith.

This paragraph closes the first major division of Acts, in which the Christian movement found expression within Judaism. Though it had traveled far in all directions, it seems to have embraced Jews only. (The proselytes had become Jews before they became Christians.) These Christian Jews were at home in the synagogues and temple, and were true to the law. There is no evidence that they had contemplated the inclusion of uncircumcised Gentiles. Jesus could be preached as the Christ in the synagogues and the temple. Though the Sadducees had

---

[56] Knowling, *op. cit.*, p. 172.

92   THE BOOK OF ACTS

sought to curb the movement, their very alarm and frustration
but emphasized the magnitude of the movement and its popularity with the Jews. Luke now observes that "the disciples
multiplied greatly in Jerusalem" and that "a great company of
the priests were obedient to the faith" (6: 7). These were most
likely the lower priests, who had little love for the high priests.
In view of the fact that the apostles continued to participate in
the temple services (3: 1), it is not improbable that these priests
continued their ministries in the Temple. This was "Christian
Judaism," and its progress had been gaining momentum to this
point.

Then, suddenly, new issues were introduced into the movement, with far-reaching results for the movement and for the
Jews. Stephen and Philip, perhaps with others, introduced ideas
which rocked the whole movement and the Jewish people. These
Grecian Jews asserted the universalism and spiritual character
of the gospel; the apostles came gradually to recognize it. The
ultimate outcome was the inclusion of uncircumcised Gentiles
and the self-exclusion of the Jews.

PART TWO

Universalism of Christianity Asserted by Grecian Jews and Gradually Recognized by Apostles
[6: 8 to 12: 25]

STEPHEN: PIONEER IN UNIVERSALISM AND MARTYR FOR IT [6: 8 to 8: 1a]

8 And Stephen, full of grace and power, did great wonders and signs among the people. 9 Then some of those who belonged to the synagogue of the Freedmen (as it was called), and of the Cyrenians, and of the Alexandrians, and of those from Cilicia and Asia, arose and disputed with Stephen. 10 But they could not withstand the wisdom and the Spirit with which he spoke. 11 Then they secretly instigated men, who said, "We have heard him speak blasphemous words against Moses and God." 12 And they stirred up the people and the elders and the scribes, and they came upon him and seized him and brought him before the council, 13 and set up false witnesses who said, "This man never ceases to speak words against this holy place and the law; 14 for we have heard him say that this Jesus of Nazareth will destroy this place, and will change the customs which Moses delivered to us." 15 And gazing at him, all who sat in the council saw that his face was like the face of an angel. 7: 1 And the high priest said, "Is this so?" 2 And Stephen said: "Brethren and fathers, hear me. The God of glory appeared to our father Abraham, when he was in Mesopotamia, before he lived in Haran, 3 and said to him, 'Depart from your land and from your kindred and go into the land which I will show you.' 4 Then he departed from the land of the Chaldeans, and lived in Haran. And after his father died, God removed him from there into this land in which you are now living; 5 yet he gave him no inheritance in it, not even a foot's length, but promised to give it to him in possession and to his posterity after him, though he had no child. 6 And God spoke to this effect, that his posterity would be aliens in a land belonging to others, who would enslave them and illtreat them four hundred years. 7 'But I will judge the nation which they serve,' said God, 'and after that they shall come out and worship me in this place.' 8 And he gave him the covenant of circumcision. And so Abraham became the father of Isaac, and circumcised him on the eighth day; and Isaac became the father of Jacob, and Jacob of the twelve patriarchs.

93

9 "And the patriarchs, jealous of Joseph, sold him into Egypt; but God was with him, 10 and rescued him out of all his afflictions, and gave him favor and wisdom before Pharaoh, king of Egypt, who made him governor over Egypt and over all his household. 11 Now there came a famine throughout all Egypt and Canaan, and great afflictions, and our fathers could find no food. 12 But when Jacob heard that there was grain in Egypt, he sent forth our fathers the first time. 13 And at the second visit Joseph made himself known to his brothers, and Joseph's family became known to Pharaoh. 14 And Joseph sent and called to him Jacob his father and all his kindred, seventy-five souls; 15 and Jacob went down into Egypt. And he died, himself and our fathers, 16 and they were carried back to Shechem and laid in the tomb that Abraham had bought for a sum of silver from the sons of Hamor in Shechem.

17 "But as the time of the promise drew near, which God had granted to Abraham, the people grew and multiplied in Egypt 18 till there arose over Egypt another king who had not known Joseph. 19 He dealt craftily with our race and forced our fathers to expose their infants, that they might not be kept alive. 20 At this time Moses was born, and was beautiful before God. And he was brought up for three months in his father's house; 21 and when he was exposed, Pharaoh's daughter adopted him and brought him up as her own son. 22 And Moses was instructed in all the wisdom of the Egyptians, and he was mighty in his words and deeds.

23 "When he was forty years old, it came into his heart to visit his brethren, the sons of Israel. 24 And seeing one of them being wronged, he defended the oppressed man and avenged him by striking the Egyptian. 25 He supposed that his brethren understood that God was giving them deliverance by his hand, but they did not understand. 26 And on the following day he appeared to them as they were quarreling and would have reconciled them saying, 'Men, you are brethren, why do you wrong each other?' 27 But the man who was wronging his neighbor thrust him aside, saying, 'Who made you a ruler and a judge over us? 28 Do you want to kill me as you killed the Egyptian yesterday?' 29 At this retort Moses fled, and became an exile, in the land of Midian, where he became the father of two sons.

30 "Now when forty years had passed, an angel appeared to him in the wilderness of Mount Sinai, in a flame of fire in a bush. 31 When Moses saw it he wondered at the sight; and as he drew near to look, the voice of the Lord came, 32 'I am the God of your fathers, the God of Abraham and of Isaac and of Jacob.' And Moses trembled and did not dare to look. 33 And the Lord said to him, 'Take off the shoes from your feet, for the place where you are standing is holy ground. 34 I have surely seen the ill-treatment of my people that are in Egypt and heard their groaning, and I have come down to deliver them. And now come, I will send you to Egypt.'

35 "This Moses whom they refused saying, 'Who made you a ruler and a judge?' God sent as both ruler and deliverer by the hand of the angel that appeared to him in the bush. 36 He led them out, having performed wonders and signs in Egypt and at the Red Sea, and in the wilderness for forty years. 37 This is the Moses who said to the Israelites, 'God will raise up for you a prophet from your brethren as he raised me up.' 38 This is he who was in the congregation in the wilderness with the angel who spoke to him at Mount Sinai, and with out fathers; and he received living oracles to give to us. 39 Our fathers refused to obey him, but thrust him aside, and in their hearts they turned to Egypt, 40 saying to Aaron, 'Make for us gods to go before us; as for this Moses who led us out from the land of Egypt, we do not know what has become of him.' 41 And they made a calf in those days, and offered a sacrifice to the idol and rejoiced in the works of their hands. 42 But God turned and gave them over to worship the host of heaven, as it is written in the book of the prophets:

> 'Did you offer to me slain beasts and sacrifices,
> forty years in the wilderness, O house of Israel?
> 43 And you took up the tent of Moloch,
> and the star of the god Rephan,
> the figures which you made to worship;
> and I will remove you beyond Babylon.'

44 "Our fathers had the tent of witness in the wilderness, even as he spoke to Moses directed him to make it, according to the pattern that he had seen. 45 Our fathers in turn brought it in with Joshua when they dispossessed the nations which God thrust out before our fathers. So it was until the days of David, 46 who found favor in the sight of God and asked leave to find a habitation for the God of Jacob. 47 But it was Solomon who built a house for him. 48 Yet the Most High does not dwell in houses made with hands; as the prophet says,

> 49 'Heaven is my throne,
> and earth my footstool.
> What house will you build for me, says the Lord,
> or what is the place of my rest?
> 50 Did not my hand make all these things?'

51 "You stiff-necked people, uncircumcised in heart and ears, you always resist the Holy Spirit. As your fathers did, so do you. 52 Which of the prophets did not your fathers persecute? And they killed those who announced before hand the coming of the Righteous One, whom you have now betrayed and murdered, 53 you who received the law as delivered by angels and did not keep it."

54 Now when they heard these things they were enraged, and they ground their teeth against him. 55 But he, full of the Holy Spirit, gazed into heaven and saw the glory of God, and Jesus standing at the right hand of God; 56 and he said, "Behold, I see the heavens opened, and the Son of man standing at the right hand of God."

57 But they cried out with a loud voice and stopped their ears and rushed together upon him. 58 Then they cast him out of the city and stoned him; and the witnesses laid down their garments at the feet of a young man named Saul. 59 And as they were stoning Stephen, he prayed, "Lord Jesus, receive my spirit." 60 And he knelt down and cried with a loud voice, "Lord, do not hold this sin against them." And when he had said this, he fell asleep. 8:1 And Saul was consenting to his death.

Stephen's ministry and arrest.—Stephen, so far as the records go, was the first of all the disciples to see Christianity in its relationship to the world; he first saw the "incidental and temporary character of the Mosaic law with the temple and all its worship." [1] He recognized that Jew and Gentile were to be united as brothers in Christ. He dared to see; he dared to speak. In so doing, he gave his life but inaugurated a new era in Christian history. His work was revolutionary against the background of his fellow disciples, but it was true to the intention of Jesus.

It is not clear whether Luke had one or several Jerusalem synagogues in mind (6: 9). The grammar does not make it clear if this was a cosmopolitan group in one synagogue or if more than one synagogue was involved. What is clear is that Stephen's insights met with violent reaction on the part of Hellenistic Jews, who then were able to arouse the people and elders against him.

Stephen was accused of "blasphemous words against Moses and God" (6: 11). It is easy for one to confuse himself with God; it is easy to cry out "blasphemy" when one's own pet ideas are challenged. National pride was offended and racial prejudice was condemned by this man Stephen. Preferring to cling to their stuffy little world, these Jews determined that Stephen must be silenced. Unable to "withstand the wisdom and the Spirit with which he spoke," they turned to violence. It is easy to appeal to the prejudices of people, and this they did. It was charged before the council that he "never ceases to speak words against this holy place and the law" (6: 13). The charge was partially true, but it was a misrepresentation of Stephen's message. His own defense (chap. 7) set forth his position on these issues.

---

[1] Rackham, *op. cit.,* p. 87.

Stephen's message.—Two distinct difficulties have been encountered by students of Stephen's speech: (1) numerous historical problems and (2) the relevancy of the speech to the charges upon which he was being tried.

It has been recognized from the earliest centuries that there are numerous problems of a historical nature in the speech. A comparison of Stephen's speech with the Old Testament discloses two problems: (1) apparent differences and (2) material in the speech of Stephen not found in the Old Testament. No satisfactory solution has been found to many of these problems.[2] Some of the differences probably indicate that the text of the Old Testament was not yet fully fixed by the first century. Stephen obviously called upon some of the rabbinical teaching of the day. Though it is not satisfactory to leave these problems unsolved, they have little to do with the meaning of the speech.

A far more important consideration is the relevancy of the speech to the occasion. Some commentators have been rather abrupt in the conclusion that the speech is pointless and that it evades the charges. This position is untenable and reflects a superficial study and unfortunate failure to see the issues with which Stephen (and Luke) was concerned.

Stephen did answer the charges, and he went beyond apology in setting forth the spiritual character and universalism of true religion. He was charged with speaking against the "holy place" and the "law," and he dealt with both of these issues. He challenged the Jews' interpretation of the "holy place" and the importance which they attached to the temple. He demonstrated that they violated the real force of the very law which they claimed to defend. The only one who had really kept it was Jesus.

Stephen, in a review of Hebrew history, demonstrated that God had never limited himself to one land and certainly not to

---

[2] For a detailed study, cf. Lake and Cadbury, *Commentary*, pp. 71–83 and Rackham, *op. cit.*, pp. 99–102: Did Terah die before or after Abraham left Haran (cf. Acts 7: 2ff. with Gen. 11: 26, 32; 12: 4)? Was Israel in Egyptian bondage 400 or 430 years (cf. Acts 7: 6 with Gen. 15: 13; Ex. 12: 40)? Were there seventy-five or seventy souls in Jacob's family (cf. Acts 7: 14 with Gen. 46: 26, Ex. 1: 5; Deut. 10: 22)? These are only a few of the problems in the chapter.

the temple in Jerusalem. "Holy ground" was any ground where God had been encountered. Many of the most cherished experiences of their fathers had taken place *outside of* Palestine. It was in Mesopotamia that God first spoke to Abraham (7: 2). Abraham never really possessed a "pace's length" of ground in Canaan (7: 5). Lake and Cadbury observe that "the point of the argument seems to be directed against the view that the promise of God entailed possession of the 'Holy Land.' " [3] The promise to Abraham was not so much that the land would be inherited as that there would be deliverance from Egypt and the freedom to worship (7: 7).[4] The patriarchs were born before Canaan was possessed. "And thus" the patriarchs were born, that is, before there was a "holy place." The English "and so" of verse 8 misses the emphasis; an adverb of manner is the Greek term, "thus," that is, "under these circumstances."

Jacob lived much of his life and died in *Egypt*, as did all his sons (7: 15). Later Jacob was buried in *Shechem*, in despised Samaria (7: 16). Moses was born in *Egypt,* reared by the Pharaoh's daughter, and instructed in the wisdom of the Egyptians (7: 20-22). One might ask if Moses, the lawgiver, was thus defiled by the land and people of Egypt! Moses sojourned in *Midian* and there begat two sons (7: 29). Stephen could have added that his wife was the daughter of a Midianite priest (Ex. 2: 16-22)! Moses lived before the Ezra reforms with their compulsory divorce for those married to foreigners (Ezra 10: 11). It was at Mount Sinai in *Arabia* that the law was given to Moses, and it was there that God spoke to him and said, "the place where you are standing is holy ground" (7: 33). Clearly, then, God had never limited himself to one land; no one land as such was "holy."

Stephen had been charged with saying that Jesus would destroy "this place," evidently referring to the temple. Without a doubt both Jesus and Stephen spoke of the overthrow of the temple, but their accusers took the statement out of its context and distorted it. Stephen drove home the fact that the temple did not represent the original plan of God; he had given instruc-

---

[3] Lake and Cadbury, *Commentary,* p. 72.
[4] *Loc. cit.*

tions for the tabernacle (7: 44), which served better as a symbol for his presence. The tabernacle was not bound to any land and served better to symbolize the universal presence of God. Solomon was permitted to build the temple; but when it was dedicated, God made it clear that he would not be limited to it (7: 48-50).

Stephen was also careful to drive home the fact that Israel had repeatedly shown the disposition to reject the Holy Spirit and the prophets. Priests reducing religion to ritual, and particularists appealing to racial pride and prejudice, always win the people who kill the prophets. Frequently there was a willful blindness to truth and a reactionary spirit in the presence of an opportunity for forward movement. The patriarchs were jealous of Joseph and sold him into Egypt (7: 9). Stephen's hearers would have little difficulty in recognizing the inference that their jealousy of Jesus had caused them to deliver him to the Romans. The brethren of Moses were strangely blind to their great deliverer (7: 25), even as those in Stephen's day were blind to Jesus, the true deliverer (cf. 7: 35-37). The law of wrath, by which stubborn blindness plunges a people into greater blindness, was operative for Israel (7: 38-43), and the same law would take its toll in Stephen's day.

Finally Stephen lashed out in the direct charge that his accusers were stubbornly blind and were violators of the very law which they professed to defend (7: 53). They, as their fathers, always resisted the prophet who dared to challenge their cherished way of life. In Jesus, the religion of the Spirit had met the religion of the letter, of ritual, of narrow nationlism and particularism. In Stephen, the message of Jesus was again being proclaimed. The Jews had said, "Crucify Jesus"; now they were saying, "Stone Stephen."

Stephen martyred.—As they "ground their teeth" against Stephen, he looked up and saw "Jesus standing at the right hand of God" (7: 54f.). Stephen referred to Jesus as "the Son of man," a most significant fact (7: 56). Only here in the New Testament does another call Jesus "the Son of man." That was the favorite self-designation of Jesus, and it is significant that Stephen thought of Jesus under that title. Jesus accepted the term "Messiah," but he did not encourage its use because it suggested to the Jews a glorification of the nation of Israel. He preferred the title which suggested his kinship to humanity. He had come as the Saviour of the world, not to set one nation in a special place of privilege.

It is generally agreed today that the basic meaning of "Son of man" was "man" in the sense of humanity. In Daniel, the figure represents the people who are the saints of the Most High or the true people of God, not identical with national Israel. This corresponds to the idea of the "remnant." But the Son of man, as was true of the remnant and the Suffering Servant, came finally to be reduced to one person, even Jesus. He, and he alone, proved to be the Son of man. At the cross he stood alone; true man existed alone in him. But not only was Jesus the Son of man; he came to create the Son of man. All those, from whatever nation or race, who are drawn into union with him constitute the Son of man. Thus by gradual elimination (mankind, national Israel, remnant, Jesus), the Son of man was fulfilled in Jesus alone. Next, by inclusion, the disciples of Jesus became with him the Son of man. There are other biblical analogies (Suffering Servant; remnant; true Israel; the church, the body of Christ) for the same idea, but this one was apparently the one most employed by Jesus and recognized by Stephen.*

It is not clear whether this was a mob "lynching" or a legal execution. Most of the atmosphere suggests mob action; the orderly laying of the clothes at Saul's feet would suggest a formal execution. The evidences are indecisive. More important is Stephen's spirit as he gives his life, saying, "Lord, do not hold this sin against them" (7: 60). It is often true that kindness and gentleness belong to the "heretics," but they are strangely lacking in many of the "defenders of the faith." Those who think they

---

*For careful study of this theme, see T. W. Manson, *The Teaching of Jesus* (second ed. reprinted; Cambridge: University Press, 1948), pp. 227–236; O. Cullmann, *Königsherrschaft Christi und Kirche im Neuen Testament* (dritte Auflage, Evangelischer Verlag A. G. Zollikon-Zürich, 1950), pp. 37f.; and C. H. Dodd, *The Interpretation of the Fourth Gospel* (Cambridge: University Press, 1953), pp. 241–249.

do God service by resorting to physical or legal force in their
persecutions of "heretics" are but egocentrics who have confused
themselves with God.

Saul of Tarsus stood by as Stephen was stoned; possibly he had
been among those who unsuccessfully debated with Stephen in
the synagogue. Saul, as a Pharisee, was infuriated by a gospel
which tampered with the "middle wall of partition," but after
his conversion he became the chief exponent of the very thing
for which Stephen gave his life.

NEW PERSECUTION BY SAUL THE PHARISEE
[8: 1b-3]

[1b] And on that day a great persecution arose against the church in
Jerusalem; and they were all scattered throughout the region of
Judea and Samaria, except the apostles. 2 Devout men buried
Stephen, and made great lamentation over him. 3 But Saul laid
waste the church, and entering house after house, he dragged off
men and women and committed them to prison.

THE PHARISEES were now aroused and were to take the lead in
the persecutions. The Sadducees had been frightened by what
they considered a potential messianic revolt against Rome. This
left the Pharisees undisturbed, but Stephen's emphasis upon the
spiritual character of religion and God's concern with humanity
above nation or race was too much for them. National pride and
racial prejudice, masquerading as orthodoxy and piety, struck
out in inquisition and persecution with animal passion. "Laid
waste" (8: 3) is a mild translation of Luke's term for Saul's action.
Saul "ravaged" the church like a savage animal. His "religious
zeal," whatever its element of sincerity, was blind passion that
mounted to sadistic expression.

Luke's statement that all were scattered "except the apostles"
(8: 1) has puzzled many readers. This datum, however, fits
perfectly into the pattern of the whole book. This new persecution under Saul was of an entirely different character and was
directed against a specific group; it was directed against those
who shared Stephen's liberal view. The twelve were probably

unmolested at this time because they were preaching nothing
to offend the exponents of the "middle wall of partition." The
twelve were still Jews—Christian Jews. They were at home in
the temple and synagogue, and they were still looking for the
Lord to "restore the kingdom to Israel" (1: 6). None of the
initiative in preaching to the Samaritans or Gentiles was taken
by the twelve. What Philip did gladly, they investigated with
anxious care. Only gradually did they grope their way—or were
forced—toward the truths for which Stephen gave his life and
which Philip was thrilled to preach.

It may be asked how this persecution could take place in a
land ruled by Rome. Lake and Cadbury made the helpful suggestion that "even if it be true that Roman law would have forbidden it, we do not know whether Roman administration would
not have connived at it."[5] Paul himself acknowledged the persecutions (Gal. 1: 13, 22f.; 1 Cor. 15: 9; Phil. 3: 6; 1 Tim. 1: 13),
though the statements in his letters do not affirm that the persecutions were "unto death." It seems that the power of capital
punishment rested with the Romans; but probably the Sanhedrin
had some authority to pass the death sentence when the issues
were religious, the sentence being subject to Roman approval.

Stephen's burial was probably by devout Jews who were not
Christians. It must not be forgotten that there were non-Christian
Jews who did not sanction the madness that martyred Stephen.
It must not be forgotten that the men who pioneered for universalism were Jews. Jesus was a Jew; the prophets before him
were of Israel,[6] and the men like Stephen who followed him
were Jews. They were Jews (or Israelites) who saw that monotheism had universalism as its inevitable corollary; one God
calls for one world. Luke tells the sad story of Jews committed to
a narrow racial creed, blinded by pride and prejudice; *but he
also tells of Jews who blazed new trails for humanity.* Anti-
Semites today need to remember this.

---

[5] Lake and Cadbury, *Commentary*, p. 86.
[6] The term "Jew" cannot be used correctly for the period before the Exile.

PHILIP FREELY PREACHES TO SAMARITANS
AND AN ETHIOPIAN [8: 4-40]

Philip in Samaria [8: 4-13]

4 Now those who were scattered went about preaching the word. 5 Philip went down to a city of Samaria, and proclaimed to them the Christ. 6 And the multitudes with one accord gave heed to what was said by Philip, when they heard him and saw the signs which he did. 6 For unclean spirits came out of many who were possessed, crying with a loud voice; and many who were paralyzed or lame were healed. 8 So there was much joy in that city.

9 But there was a man named Simon who had previously practiced magic in the city and amazed the nation of Samaria, saying that he himself was somebody great. 10 They all gave heed to him, from the least to the greatest, saying, "This man is that power of God which is called Great." 11 And they gave heed to him, because for a long time he had amazed them with his magic. 12 But when they believed Philip as he preached good news about the kingdom of God and the name of Jesus Christ, they were baptized, both men and women. 13 Even Simon himself believed, and after being baptized he continued with Philip. And seeing signs and great miracles performed, he was amazed.

THE WORD for "scattered" is the term for seed-sowing. The truth of the proverb is borne out: "The blood of the martyrs is the seed of the church." This Christian dispersion was turned to gain.

Philip, one of the Grecians, freely preached to the Samaritans. This is amazing in the light of the bitterness that obtained between Jews and Samaritans in his day. Samaritans were despised because their blood was mixed through intermarriages with those outside Israel. How is it that it was forgotten that all of the race had become mixed? The Old Testament clearly indicates that there were intermarriages down the line until the time of Ezra. Moses married a Midianitess; Jacob had children by Bilhah and Zilpah, maids to Rachel and Leah (Gen. 29: 24, 29); Judah had sons, Er and Onan, by a Canaanitess (Gen. 38: 2-4); Joseph's sons were born to Asenath, daughter of the priest (or prince) of On (Gen. 41: 45); David was descended from Ruth, a Moabitess; Solomon had innumerable foreign wives; and so the record goes. The long list of mixed marriages in the tenth chapter of Ezra indicates something of the extent of such marriages. But pride and prejudice care little for facts, preferring to further selfish interests through any convenient fiction. The Samaritan attitude was no better than that of the Jew. Neither was unique, for the stupidity of such prejudice belongs to the human race, not to just a part of it.

Simon Magus may have taught some system of emanations in which he was the "power of God," but the truth is that the exact nature of his teaching is not clear to us. He was a magician and had commanded a large following. Justin Martyr thought that there was a statue at Rome in his honor, but it is now known that he misinterpreted the inscription. The Simon of Acts was thought by church fathers in the second and third centuries to be the founder of a gnostic sect, but this cannot be established. What is certain is that Simon Magus represented a false spiritualism, and it was clearly exposed as false. True religion of the Spirit was distinguished from false spiritualism. This Simon "believed" and was baptized. He accepted the fact of the miracles accomplished by Philip and the fact of the Power behind the miracles. Simon was not "converted," however. His basic motivation, before and after he "believed," was selfish. Even in religion he sought to further selfish interests, and that is but the sublimation of the core of depravity. He knew nothing of the Cross, with its self-renunciation. He showed no willingness to "be crucified with Christ."

Peter in Samaria [8: 14-25]

14 Now when the apostles at Jerusalem heard that Samaria had received the word of God, they sent to them Peter and John, 15 who came down and prayed for them that they might receive the Holy Spirit; 16 for it had not yet fallen on any of them, but they had only been baptized in the name of the Lord Jesus. 17 Then they laid their hands on them and they received the Holy Spirit. 18 Now when Simon saw that the Spirit was given through the laying on of the apostles' hands, he offered them money, 19 saying, "Give me also this power, that any one on whom I lay my hands may receive the Holy Spirit." 20 But Peter said to him, "Your silver perish with you, because you thought you could obtain the gift of God with money! 21 You have neither part nor lot in this matter, for your heart is not right before God. 22 Repent therefore of this wickedness of yours, and pray to the Lord that, if possible, the intent of

your heart may be forgiven you. 23 For I see that you are in the gall of bitterness and in the bond of iniquity." 24 And Simon answered, "Pray for me to the Lord, that nothing of what you have said may come upon me."
25 Now when they had testified and spoken the word of the Lord, they returned to Jerusalem, preaching the gospel to many villages of the Samaritans.

The apostles were still in Jerusalem when Philip was extending the gospel to the Samaritans. Though apparently sympathetic with the development, they did not initiate it. The statement is puzzling that these Samaritans had believed and "been baptized in the name of the Lord Jesus" (8: 12, 16), but had not received the Holy Spirit (8: 15f.). Any conviction of sin or willingness to trust Jesus would reflect a striving of the Spirit with man's spirit. Possibly Luke means that there was no manifestation of the Spirit comparable to that at Pentecost until Peter and John had laid their hands upon them. If this is true, then a pattern can be seen: there was a great outpouring of the Holy Spirit at Jerusalem on the day of Pentecost; and there were similar outpourings when Samaritans were reached, when God-fearing Greeks at Caesarea were reached, and when disciples of John the Baptist at Ephesus were reached.[7] Each of the significant stages of development was divinely authenticated. That the laying on of hands by the apostles was indispensable to the receiving of the Holy Spirit is not supported in Acts. The very next story is of the conversion of the Ethiopian, with no apostle present, and no mention of laying on of hands; yet the Holy Spirit must certainly have come upon him. Definitely, the Holy Spirit came upon Cornelius and those with him apart from any laying on of hands.

Although God was willing to honor simple faith and the symbolic act of laying on of hands, this gift of God could not be bought (8: 20). Simon's attempt to buy this power made it clear that his heart was not right before God; he had not repented. Simon had reached such depths of depravity that in his self-centeredness, he even tried to gain the power of God for the furthering of selfish interests. The core of depravity is the disposition to give to self the place that belongs to God; it has its

---

[7] Cf. Rackham, *op. cit.*, p. 117.

crudest expression when it even invades religion to enlist that help in the exalting of self.

It is an evidence of progress in Peter and John that they preached the gospel to many villages of the Samaritans (8: 25). John once wanted to burn them up (Luke 9: 54). The Greek indicates that this is the beginning of a new paragraph and that verses 25 and 26 are joined together. This means that the "they" includes Philip.[8] This probably accounts for the additional work among the Samaritans.

Unhindered: The Ethiopian Eunuch, a God-fearing Greek
[8: 26-40]

26 But an angel of the Lord said to Philip, "Rise and go toward the south to the road that goes down from Jerusalem to Gaza." This is a desert road. 27 And he rose and went. And behold, an Ethiopian, a eunuch, a minister of Candace the queen of the Ethiopians, in charge of all her treasure, had come to Jerusalem to worship 28 and was returning; seated in his chariot, he was reading the prophet Isaiah. 29 And the Spirit said to Philip, "Go up and join this chariot." 30 So Philip ran to him, and heard him reading Isaiah the prophet, and asked, "Do you understand what you are reading?" 31 And he said, "How can I, unless some one guides me?" And he invited Philip to come up and sit with him. 32 Now the passage of the scripture which he was reading was this:
"As a sheep led to the slaughter
or a lamb before its shearer is dumb,
so he opens not his mouth.
33 In his humiliation justice was denied him.
Who can describe his generation?
For his life is taken up from the earth."
34 And the eunuch said to Philip, "About whom, pray, does the prophet say this, about himself or about some one else?" 35 Then Philip opened his mouth, and beginning with this scripture he told him the good news of Jesus. 36 And as they went along the road they came to some water, and the eunuch said, "See, here is water! What is to prevent my being baptized?" 38 And he commanded the chariot to stop, and they both went down into the water, Philip and the eunuch, and he baptized him. 39 And when they came up out of the water, the Spirit of the Lord caught up Philip; and the eunuch saw him no more, and went on his way rejoicing. 40 But Philip was found at Azotus, and passing on he preached the gospel to all the towns till he came to Caesarea.

---

[8] Cf. Lake and Cadbury, *Commentary*, p. 95.

This marks the third major area into which the gospel has reached: first Jews only; then Samaritans, who were of mixed blood; and now God-fearing Greeks. The Ethiopian and Cornelius are representatives of this third group. They were Gentiles who were students of Judaism but who had not actually become proselytes. The fourth group, the pagans with no training in Judaism, is yet to be reached; the Philippian jailer will be the first of this group to be presented.

The Ethiopian was a God-fearing Greek; that he was not a Jew is not explicitly stated but is certainly implied. He had gone to Jerusalem for the purpose of worship (8: 27) and was reading the Septuagint, the Old Testament in Greek, while returning to Ethiopia.

There was a large group of Gentiles who were termed "God-fearers." They were attracted to Judaism because of its monotheism and its high moral and ethical teachings. Many had lost faith in the gods of the empire, and they were disturbed by the immorality which was promoted by heathen cults. Great numbers of Gentiles turned to the synagogues. Some of these came into Judaism as proselytes, but others stopped short of that step. To become a proselyte involved circumcision, Jewish baptism, and the offering of certain sacrifices. It also involved the proposition that Judaism was a nation as well as a religion. To become a proselyte was to become a part of the nation as well as of the religion of the Jews. The Ethiopian and Cornelius belonged rather to the group of God-fearers. Much of the early expansion of Christianity was through this group. Christianity offered the same monotheism, the moral and ethical standard, and more; yet it did not require one to identify himself with a particular national group.

The eagerness of Philip in preaching to the Ethiopian is in striking contrast with the reluctance of Peter in preaching to Cornelius. Philip "ran to him" (8: 30) and lost no time in telling him "the good news of Jesus" (8: 35), beginning with the passage in Isaiah.

The major point which Luke is concerned to develop probably comes out in the Ethiopian's question: "See, here is water!

What is to prevent my being baptized?" The Ethiopian had doubtless been "prevented" from being circumcised and becoming a Jew. He was a eunuch, and because of this physical mutilation he probably had been denied the privilege of becoming a proselyte to Judaism. This would be in keeping with the priestly view expressed in Deuteronomy 23: 1. The prophetic view was quite different (Isa. 56: 3ff.), but probably did not prevail over the priestly view. The position in Isaiah did not guarantee full admission as a proselyte but rather a special blessing for those who observed the sabbath. The eunuch's concern now, as Philip led him into a new religious experience, would be about the technicality which might prevent his baptism: "What is to prevent my being baptized?" Philip had nothing to say about race, nationality, physical mutilation, or any other consideration of an external, artificial, or superficial nature. All that Philip awaited was evidence of the man's trust in Jesus, and thus he baptized him.[9] A God-fearing Gentile, barred from becoming a Jew because of a physical mutilation, could become a disciple of Jesus. It was a matter of spiritual experience instead of race or ritual.

"Unhindered!" is the concluding shout of Luke's two volumes. The Ethiopian, too, was "unhindered" in his request for baptism. The very word, "What *prevents* me?" is basically the same word in the Greek with which Acts is closed. The word here is a verb, *kōluei*; the closing word of Acts is an adverb, *akōlutōs*. The idea expressed by these words is precisely the thing with which Luke was most concerned. He traced the story of how the gospel was *liberated* and how men of all classes and races were liberated by it. "Unhindered" was his thrilling theme. No one can truly appreciate it, except as he too is liberated—from sin, from self, from narrow nationalism, from provincialism and particularism, from racial pride and prejudice—and as he finds himself in Christ Jesus related to humanity and to eternity!

---

[9] It is recognized by all students of textual criticism that verse thirty-seven is not supported by the best manuscripts. The verse reads (with variation in the manuscripts): "And Philip said, 'If you believe with all your heart, you may.' And he replied, 'I believe that Jesus Christ is the Son of God.'" Though the verse is doubtless a scribe's addition to the text, it does accurately interpret the thought of Philip and the Ethiopian.

Had Luke been concerned to trace Christianity's geographical expansion, this would have been a good opportunity. What developed in Ethiopia? Luke let the curtain fall on that because his interest was elsewhere. The barriers with which he was concerned were not geographical, but national, racial, legal, ritual.

SAUL'S CONVERSION, COMMISSION, AND RECEPTION
[9: 1-30]

Saul's Conversion [9: 1-9]

1 But Saul, still breathing threats and murder against the disciples of the Lord, went to the high priest 2 and asked him for letters to the synagogues at Damascus, so that if he found any belonging to the Way, men or women, he might bring them bound to Jerusalem. 3 Now as he journeyed he approached Damascus, and suddenly a light from heaven flashed about him. 4 And he fell to the ground and heard a voice saying to him, "Saul, Saul, why do you persecute me?" 5 And he said, "Who are you, Lord?" And he said, "I am Jesus, whom you are persecuting; 6 but rise and enter the city, and you will be told what you are to do." 7 The men who were traveling with him stood speechless, hearing the voice but seeing no one. 8 Saul arose from the ground; and when his eyes were opened, he could see nothing; so they led him by the hand and brought him into Damascus. 9 And for three days he was without sight, and neither ate nor drank.

THIS IS THE FIRST of three accounts in Acts of Saul's conversion (cf. chaps. 22 and 26). In his letters Paul acknowledges that he had "persecuted the church of God violently and tried to destroy it" (Gal. 1: 13; Phil. 3:6), that he had been extremely zealous for the traditions of his fathers (Gal. 1: 14), that his early days as a Christian were around Damascus (Gal. 1: 17), that he had seen Jesus our Lord (1 Cor. 9:1; 15: 8), and that he had experienced a remarkable vision (2 Cor. 12: 1ff.). Though there are minor differences in the accounts,[10] there can be no reasonable

---

[10] There is an apparent problem in the comparison of Acts 9: 7, "hearing the voice but seeing no one," and Acts 22: 9, "did not hear the voice of the one who was speaking to me." This problem may be cleared up by Greek grammar: in 9: 7 the genitive case follows the word "hearing"; in 22: 9 it is the accusative case, with the verb for hearing. The accusative usually carries the idea of understanding, and the genitive may reflect only the awareness of the sound. This distinction can be made in the Greek and possibly was intended in Acts, but it must be admitted that in the Greek New Testament this distinction is not always maintained.

doubt that Saul encountered the risen Lord near Damascus and
that there his character and life were changed. The "old man"
was shattered and the new man in Christ came into being.

Saul was a Jew of Tarsus, a city of great culture, excelled in the
empire only by Athens and Alexandria. He could there hardly
have escaped the influence of Greek culture, though as a Pharisee
(Phil. 3: 5) it is improbable that he would have studied in Greek
schools. Though a Hellenistic Jew by virtue of the Greek culture
which he could not escape, he was by choice and family tradition
a "Hebrew born of Hebrews" (Phil. 3: 5). He had facility in
Hebrew, Aramaic, and Greek. His family had enough wealth
and prominence to gain for him the privilege of studying under
Gamaliel, the great Pharisee in Jerusalem. His sister lived in
Jerusalem and evidently had access to the high priestly families
(Acts 23: 16ff.). He was a Roman citizen by birth; probably his
father had been honored with this citizenship as a reward for
outstanding service. His Hebrew name was Saul, which was
closely resembled by the Latin name, "Paulus," which he would
bear as a Roman citizen. As was true of any properly reared
Jewish son, he had a trade; his was possibly that of tentmaker.[11]

Surely many influences contributed to the making of the
Apostle Paul: his Jewish background, the Greek influence, his
pre-conversion contact with the followers of Jesus, and other
forces and factors. Doubtless the most important element by far
in his conversion and subsequent life was the personal encounter
with Jesus himself. The core of Paul's theology was the "in
Christ" or "Christ in you" relationship.[12] To Paul, as to John, the
vital union between Christ and the believer was real and all-
important. That conviction was rooted in the experience with
Jesus at Damascus.

The question is often raised about the possibility of arrests
being made in Damascus by a representative of the Jerusalem
Sanhedrin. This does seem to have been permissible as Rome
had given the Jews the right of extradition of Jewish malefac-

---

[11] See below, p. 189.
[12] For an excellent study of this theme, cf. James S. Stewart, *A Man In Christ*
(London: Hodder & Stoughton, 1935).

tors.[13] If 1 Maccabees 15: 15-21 may be trusted, a letter was written by Lucius, consul of the Romans, to King Ptolemy saying that "if any miscreants flee from their country [that of the Jews] to you, hand them over to Simon, the high priest, so that he may punish them in accordance with their law."* True, this related to the time of the Maccabees, but it is possible that this same power to extract fugitive Jews remained with the Sanhedrin in Saul's day. Josephus (*Antiquities* xiv, 10, 2) preserves a letter showing that Julius Caesar extended the privileges of the office of high priest to Hyrcanus. Possibly the followers of Jesus which Saul expected to arrest were some of those who fled the persecution in Jerusalem.

Saul Commissioned and Baptized [9: 10-19a]

10 Now there was a disciple at Damascus named Ananias. The Lord said to him in a vision, "Ananias." And he said, "Here I am, Lord." [11] And the Lord said to him, "Rise and go to the street called Straight, and inquire in the house of Judas for a man of Tarsus named Saul; for behold, he is praying, [12] and he has seen a man named Ananias come in and lay his hands on him so that he might regain his sight." [13] But Ananias answered, "Lord, I have heard from many about this man, how much evil he has done to thy saints at Jerusalem; [14] and here he has authority from the chief priests to bind all who call upon thy name." [15] But the Lord said to him, "Go, for he is a chosen instrument of mine to carry my name before the Gentiles and kings and the sons of Israel; [16] for I will show him how much he must suffer for the sake of my name." [17] So Ananias departed and entered the house. And laying his hands on him he said, "Brother Saul, the Lord Jesus who appeared to you on the road by which you came, has sent me that you may regain your sight and be filled with the Holy Spirit." [18] And immediately something like scales fell from his eyes and he regained his sight. Then he rose and was baptized, [19] and took food and was strengthened.

The followers of Jesus at Damascus were not yet separated from the synagogues. Ananias, who was sent to Saul, was "a devout man according to the law, well spoken of by all the Jews who lived there" (22: 12). Hostility there between Jews and the disciples seems not to have started until later.

---

[13] Cf. Lake and Cadbury, *Commentary*, p. 99.
*V. 21. Edgar J. Goodspeed, *The Apocrypha, an American Translation* (Chicago: The University of Chicago Press, 1939).

Saul's commission is significant: he was to carry the gospel to "Gentiles and kings and the sons of Israel" (9: 15). His ministry was to be pre-eminently to the Gentiles, but not to the exclusion of the Jews. Paul never lost his concern for the Jews, and he never ceased trying to win them. Only when he was forced to choose between Jew and Gentile would he turn to the latter. His desire was to minister to the two as one people. His ministry was also destined to carry the gospel before kings, proconsuls, Asiarchs, and possibly before the emperor. Paul seemed equally at home with the humble people of everyday life and the rulers of the nations. His commission included the cross; he would suffer for his Lord (9: 16).

"Something like scales fell from his eyes" (9: 18) at Damascus. Saul saw Jesus aright for the first time. He also saw humanity in a new light. The one whose following he had sought to destroy now became his Lord. But also of immeasurable significance, his eyes were opened to the fallacy of the "middle wall of partition" which he had sought to preserve.

Saul's Reception at Damascus and Jerusalem [9: 19b-30]

[19b] For several days he was with the disciples at Damascus. 20 And in the synagogues immediately he proclaimed Jesus, saying, "He is the Son of God." 21 And all who heard him were amazed, and said, "Is not this the man who made havoc in Jerusalem of those who called on this name? And he has come here for this purpose, to bring them bound before the chief priest." 22 But Saul increased all the more in strength, and confounded the Jews who lived in Damascus by proving that Jesus was the Christ.

23 When many days had passed, the Jews plotted to kill him, 24 but their plot became known to Saul. They were watching the gates day and night, to kill him; 25 but his disciples took him by night and let him down over the wall, lowering him in a basket.

26 And when he had come to Jerusalem he attempted to join the disciples; and they were all afraid of him, for they did not believe that he was a disicple. 27 But Barnabas took him, and brought him to the apostles, and declared to them how on the road he had seen the Lord, who spoke to him, and how at Damascus he had preached boldly in the name of Jesus. 28 So he went in and out among them at Jerusalem, 29 preaching boldly in the name of the Lord. And he spoke and disputed against the Hellenists; but they were seeking to kill him. 30 And when the brethren knew it, they brought him down to Caesarea, and sent him off to Tarsus.

After some days, probably days of adjustment and getting acquainted with his new colleagues, Saul *in the synagogues* proclaimed Jesus as the Son of God (9: 20). Those who heard him were amazed at this complete reversal in Saul. Evidently those who were "amazed" were unbelieving Jews. It is important to observe that at this point in Damascus, as at Jerusalem, the disciples worshipped in the synagogues and at this point Jesus could be preached in the synagogues as the Son of God and the Christ.

The situation changed, however, "when many days had passed" (9: 23); there developed a plot to kill Saul.[14] Why this change of attitude of the unbelieving Jews? Saul had evidently injected a new issue into the preaching at Damascus. Preaching Jesus as the Christ, the Son of God, had not precipitated persecution, but at this point something in Paul's preaching made the difference. Was Saul injecting something of Stephen's great insights into the Damascus situation? This issue which finally parted Jews and Christians was not that he was preached as the Christ, the Son of God, but that he was preached as the Son of man in whom differences of race were superseded.

The fear of Saul on the part of the Jerusalem disciples supports the other evidences that the persecutions he had led were fierce. Barnabas played his usual role of courage and fairness, and to him Saul had a great debt. Saul's sharpest conflict in Jerusalem was precisely where it could have been expected, with the Hellenists. As shown earlier, the influences under which the Hellenistic Jews had lived could make them more liberal in attitude toward Gentiles or could bring about a reactionary spirit in which they would become the most fanatical champions of separation.

PEACE AND GROWTH [9: 31]

31 So the church throughout all Judea and Galilee and Samaria had peace and was built up; and walking in the fear of the Lord and in the comfort of the Holy Spirit it was multiplied.

---

[14] Luke omits reference to the years in Arabia (Gal. 1: 17), just as he is silent about the years at Tarsus. Luke is not tracing the life of Paul. Verse twenty-three may be a veiled reference to the time spent in Arabia.

SEVERAL FACTORS could have combined to give peace to "the church throughout all Judea and Galilee and Samaria." In the year 38 there was an outbreak of persecution against the Jews in Alexandria, and in 39 the Emperor Caligula ordered that his image be placed in the temple. These terrible events would naturally divert attention from the Christians. But Saul's removal to Tarsus was perhaps the major factor. When men like Stephen, Philip, and Paul were off the scene the disciples had little difficulty with the unbelieving Jews (cf. Acts 21: 17-26).

The best manuscripts have the singular, "church," though there is strong support for the plural, "churches." The singular views the disciples as a new humanity in Christ, or body of Christ, with no reference to an ecclesiastical system. The plural points to separate local bodies. The New Testament uses "church" in these two ways only: either for the local assembly or for the whole of Christendom, with no reference to organization.

THE APOSTLES BROUGHT TO RECOGNITION OF UNCIRCUMCISED GENTILES [9: 32 to 11: 18]

Peter at Lydda and Joppa [9: 32-43]

32 Now as Peter went here and there among them all, he came down also to the saints that lived at Lydda. 33 There he found a man named Aeneas, who had been bedridden for eight years and was paralyzed. 34 And Peter said to him, "Aeneas, Jesus Christ heals you; rise and make your bed." And immediately he rose. 35 And all the residents of Lydda and Sharon saw him, and they turned to the Lord.

36 Now there was at Joppa a disciple named Tabitha, which means Dorcas or Gazelle. She was full of good works and acts of charity. 37 In those days she fell sick and died; and when they had washed her, they laid her in an upper room. 38 Since Lydda was near Joppa, the disciples, hearing that Peter was there, sent two men to him entreating him, "Please come to us without delay." 39 So Peter rose and went with them. And when he had come, they took him to the upper room. All the widows stood beside him weeping, and showing coats and garments which Dorcas made while she was with them. 40 But Peter put them all outside and knelt down and prayed; then turning to the body he said, Tabitha, rise." And she opened her eyes, and when she saw Peter

she sat up. [41] And he gave her his hand and lifted her up. Then calling the saints and widows he presented her alive. [42] And it became known throughout all Joppa, and many believed in the Lord. [43] And he stayed in Joppa for many days with one Simon, a tanner.

THE MINISTRY OF HEALING serves to turn attention again to Peter and those with whom he was closely associated. The miracles were acts of mercy and they were instrumental in the making of converts. No disturbing issues are reported in this phase of the work. In lodging with a tanner, whose work with hides would be "defiling," Peter reflects either some progress in attitude in the matter of ritual purity or a native indifference to scruples so important to the ritualists. This may be another indication that when away from the influence of those who insisted upon strict observance of the law, Peter was rather liberal.

Cornelius' Vision [10: 1-8]

1 At Caesarea there was a man named Cornelius, a centurion of what was known as the Italian Cohort, 2 a devout man who feared God with all his household, gave alms liberally to the people, and prayed constantly to God. 3 About the ninth hour of the day he saw clearly in a vision an angel of God coming in and saying to him, "Cornelius." 4 And he stared at him in terror, and said, "What is it, Lord?" And he said to him, "Your prayers and your alms have ascended as a memorial before God. 5 And now send men to Joppa, and bring one Simon who is called Peter; 6 he is lodging with Simon, a tanner, whose house is by the seaside." 7 When the angel who spoke to him had departed, he called two of his servants and a devout soldier from among those that waited on him, 8 and having related everything to them, he sent them to Joppa.

It is often asserted that in preaching to Cornelius Peter opened the door to the Gentiles.[15] This statement is filled with untruths and half-truths. It inexcusably overlooks many of the facts made most emphatic by Luke. It should be observed that (1) Cornelius, though a Gentile, was also a God-fearer like the Ethiopian eunuch, not a pagan like the Philippian jailer; (2) Peter was not the first to win a God-fearer, for Philip did that with an eagerness

---

[15] Cf. Rackham, *op. cit.*, pp. 141f.; Bruce, *op. cit.*, pp. 227f. for typical confusions of this matter.

and joy that put Peter's reluctance and fear to shame; (3) Stephen gave his life for the proposition of universalism and the spiritual character of true religion long before Peter timidly preached to Cornelius.

Cornelius belonged to the third great group reached by the gospel. Having begun with Jews and proselytes to Judaism, it next reached the Samaritans, then went on to the God-fearers like the Ethiopian and Cornelius. Luke is yet to trace its entrance into the last group, those in raw paganism, unconditioned by the synagogue discipline.

Cornelius was a Roman centurion who was a devout student of Judaism, but not a proselyte; he was not circumcised (cf. 11: 3). Centurions have a good name in the New Testament as well as in Roman history. He was in charge of one hundred men in the Italian Cohort; a cohort numbered six hundred at full strength. Cornelius made no secret of his religious devotion and had influenced those near him for good. He gave alms liberally to "the people," that is, to the Jews, and he prayed constantly to God (10: 2).

Peter's Vision in Joppa [10: 9-23a]

9 The next day, as they were on their journey and coming near the city, Peter went up on the housetop to pray, about the sixth hour. 10 And he became hungry and desired something to eat; but while they were preparing it, he fell into a trance 11 and saw the heaven opened, and something descending, like a great sheet, let down by four corners upon the earth. 12 In it were all kinds of animals and reptiles and birds of the air. 13 And there came a voice to him, "Rise, Peter; kill and eat." 14 But Peter said, "No Lord; for I have never eaten anything that is common or unclean." 15 And the voice came to him again a second time, "What God has cleansed, you must not call common." 16 This happened three times, and the thing was taken up at once to heaven.

17 Now while Peter was inwardly perplexed as to what the vision which he had seen might mean, behold, the men that were sent by Cornelius, having made inquiry for Simon's house, stood before the gate 18 and called out to ask whether Simon who was called Peter was lodging there. 19 And while Peter was pondering the vision, the Spirit said to him, "Behold, three men are looking for you. 20 Rise and go down and accompany them without hesitation; for I have sent them." 21 And Peter went down to the men and said, "I am the one you are looking for; what is the reason for

your coming?" ²² And they said, "Cornelius, a centurion, an up-
right and God-fearing man, who is well spoken of by the whole
Jewish nation, was directed by a holy angel to send for you to
come to his house, and to hear what you have to say." ²³ So he
called them in to be his guests.

It was to Joppa that Jonah fled, trying to escape a mission to
Nineveh, whose destruction he desired. Jonah took no initiative
in preaching to the Gentiles but was forced to do so. Peter found
himself at Joppa in much the same situation. Through the
activities of others and the growth of the movement, he was being
forced into the consideration of the Gentile issue.

When the vision came and the voice commanded that he eat
from the mixture of "clean" and "unclean" animals, Peter
bluntly protested that he had never eaten anything "common
or unclean" (10: 14). Had he learned nothing from Jesus who
insisted that "there is nothing outside a man which by going
into him can defile him" (Mark 7: 15)? From this statement of
Jesus it had been concluded that he thus "declared all foods
clean" (Mark 7: 19), but Peter used in disparagement the word
"common" which with another significance had described a beautiful brotherhood among the saints in Jerusalem: "And all who
believed were together and had all things in *common*" (2: 44).

Peter is told to "stop calling common" (so the force of the
Greek) what God has cleansed (10: 15). Though the vision was
thrice repeated, Peter was perplexed as to its meaning. For all
the opportunity he had encountered as a follower of Jesus, and
for all the pioneering of men like Stephen and Philip, he yielded
to the light only after the greatest pressure was brought to bear
upon him. His progress was painfully slow, even then.

Peter and Cornelius [10: 23b-48]

[23b] The next day he rose and went off with them, and some of the
brethren from Joppa accompanied him. ²⁴ And on the following
day they entered Caesarea. Cornelius was expecting them and had
called together his kinsmen and close friends. ²⁵ When Peter
entered, Cornelius met him and fell down at his feet and wor-
shiped him. ²⁶ But Peter lifted him up, saying, "Stand up; I too
am a man." ²⁷ And as he talked with him, he went in and found
many persons gathered; ²⁸ and he said to them, "You yourselves

know how unlawful it is for a Jew to associate with or to visit any one of another nation; but God has shown me that I should not call any man common or unclean. 29 So when I was sent for, I came without objection. I ask then why you sent for me."

30 And Cornelius said, "Four days ago, about this hour, I was keeping the ninth hour of prayer in my house; and behold, a man stood before me in bright apparel, 31 saying, 'Cornelius, your prayer has been heard and your alms have been remembered before God. 32 Send therefore to Joppa and ask for Simon who is called Peter; he is lodging in the house of Simon, a tanner, by the seaside.' 33 So I sent to you at once, and you have been kind enough to come. Now therefore we are all here present in the sight of God, to hear all that you have been commanded by the Lord."

34 And Peter opened his mouth and said: "Truly I perceive that God shows no partiality, 35 but in every nation any one who fears him and does what is right is acceptable to him. 36 You know the word which he sent to Israel, preaching good news of peace by Jesus Christ (he is Lord of all), 37 the word which was proclaimed throughout all Judea, beginning from Galilee after the baptism which John preached: 38 how God anointed Jesus of Nazareth with the Holy Spirit and with power; how he went about doing good and healing all that were oppressed by the devil, for God was with him. 39 And we are witnesses to all that he did both in the country of the Jews and in Jerusalem. They put him to death by hanging him on a tree; 40 but God raised him on the third day and made him manifest: 41 not to all the people but to us who were chosen by God as witnesses, who ate and drank with him after he rose from the dead. 42 And he commanded us to preach to the people, and to testify that he is the one ordained by God to be judge of the living and the dead. 43 To him all the prophets bear witness that every one who believes in him receives forgiveness of sins through his name."

44 While Peter was still saying this, the Holy Spirit fell on all who heard the word. 45 And the believers from among the circumcised who came with Peter were amazed, because the gift of the Holy Spirit had been poured out even on the Gentiles. 46 For they heard them speaking in tongues and extolling God. Then Peter declared, 47 "Can any one forbid water for baptizing these people who have received the Holy Spirit just as we have?" 48 And he commanded them to be baptized in the name of Jesus Christ. Then they asked him to remain for some days.

The eagerness of Cornelius and the reluctance of Peter are set against each other in sharpest contrast. Cornelius received his vision about the ninth hour (3:00 P.M.) and dispatched his messengers at once. They traveled from Caesarea to Joppa (about thirty miles) by noon the next day. Cornelius set aside all other concerns and for four days awaited Peter's arrival (10: 30). He was concerned sufficiently to gather about him his kinsmen and intimate friends (10: 24). Peter, in contrast, moved on only as he must. The initial delay until the day following can be justified; the messengers from Cornelius would need rest, and Peter would need to get ready for the journey. But almost two days were required for the journey from Joppa to Caesarea. Whereas Cornelius was concerned to assemble others to hear the gospel, Peter was concerned to round up defense witnesses to protect his reputation; these he took to Caesarea and later to Jerusalem (cf. 10: 23; 11: 12).

Peter's reluctance to go in to Cornelius is in sharp contrast to Philip's joy in getting into the chariot with the Ethiopian. Peter pointed out the irregularity of this meeting: "You yourselves know how unlawful it is for a Jew to associate with or to visit any one of another nation." (10: 28). The Greek word translated "unlawful" really suggests the violation of "the divinely constituted order of things" or "breaking a taboo." [16] The translation obscures another contrast between Philip and Peter. The Spirit said to Philip, "Go up and *join* this chariot" (8: 29). Peter protested that it was profane (or taboo) for a Jew "to be *joined*" to one of another nation. The identical word is used. Philip rejoiced to be *joined* to the chariot of the Ethiopian, but Peter explained the irregularity of being *joined* to these "aliens." Note, too, that Peter identifies himself as a "Jew" (10: 28).

Peter justified his presence at the house of Cornelius, contrary to Jewish custom, by pointing out that God had shown him that he "should not call any man common or unclean" (10: 28). His next statement is astounding: "So when I was sent for, I came without objection. *I ask then why you sent for me.*" Such evangelism! And yet, there are those who continue to say that Peter opened the door to the Gentiles; it would be closer to the truth to say that the Gentiles opened a door to a larger world for Peter!

After Cornelius related his experience and affirmed that the household was all gathered to hear what the Lord had com-

[16] Lake and Cadbury, *Commentary*, p. 117.

manded, Peter started his message. He acknowledged that he
was perceiving (literally, "I am catching on") that God shows
no partiality (10: 34). Stephen had already been martyred for
seeing that. While he was preaching, "the Holy Spirit fell on all
who heard the word" (10: 44). The "believers from among the
circumcised . . . were amazed, because the gift of the Holy Spirit
had been poured out even on the Gentiles" (10: 45).

"Unhindered" is again the glorious climax. Peter, hearing
them speaking in tongues and praising God, asked: "Can any
one forbid water for baptizing these people who have received
the Holy Spirit just as we have?" (10: 47). The word "forbid"
is an infinitive (*kōlusai*), corresponding to the adverb (*akōlutōs*)
with which Acts is closed. The same idea was brought out in the
Ethiopian's question: "What hinders (*kōluei*) me from being
baptized?" The Ethiopian was unhindered. Here Peter concludes that these with Cornelius are not to be hindered. Luke's
final and glorious shout is "unhindered!"

Peter's message (10: 34-43) is one of the best examples of the
earliest apostolic preaching. Its essential elements were in all
likelihood those around which all the early preaching was built:
the ministry that was linked to that of John the Baptist, the
death by crucifixion, the resurrection by which it was reinterpreted, the appearances to chosen witnesses, the judgment, the
witness of the prophets, the call for decision in faith, and the
offer of forgiveness.[17]

The "tongues" at Caesarea probably may be best understood
as similar to the "tongues" at Corinth; they were probably ecstatic
utterances. At Pentecost the tongues were intelligible to those
who responded to the Spirit, and they were understood by many
linguistic groups. There would have been no need for this at
Caesarea, for all would understand the same language. This outpouring of the Holy Spirit is perhaps to be understood, though,
as the parallel for the God-fearers of the Pentecost outpouring for
the Jews.

One further observation should be made: the Holy Spirit

---

[17] For an excellent study of this see C. H. Dodd, *The Apostolic Preaching and Its
Developments* (New York: Harper and Brothers, 1936).

came upon the God-fearers before they were baptized and without the laying on of hands. The baptism was a recognition of their conversion, not the means for effecting it. The major concern of Luke is to demonstrate that circumcision is not necessary to salvation, but he incidentally demonstrates the same thing about baptism. Both circumcision and baptism are symbolic rites; it would be "tweedledum and tweedledee" to say that circumcision is not necessary but baptism is.

Peter Challenged for Eating with Gentiles [11:1-18]

1 Now the apostles and the brethren who were in Judea heard that the Gentiles also had received the word of God. 2 So when Peter went up to Jerusalem, the circumcision party criticized him, 3 saying, "Why did you go to uncircumcised men and eat with them?" 4 But Peter began and explained to them in order: 5 "I was in the city of Joppa praying; and in a trance I saw a vision, something descending like a great sheet, let down from heaven by four corners; and it came down to me. 6 Looking at it closely I observed animals and beasts of prey and reptiles and birds of the air. 7 And I heard a voice saying to me, 'Rise, Peter; kill and eat.' 8 But I said, 'No Lord: for nothing common or unclean has ever entered my mouth.' 9 But the voice answered a second time from heaven, 'What God has cleansed you must not call common.' 10 This happened three times, and all was drawn up again into heaven. 11 At that very moment three men arrived at the house in which we were, sent to me from Caesarea. 12 And the Spirit told me to go with them without hesitation. These six brethren also accompanied me, and we entered the man's house. 13 And he told us how he had seen the angel standing in his house and saying, 'Send to Joppa and bring Simon called Peter; 14 he will declare to you a message by which you will be saved, you and all your household.' 15 As I began to speak, the Holy Spirit fell on them just as on us at the beginning. 16 And I remembered the word of the Lord, how he said, 'John baptized with water, but you shall be baptized with the Holy Spirit.' 17 If then God gave the same gift to them as he gave to us when we believed in the Lord Jesus Christ, who was I that I could withstand God?" 18 When they heard this they were silenced. And they glorified God, saying, "Then to the Gentiles also God has granted repentance unto life."

The disturbing report soon reached Jerusalem that Peter had eaten with uncircumcised men! The liberal views of Stephen had introduced a new era for the followers of Jesus; Philip's Samari-

tan mission was cause for sending Peter and John to investigate
the strange development; Philip's further work in baptizing the
Ethiopian created less stir because it did not involve social customs and because the Ethiopian went on to Ethiopia; but Peter's
action in eating with uncircumcised men was most disturbing to
those in Jerusalem of the "circumcision party."

The Ethiopian and Cornelius were both God-fearers; they
were Gentile students of Judaism, but uncircumcised. The cases
were not quite parallel, however, for in the case of Cornelius
social intercourse, as well as the conditions of salvation, was involved.[18] Two distinct questions emerge: (1) can Gentiles be
saved without circumcision and (2) may a Jewish Christian eat
with an uncircumcised Gentile Christian?

At this point a definite party in the Jerusalem church was forming, out of which came the Judaizers who fought Paul so bitterly.
"Those out of the circumcision" in 11: 2 are doubtless to be
distinguished from those described by the same phrase in 10: 45.[19]
In 10: 45 the reference is simply to Jewish Christians, but in
11: 2 the reference is to a definite group which was forming; and,
as Rackham suggests, "their watchword would be 'circumcision.'"[20]

Though Peter "went" to Jerusalem, there is the possible implication that "the apostles and brethren who were in Judea"
asked him to return to Jerusalem to explain his conduct.[21] At
least it is clear that Peter fully realized that he would be called
on to explain this violation of Jewish custom. Accordingly, he
delayed his visit to Cornelius until he had rounded up "brethren
from Joppa" to accompany him (10: 23), whom he later took
with him to Jerusalem and called on as witnesses (11: 12).

Peter took a courageous stand before the Jerusalem Christians
in maintaining that those uncircumcised men had actually re-

---

[18] Cf. Knowling, op. cit., p. 263.

[19] The RSV is no doubt correct in its interpretation of the two passages, "the believers from among the circumcised" (10: 45) and "the circumcision party" (11: 2),
even though the Greek phrases are almost identical.

[20] Op. Cit., p. 160.

[21] Lake and Cadbury suggest that possibly the expanded Western text, which
represents Peter as wishing to go to Jerusalem, was designed "to minimize the suggestion that Peter was recalled to Jerusalem to answer to the church." Cf. Commentary, p. 124.

ceived the Holy Spirit and that their conversion was the work of God (11: 15-17). He made it equally clear that *at no point was the initiative his own,* going into great detail to demonstrate that he acted only as God directed him. He pointed out that to reject the validity of this experience would be to "withstand God" (11: 17). The Greek word used is *kōlusai,* to hinder. Peter recognized that God must be "unhindered." Up to this point, however, there is no evidence that any one of the apostles was ready *to encourage* a Gentile mission.

In the light of irrefutable evidence the Jerusalem Christians were "silenced," and they "glorified God" (11: 18). They said, "Then to the Gentiles also God has granted repentance unto life" (11: 18). This translation is faulty at a vital point; the aorist tense of the Greek (*edōken*) has been translated as though it were the perfect tense. They concluded only that to the Gentiles God "did grant" repentance unto life. All of the evidences are to the effect that, as the grammar suggests, the experience in the home of Cornelius was viewed as exceptional, an isolated case like that of Naaman in the Old Testament.[22] At the Jerusalem conference later (Acts 15), this incident was looked back upon as something almost forgotten, and it evidently was not followed up by the apostles.[23] Peter's subsequent work was presumably not among Gentiles, for he was known as the "apostle of the circumcision."

This slowness of the apostles to see the equality of Gentile with Jew is not unique in history; one needs only to remember recent and present guilt of Christians of many lands. Rackham observes:

It is almost inconceivable how in the seventeenth century a good protestant English captain could be praying and reading the Bible on deck, while beneath the hatches he was carrying a cargo of negro slaves to work on American plantations.[24]

One may recall the many sermons from pulpits "proving" from the Bible that God intended for the Negroes to be slaves. One

---

[22] Cf. Knowling, *op. cit.,* p. 264; Bruce, *op. cit.,* p. 230; Rackham, *op. cit.,* p. 163.
[23] Cf. Rackham, *op. cit.,* p. 162.
[24] *Ibid.,* p. 162.

may hear with shame today men of the state and the church
protesting the progress of the Negro in human rights. It is possible that future historians may declare the irony of ironies—
that in the middle of the twentieth century, fight promoters and
baseball managers did more for emancipating the Negro than
did the churchmen? To say that these have done it for money
removes none of the sting, for it is a humiliation if a pagan for
money effects good which a Christian fails to effect for love. There
are even evidences that segregation may make its last stand in
the churches.

UNNAMED MEN OF CYPRUS AND CYRENE PREACH
TO GREEKS AT ANTIOCH [11: 19-26]

19 Now those who were scattered because of the persecution that
arose over Stephen traveled as far as Phoenicia and Cyprus and Antioch, speaking the word to none except Jews. 20 But there were
some of them, men of Cyprus and Cyrene, who on coming to Antioch spoke to the Greeks also, preaching the Lord Jesus. 21 And
the hand of the Lord was with them, and a great number that believed turned to the Lord. 22 News of this came to the ears of the
church in Jerusalem, and they sent Barnabas to Antioch. 23 When
he came and saw the grace of God, he was glad; and he exhorted
them all to remain faithful to the Lord with steadfast purpose;
24 for he was a good man, full of the Holy Spirit and of faith. And
a large company was added to the Lord. 25 So Barnabas went to
Tarsus to look for Saul; 26 and when he had found him, he brought
him to Antioch. For a whole year they met with the church, and
taught a large company of people; and in Antioch the disciples
were for the first time called Christians.

LUKE significantly connects the revival at Antioch with Stephen.
At least the revival was begun by men influenced by Stephen
(11: 19). The great missionary impulse at Antioch was a part
of the impact of this great man upon the Christian movement.
Not only Saul's conversion but the so-called "first missionary
journey" of Paul was the indirect influence of Stephen.

There are evidences that the gospel was planted in North
Africa and Cyprus years before Barnabas and Saul embarked
on their "first missionary journey." Men seem to have traveled

from Cyrene in Africa and Cyprus in the Mediterranean to start
a revival in Antioch, out of which later Barnabas and Saul went
as missionaries to Cyprus and Asia Minor. It is not said explicitly
that these men came directly from Cyprus and Cyrene to Antioch;
it is only said that they were Cypriotes and Cyrenians. However,
it is altogether possible that they were in Cyprus and Cyrene as
Christians before traveling to Antioch. If so, it is additional
evidence that Luke is not concerned with the geographical expansion of Christianity but rather with its crossing of national
and racial lines. The strong evidence is that Christianity reached
Cyprus before Barnabas and Saul went there together on the
"first missionary journey." Those who "spoke to Greeks also"
were men influenced by Stephen, not by the Hebrews.

Several years must be allowed between 11:19 and 11:20. Verse
19 goes back to the martyrdom of Stephen, but verse 20 refers
to a time when Saul had been in Tarsus as a Christian. Saul's
conversion and his years in Arabia, Jerusalem, and Tarsus must
be allowed for between the events of 11:19 and 11:20. Saul's
conversion was not later than A.D. 35, and the year with Barnabas
at Antioch was some time during the reign of Claudius (A.D.
41-54). Without attempting to fix either of these dates, it is obvious that several years are to be accounted for. Doubtless the
gospel had traveled far in these years, for the most part being
preached to "none except Jews"; yet men from Cyprus and
Cyrene upon coming to Antioch (of Syria) preached to Greeks
also (11:19-20).

The manuscripts are divided between "Greeks" and "Grecians" in verse 20. Lake and Cadbury are probably correct in
saying that the context is decisive for the reference being to non-
Jews, whichever word is used, for these people were contrasted
with Jews.[25] Rackham may be correct in contending that these
Greeks are "God-fearers," the third class of the four distinguished
in Acts: Hebrews (Jews), Hellenists (Jews), God-fearing Greeks
(Gentiles influenced by Judaism), and the pagans.[26]

The church at Jerusalem, after more than a decade, was still

---

[25] *Commentary*, p. 128.
[26] *Op. cit.*, p. 166.

playing the role of cautious observer (11: 29). The selection of
Barnabas, however, indicated a fairness in the church, for a more
sympathetic observer could not have been sent. Barnabas was
made glad by what he saw, and he encouraged the converts. Because of the magnitude of the work, additional help was needed.
Barnabas sought out Saul at Tarsus, as one ideally suited for the
ministry at Antioch. Calvin made the interesting observation
that the greatness of Barnabas is reflected in his concern only
that Christ be pre-eminent—he could have retained first place
for himself, but he brought Saul into the picture.[27]

It was at Antioch that the disciples were first called Christians,
whether in derision or simply because that best characterized
them is not known. The new name was well suited to a movement rapidly asserting its universal character. The term is basically Greek, expressing a Hebrew idea (Messiah), and its form
(suffix) is Latin.[28] It may also reflect the transition from being
a sect within Judaism to becoming a separate movement.

THREAT OF FAMINE AN OCCASION FOR FELLOWSHIP
[11: 27-30]

> 27 Now in these days prophets came down from Jerusalem to An-
> tioch. 28 And one of them named Agabus stood up and foretold
> by the Spirit that there would be a great famine over all the
> world; and this took place in the days of Claudius. 29 And the
> disciples determined, every one according to his ability, to send
> relief to the brethren who lived in Judea; 30 and they did so,
> sending it to the elders by the hand of Barnabas and Saul.

THE PROBLEM of chronology is extremely difficult here, but probably the visit of Barnabas and Saul to Judea was before the death
of Herod Agrippa I (A.D. 44); this, at least, is the implication
of Acts. Luke states that the famine took place during the days
of Claudius; his reign was from A.D. 41 to A.D. 54. The Roman
historians Suetonius (*Claudius,* xix) and Tacitus (*Ann.* xii. 43)
indicate that famines did occur in the reign of Claudius. The

---

[27] Cf. Knowling, *op. cit.,* p. 268.
[28] Cf. Rackham, *op. cit.,* p. 170.

matter is complicated in that Josephus (*Ant.* iii. 15. 3; xx. 2. 5; xx 5. 2) locates a famine in Judea during the time of the procurators Cuspius Fadus (*ca.* 44-46) and Tiberius Alexander (*ca.* 46-48), which would be after the death of Agrippa I in 44. But the famine which Suetonius (*Claudius*, xix) represents as having been occasioned by several successive years of poor crops, was evidently just coming on when Agabus visited Antioch and when Barnabas and Saul were sent to Judea (evidently to Jerusalem). From earliest times the church had its poor, and the policy of sharing possessions may have depleted the material resources of the disciples in Jerusalem. It is not difficult to imagine that the dearth was felt first by just such communities, and that the Christians would be quick to do something about it. Of course, "all the world" (11: 28) would be understood as the Roman world, not the whole geographical world.

Luke's primary interest may be to submit evidence that fellowship between the great communities of Antioch and Jerusalem was genuine, for all the differences. The inclusion of the God-fearers had strained fellowship at times but had not broken it.

"Prophets" are prominent in Acts, as many are so described: Silas and Judas (15: 32), numerous "prophets and teachers" at Antioch (13: 1), the daughters of Philip (21: 8), as well as Agabus (11: 27; 21: 10) and his companions. In the gospels John the Baptist and Jesus were considered prophets. Though the predictive function was only a minor one in the prophetic ministry, it was included. The major function was bringing a fresh message from God. A prophet sought to interpret the mind of God to the people and to interpret the people to themselves.

The "elders" (11: 30) cannot be identified with certainty. In Acts and the Pastoral Epistles the term "elder" is interchangeable with "bishop" (cf. Acts 20: 17 with 20: 28 [29] and Titus 1:5 with 1: 7). It is not certain whether the "elders" here are to be identified with or distinguished from the apostles; probably the latter is true.

---

[29] The RSV somewhat obscures the point here by translating the term "guardians"; this is the term elsewhere rendered "bishops."

HERODIAN PERSECUTION AND DEATH OF HEROD
[12: 1-23]

Herodian Persecution [12: 1-5]

1 About that time Herod the king laid violent hands upon some who belonged to the church. 2 He killed James the brother of John with the sword; 3 and when he saw that it pleased the Jews, he proceeded to arrest Peter also. This was during the days of Un-leavened Bread. 4 And when he had seized him, he put him in prison, and delivered him to four squads of soldiers to guard him, intending after the Passover to bring him out to the people. 5 So Peter was kept in prison; but earnest prayer for him was made to God by the church.

THE PERSECUTION under Herod Agrippa I was the third major assault upon the disciples, the first being by the Sadducees and the next by the Pharisees. Herod lost no opportunity to strengthen himself with the Jews; and when the Jerusalem disciples approved of Peter's conduct in the home of Cornelius, he may have seen an opening for increasing his favor with the Jews. The twelve had escaped persecution at the time of Stephen's martyrdom because of their loyalty to the law, but for one of their number to eat with an uncircumcised Gentile would be viewed as inexcusable compromise.

Herod Agrippa was the son of Aristobulus and grandson of Herod the Great. The latter executed his son Aristobulus in 7 B.C., and Herod Agrippa was brought up in Rome in imperial society. He helped Caligula (A.D. 37-41) become emperor at the death of Tiberius; and Caligula rewarded him with the title of king and the tetrarchy of Philip, adding Galilee and Perea to it shortly after. When Caligula was killed, Agrippa helped Claudius (A.D. 41-54) win the approval of the Roman Senate; and the new emperor added Judea and Samaria to his kingdom. Herod Agrippa was of Edomite as well as Jewish ancestry but wanted to be received by the Jews. The execution of James and arrest of Peter represented a part of his strategy. The scrupulous observance of the Passover season was a part of the precaution of the tyrant in seeking Jewish favor.

It is assumed by many today that John was martyred with his brother James. This has no support in the New Testament and rests upon exactly the kind of "evidence" which is thrown out of court when in support of a traditional position. The argument depends on statements of George the Sinner (seventh century) and Philip of Side (fourth century) to the effect that Papias (second century) reported that James and John were killed by the Jews. Even if this questionable tradition be accepted, it still must be observed that Papias did not say that James and John were martyred *at the same time*. The tradition preserved by Eusebius, and attributed by him to Irenaeus, to the effect that John lived to an old age and died a natural death is much stronger. This is not conclusive for the tradition that John lived on toward the end of the century (and wrote the books bearing his name), but the dogmatic view that John was killed by Herod along with James must be challenged.

Peter's Deliverance [12: 6-19]

6 The very night when Herod was about to bring him out, Peter was sleeping between two soldiers, bound with two chains, and sentries before the door were guarding the prison; 7 and behold, an angel of the Lord appeared, and a light shone in the cell; and he struck Peter on the side and woke him, saying, "Get up quickly." And the chains fell off his hands. 8 And the angel said to him, "Dress yourself and put on your sandals." And he did so. And he said to him, "Wrap your mantle around you and follow me." 9 And he went out and followed him; he did not know that what was done by the angel was real, but thought he was seeing a vision. 10 When they had passed the first and the second guard, they came to the iron gate leading into the city. It opened to them of its own accord, and they went out and passed on through one street; and immediately the angel left him. 11 And Peter came to himself, and said, "Now I am sure that the Lord has sent his angel and rescued me from the hand of Herod and from all that the Jewish people were expecting."

12 When he realized this, he went to the house of Mary, the mother of John whose other name was Mark, where many were gathered together and were praying. 13 And when he knocked at the door of the gateway, a maid named Rhoda came to answer. 14 Recognizing Peter's voice, in her joy she did not open the gate but ran in and told that Peter was standing at the gate. 15 They said to her, "You are mad." But she insisted that it was so. They said, "It is his

angel!" 16 But Peter continued knocking; and when they opened,
they saw him and were amazed. 17 But motioning to them with
his hand to be silent, he described to them how the Lord had
brought him out of the prison. And he said, "Tell this to James
and to the brethren." Then he departed and went to another
place.
18 Now when day came, there was no small stir among the soldiers
over what had become of Peter. 19 And when Herod had sought
for him and could not find him, he examined the sentries and
ordered that they should be put to death. Then he went down
from Judea to Caesarea, and remained there.

This is one of the happiest pictures we have of Peter; here some
of his best qualities are in evidence. On the very night before
his scheduled execution, Peter slept soundly. His physical courage was always equal to the test. Instead of nervously pacing the
floor (with chains and all) through a sleepless night, Peter prepared for a night's sleep and was well on his way toward it when
the deliverance came. He had removed his sandals and mantle
and had gone soundly to sleep; the angel had to prod him in the
side to awaken him. This corresponds to the pattern seen elsewhere. In Gethsemane, Peter showed no fear in the presence
of physical danger, but later was unnerved by the questions of
a girl who recognized him to be a follower of Jesus. Peter's courage failed in situations where there was no immediate physical
danger, as at Antioch when Jerusalem brethren caught him
eating with uncircumcised Christians (Gal. 2: 11ff.). He feared
disapproval more than bodily injury.

The house of Mary, John Mark's mother, was the meeting
place of many who had gathered to pray. Mark could easily have
been Luke's informant for this and other incidents. This story
is delightfully told and has all the marks of genuineness. There
is no evidence that others of the twelve were in Jerusalem, unless
they are the "brethren" of verse 17. James, the brother of Jesus,
seems already to be the recognized leader at Jerusalem and continued to be for some years.

Luke states that Peter "departed and went to another place"
(12: 17). It is simply not known where this place was. This is
another indication that Luke's interest was not primarily in
the acts of the apostles or in places. The Roman Church has been

built on the late tradition that the place was Rome, where it is claimed Peter became the first bishop.[30] Only on dogmatic grounds can this position be held; the evidences are against it. To begin with, there is no evidence that Peter was at this time committed to a mission outside Palestine; he found it difficult enough to deal with God-fearers nearby. When Paul wrote the Romans (ca. A.D. 55), Peter certainly had not been in Rome. Peter was in Jerusalem during the conference (Acts 15) about A.D. 48 or 49. When Paul reached Rome (ca. 57 or 58), evidently no apostle had been there, for the Jews came to him for a dependable account of "this sect" everywhere spoken against (28: 22). Had Peter been there for nearly two decades (since 42 as the tradition has it) there would have been no need for seeking such information from Paul. Peter may have departed from Jerusalem only until the death of Agrippa (A.D. 44). He is but self-deceived who builds his faith on arbitrary dogma.

Herod's Death [12: 20-23]

20 Now Herod was angry with the people of Tyre and Sidon; and they came to him in a body, and having persuaded Blastus, the king's chamberlain, they asked for peace, because their country depended on the king's country for food. 21 On an appointed day Herod put on his royal robes, took his seat upon the throne, and made an oration to them. 22 And the people shouted, "The voice of a god, and not of man!" 23 Immediately an angel of the Lord smote him, because he did not give God the glory; and he was eaten by worms and died.

Josephus (*Ant.* xix, 8, 2) gives substantially the same story as does Luke, but with greater detail. Without the account of Josephus it would be assumed that Agrippa died immediately, though Luke does not say this. From Josephus it is learned that he lingered in great pain for five days and died a horrible death. According to Josephus, the Greeks and Syrians celebrated the death of Agrippa. Their delight at his death may have been due, at least in part, to the many favors Agrippa had shown to the Jews.

---

[30] For an excellent study of the traditions about Peter, see F. J. Foakes-Jackson, *Peter: Prince of Apostles* (New York: George H. Doran Co., 1927) and Oscar Cullmann, *Peter: Disciple, Apostle, Martyr.*

GROWTH AND THE MISSION OF BARNABAS AND SAUL
[12: 24-25]

24 But the word of God grew and multiplied.
25 And Barnabas and Saul returned from Jerusalem when they had
fulfilled their mission, bringing with them John whose other
name was Mark.

VERSE 24 is another of Luke's summary statements, marking the
transition to a new phase of the work and a natural division of
his book. At the death of Agrippa, Palestine was again made a
Roman province. Rackham's plausible suggestion is that Roman
power restored peace and afforded a new opportunity for growth.[31]
A textual uncertainty adds to the difficulty in understanding
the time of the mission of Barnabas and Saul. The best manuscripts read, "and Barnabas and Saul returned *into* Jerusalem."
The reading "into Jerusalem" not only has the best manuscript support but would ease one problem, if correct. Josephus
(xx, 2, 5) places the famine about A.D. 45, after Herod's death.
If Luke means that the mission of Barnabas and Saul followed
the death of Herod, then it is easier to harmonize Josephus and
Luke. On the other hand, Josephus and Luke are not necessarily
in conflict even if Luke places the mission to Jerusalem *before*
Herod's death; the first pinch of the coming famine could have
been felt in Jerusalem before its full force in A.D. 45 (see above).
It seems more natural, too, to understand from Acts 11: 27-30
that Barnabas and Saul were sent to Jerusalem *before* Herod's
death, though this is not stated explicitly; in turning from the
events in Antioch to Herod, Luke merely says "about that time"
(12: 1). The Greek participles in the sentence are decidely against
the reading "into." Though the "into Jerusalem" reading has
the best manuscript support, and though it has able defenders
today, it seems to be ruled out by the context. In 11: 27-30
Barnabas and Saul seem to be on their way to Jerusalem; in
13: 1-3 they are in Antioch; evidently 12: 25 intends to represent
them as going "from," not "to," Jerusalem.

---

[31] *Op. cit.,* p. 182.

PART THREE

Triumph and Tragedy:
The Unhindered Preaching of the Gospel
and the Self-exclusion of the Jews
[13:1 to 28:31]

THE THIRD MAJOR PHASE of Christian development is traced from chapter 13 to the end of Acts. At the outset the movement was exclusively Jewish and was dominated by the Hebrew element; in the second phase the Hellenists or Grecian Jews introduced far-reaching ideas and extended the gospel to Samaritans and God-fearing Greeks; in the last phase the gospel was carried directly to the pagans, and after a bitter struggle freed itself, "unhindered," but at tremendous cost—the self-exclusion of the Jews.

In the most primitive stage (1:6-6:7), the Christian movement was centered in Jerusalem and was Jewish in character. The Hebrews dominated the movement, and they thought of it as something which could have its development within the framework of Judaism. They were at home in the temple and synagogue, continued to live as Jews, and were viewed as a sect of Judaism. The twelve were the recognized leaders and gave little evidence of a vision beyond a kingdom restored to Israel.

The second major phase (6:8 to 12:25) was introduced by the Hellenists, chief of whom at the outset were Stephen and Philip. These were followed by unnamed men of Cyprus and Cyrene, Saul, and others, who set the patterns and blazed new trails. The Hebrews and the twelve were judging and adjusting. The seven provided the leadership at the outset of this stage of development even as the twelve provided the leadership in the earlier stage. In this second period, Christianity began to assert its spiritual character and inherent universalism, and it be-

133

gan to break through barriers of race and ritual. With the Hellenists in the vanguard, many God-fearing Greeks were won.

The final phase of development (chapters 13 to 28) is introduced with the five, possibly paralleling the twelve and the seven. As was true of the twelve and the seven, the majority are only named and not featured. Events were centered at Antioch and outside Palestine, rather than at Jerusalem and in Palestine. Though Jews were still being won to the movement, the most significant gains were among the pagans. Attempt was made to win Jews and Gentiles through the synagogue, but it was soon found necessary to by-pass the synagogue and go directly to the Gentiles. With this development certain issues pertaining to the Jew-Gentile relationship became acute. The final outcome was the full liberation of the gospel, "unhindered," but the self-exclusion of the Jews.

JEWS AND GENTILES APPROACHED CHIEFLY THROUGH THE SYNAGOGUES; DOOR OF FAITH FOR GENTILES ACKNOWLEDGED
[13: 1 to 16: 5]

IN THIS SECTION there is much travel by land and sea, but Luke's primary interest was not in the geographical expansion of Christianity. *The gospel was preached in Cyprus and Asia Minor before this "first missionary journey."* Cyprus and Cyrene had been prominent in Christian beginnings, and Paul had already spent about seven years at Tarsus as a Christian. Certainly Paul's lips were not sealed during those years. Luke made it clear that the gospel reached out far and wide soon after Pentecost.

Luke is now showing how the gospel finally went directly to the Gentiles along with the results and repercussions that followed. He will show the consistent effort of the missionaries to take the natural approach through the synagogues, and the fact that those who contended for equality of Gentile with the Jew were finally driven out of the synagogues. Ultimately the church became separated from the synagogue, and the Jews turned from Christianity.

Two major campaigns are sketched. What are termed three missionary journeys were really two great campaigns. The first (13:1 to 16:5) was conducted chiefly through the synagogues under the leadership of Barnabas and Saul. The second campaign (16:6 to 20:2) was led by Paul and many companions, and it was conducted in the great Greco-Roman cultural center which embraced Roman provinces around the Aegean Sea (Macedonia, Achaia, and Asia). During this campaign the attempt was still made to reach Jew and Gentile through the synagogues, but synagogue doors were rapidly closing to the movement.

Campaign of Barnabas and Saul [13:1 to 14:28]

Barnabas and Saul separated for appointed work [13: 1-3]

> 1 Now in the church at Antioch there were prophets and teachers, Barnabas, Symeon who was called Niger, Lucius of Cyrene, Manaen a member of the court of Herod the tetrarch, and Saul. 2 While they were worshiping the Lord and fasting, the Holy Spirit said, "Set apart for me Barnabas and Saul for the work to which I have called them." 3 Then after fasting and praying they laid their hands on them and sent them off.

The church at Antioch proved to be the strong base of operations for some years. It should be remembered that through the unnamed men of Cyprus and Cyrene, "scattered because of the persecution that arose over Stephen" (11:19-20), this great missionary church was under the influence of Stephen. It is not incidental that Luke linked the Antioch revival, out of which grew this missionary campaign, to Stephen.

Some of the most critical scholars understand 13:1 to refer to "the local church" at Antioch, and they so translate. The Greek construction, involving the articular use of the participle of the verb "to be," seems to be used frequently in Acts in an idiomatic sense, conveying the idea of "local," "current," or "existing." [1] It is made clear that this church at Antioch was a genuine church, independent of the church at Jerusalem, and that the new work originating there was under the direct inspiration of the Holy Spirit.

---

[1] Cf. Lake and Cadbury, *Commentary*, pp. 56–57, 141; Bruce, *op. cit.*, pp. 140, 252.

The church "laid hands" on the missionaries and "released them" (13: 3), but the commission was directly from the Holy Spirit. It is held by many that the "prophets and teachers" were the ones who laid hands on the missionaries, but it is not conclusive that this was so. Barnabas and Saul were two of the five prophets and teachers, so it may be asked what the three would have conferred on the two. Rackham asserts that "the only antecedent to the pronouns in verse 3 are the *prophets* and *teachers* of verse 1; and so they uttered the prayer and laid on hands." [2] That is true if the Greek grammar is observed strictly; but if that be true then all the action of 13: 1-3 relates to the five and not to the church: the worshipping, fasting, setting apart, praying, laying on hands, and releasing. All that Rackham has said about the importance of the Antioch church would be nullified. Furthermore, if Rackham's principle of grammar is to be rigidly observed here, it should also apply to Acts 6: 5-6 where it would establish conclusively that "all the multitude" (6: 5), not the twelve, laid hands on the seven. Rackham does not apply the rule of antecedents there! Knowling views "the church" as the grammatical antecedent rather than the "prophets and teachers," but concludes that the subject is changed as in 6: 6. [3] But who changed the subject: Luke or his interpreter?

It is probably best to conclude that there is no agreement in case between the pronouns implied in verse 3 and the antecedent in verse 1, and that the antecedent is "the local church" rather than the "prophets and teachers"; it is often true in New Testament Greek that concord in case, number, or gender is lacking. At least it is the possible meaning that the church laid hands on Barnabas and Saul. (There is strong evidence that the function of laying on of hands belongs to the congregation and not to a "presbytery.") Bruce aptly sums it up:

Not that they could by this act qualify Barnabas and Saul for the work to which God had called them; but by this means they [the whole church] expressed their fellowship with the two and their recognition of the divine call. [4]

[2] *Op. cit.,* p. 191.
[3] *Op. cit.,* pp. 172, 283.
[4] *Op. cit.,* p. 254.

To say that here Barnabas and Saul were made apostles is to contradict Paul's claim to the contrary (Gal. 1: 1).

The translation "sent them off" is hardly correct; "released them" or "let them go" is better. The church simply recognized the directive of the Holy Spirit and co–operated with it. Bruce observed that those "released for missionary service were the most gifted and outstanding in the church." [5]

Of the "prophets and teachers" mentioned, Barnabas and Saul are already familiar to the reader. Lucius of Cyrene may have been one of those from Cyrene who helped initiate the revival in preaching to "Greeks also" (11: 20). Symeon (Hebrew name) was doubtless from Africa as his surname, Niger, suggests. Niger means "Black," and it is Latin in origin; both of these factors would suggest Africa. He may have been one of those from Cyrene (in Africa) who shared with those from Cyprus in initiating the revival at Antioch. Manaen is described by a Greek term used for a youth of the age of princes and brought up at court with them. The term is somewhat uncertain as used here, but at least Manaen had some close connection with the family of Herod Antipas. This Manaen may have been a descendant of the Manaen who won the favor of Herod the Great by foretelling his rise to power (Josephus, *Ant.* xv, 10, 5).

Christianity distinguished from false philosophy before official Rome [13: 4-12]

4 So, being sent out by the Holy Spirit, they went down to Seleucia; and from there they sailed to Cyprus. 5 When they arrived at Salamis, they proclaimed the word of God in the synagogues of the Jews. And they had John to assist them. 6 When they had gone through the whole island as far as Paphos, they came upon a certain magician, a Jewish false prophet, named Bar-Jesus. 7 He was with the proconsul, Sergius Paulus, a man of intelligence, who summoned Barnabas and Saul and sought to hear the word of God. 8 But Elymas the magician (for that is the meaning of his name) withstood them, seeking to turn away the proconsul from the faith. 9 But Saul, who is also called Paul, filled with the Holy Spirit, looked intently at him 10 and said, "You son of the devil, you enemy of all righteousness, full of all deceit and villainy, will you not stop making crooked the straight paths of the Lord? 11 And

[5] *Op. cit.*, p. 253.

now, behold, the hand of the Lord is upon you, and you shall be blind and unable to see the sun for a time." Immediately mist and darkness fell upon him and he went about seeking people to lead him by the hand. 12 Then the proconsul believed, when he saw what had occurred, for he was astonished at the teaching of the Lord.

Barnabas, Saul, and their companions sailed to Cyprus; but Christianity was not new to Cyprus. Barnabas and other unnamed disciples were from Cyprus; and, as already pointed out, Cypriotes and Cyrenians kindled the revival fires in Antioch. Mnason, too, was from Cyprus and is described as "an early disciple," or "an original disciple" (21: 16). Luke's interest seems to be in showing how Christianity was distinguished from false religion and philosophy and how it impressed a Roman proconsul. He may also be concerned with the effect this response of the proconsul had on Paul.

Though synagogues are mentioned, Luke gives nothing of the development on the island apart from the meeting with Sergius Paulus and Bar-Jesus. There were many communities on this large island, with many Jewish synagogues. Luke is content to say merely that "they proclaimed the word of God in the synagogues of the Jews" (13: 5). The number of outstanding Cypriote believers already active as missionaries would suggest that the island was a ready field. The favorable response of Sergius Paulus doubtless provided an open door for the missionaries. Luke gives no hint as to how long they remained in Cyprus or of the extent of the work. The fact that Barnabas and Mark returned to Cyprus later (15: 39) would suggest that they must have had some encouragement there. What is obvious is that Luke was not primarily concerned with multiplying of disciples or churches as such, nor was he interested in showing geographical progress. He was interested in ideas and issues of another sort.

John Mark is described as an "assistant." The Greek term employed appears significantly in Luke 1: 2, where Luke asserts his dependence upon "ministers" of the word. Presumably those thus described had some special function. Possibly this included drill work in the Christian tradition. Converts would need to be taught the fundamental facts of the faith, including the things Jesus did and said. John Mark may have been employed in this capacity. His residence in Jerusalem would have fitted him well for this work. If, as is most likely, he was indeed the author of the earliest gospel, then the suggestion is all the more plausible.[6] He may have done the baptizing for Barnabas and Saul, but was more likely a drillmaster in the tradition.

Bar-Jesus was a Jew, a "magician," and a false prophet. The prophetic function is not primarily prediction but interpretation of the mind of God; this man claimed "falsely to be a medium of divine revelations." [7] Foakes-Jackson suggests that he was "one who combined his 'philosophy' (for so it would be called) with the exercise of magic or divination." [8] Bar-Jesus means "Son of Jesus (Joshua)," but it is not clear how that is connected with the name "Elymas." What is clear is that he feared that he would lose his standing with the proconsul, so he attempted to discredit the missionaries. Paul perhaps saw that it was all-important to dissociate the faith from this spiritualism of Elymas, and hence the sternness of his response. Bar-Jesus (Son of Jesus) is termed "Son of the devil" and the enemy of righteousness. A true "Jewish prophet" was primarily concerned for righteousness; Bar-Jesus was its enemy.

Sergius Paulus "believed," but it is not said that he was or was not converted. He may simply have believed that the missionaries were men of God and true prophets. Had a Roman proconsul been converted at this early date it is likely that some word of it would have come down in Christian tradition.

It is significant that at this point Saul is said also to be called Paul (13: 9), which was his Roman name. The suggestion that he assumed the name at this point because the proconsul was named Paulus cannot be established; it is not known whether he received the Roman name at birth or later. Certainly Paul must have gotten a new vision for missions. The favorable response of the proconsul probably suggested to him the pos-

---

[6] See R. O. P. Taylor, *The Groundwork of the Gospels* (Oxford: Basil Blackwell, 1946), pp. 21–30.
[7] Bruce, *op. cit.*, p. 256.
[8] *The Acts of the Apostles*, p. 111.

sibility of winning the empire to Christ and set him afire for
that task.

Paul and his company reach Pisidian Antioch [13: 13-15]

13 Now Paul and his company set sail from Paphos, and came to
Perga in Pamphylia. And John left them and returned to Jerusalem; 14 but they passed on from Perga and came to Antioch of
Pisidia. And on the sabbath day they went into the synagogue and
sat down. 15 After the reading of the law and the prophets, the
rulers of the synagogue sent to them, saying, "Brethren, if you
have any word of exhortation for the people, say it."

Paul became the dominant leader in the missionary group, and
Barnabas evidently showed no resentment. Whether or not it
influenced John Mark's decision to return to Jerusalem is not
known. Many explanations have been offered but none is conclusive; some should never have found their way into serious
literature on the subject. Mark has been charged with fear of
the mountains or robbers, jealousy of Paul, laziness, homesick-
ness, and lovesickness. On the other hand, he had grown up at
Jerusalem amidst mountains and robbers; his home, as one
having provided hospitality for Jesus and early disciples, should
not be spoken of lightly.[9] Paul was as susceptible to error as was
Mark. It may be that the *courage* of Mark enabled him to turn
back at Perga. Possibly Mark left because he dared to live his
own life. Mark's life achievements may have been made possible
by escape from the dominating, if not domineering, personality
of Paul.[10] Highly plausible is the suggestion of Rackham that the
separation concerned policy and not personalities.[11] Mark is here
called by his Hebrew name, "John," and it may be that he had
not yet come to a full adjustment on the Gentile issue.

There are evidences that Paul's heart was set on Ephesus and
Rome for many years before he actually preached in those cities.
Possibly he purposed to travel to Ephesus when he left Cyprus;
certainly he wanted to go to Ephesus on the next journey when

---

[9] Cf. P. H. Anderson, *John Mark, Servant of Christ* (Boston: The Christopher
Publishing House, 1949) for a valuable and intriguing study of this subject.
[10] For a development of this possibility one may see the author's article, "John
Mark: Who Dared to Live His Own Life," *The Baptist Student* (Nashville: The
Baptist Sunday School Board, February, 1951) XXX, 5, 12.
[11] *Op. cit.*, pp. 203f.

they were "forbidden by the Holy Spirit to speak the word in Asia" (16: 6). In turning to Antioch of Pisidia, he may have been headed for Ephesus. If the letter to the Galatians was directed to "South Galatia" (including Pisidian Antioch, Iconium, Lystra, and Derbe),[12] then there is conclusive evidence that Paul had not purposed to preach in these towns (Gal. 4: 13). The occasion for his first preaching in these towns was evidently some "bodily ailment" which had caused him to give up plans for preaching elsewhere. Though the nature of the ailment is unknown to us, the suggestion that it was a destestable eye-disease has some support from Paul's own writing (Gal. 4: 14f.). The illness probably came at Antioch as he was on his way toward Ephesus.

The synagogue services were orderly, yet somewhat informal. They included (1) the Shema, a recitation of Deuteronomy 6: 4; (2) prayer; (3) readings from the law and prophets with necessary translations; (4) sermon by any man in the congregation; and (5) benediction. It was normal procedure, then, for a visitor to be called on for the sermon. It was normal, too, for these Christians to share in a synagogue service. To Paul, as to Jesus, Christianity was the consummation, and not the competitor of Judaism.

Paul's sermon to Jews and God-fearers [13: 16-41]

16 So Paul stood up, and motioning with his hand said: "Men of Israel, and you that fear God, listen. 17 The God of this people Israel chose our fathers and made the people great during their stay in the land of Egypt, and with uplifted arm he led them out of it. 18 And for about forty years he bore with them in the wilderness. 19 And when he had destroyed seven nations in the land of Canaan, he gave them their land as an inheritance, for about four hundred and fifty years. 20 And after that he gave them judges until Samuel the prophet. 21 Then they asked for a king; and God gave them Saul the son of Kish, a man of the tribe of Benjamin, for forty years. 22 And when he had removed him, he raised up David to be their king; of whom he testified and said, 'I have found in David the son of Jesse a man after my heart, who will do all my will.' 23 Of this man's posterity God has brought to

---

[12] The literature is abundant on the controversy about "North" and "South Galatia." To this writer the South Galatian theory is the more plausible.

142

Israel a Savior, Jesus, as he promised. 24 Before his coming John had preached a baptism of repentance to all the people of Israel. 25 And as John was finishing his course, he said, 'What do you suppose that I am? I am not he. No, but after me one is coming, the sandals of whose feet I am not worthy to untie.'
26 "Brethren, sons of the family of Abraham, and those among you that fear God, to us has been sent the message of this salvation. 27 For those who live in Jerusalem and their rulers, because they did not recognize him nor understand the utterances of the prophets which are read every sabbath, fulfilled these by condemning him. 28 Though they could charge him with nothing deserving death, yet they asked Pilate to have him killed. 29 And when they had fulfilled all that was written of him, they took him down from the tree, and laid him in a tomb. 30 But God raised him from the dead; 31 and for many days he appeared to those who came up with him from Galilee to Jerusalem, who are now his witnesses to the people. 32 And we bring you the good news that what God promised to the fathers, 33 this he has fulfilled to us their children by raising Jesus; as also it is written in the second psalm,
'Thou art my Son,
today I have begotten thee.'
34 And as for the fact that he raised him from the dead, no more to return to corruption, he spoke in this way,
'I will give you the holy and sure blessings of David.'
35 Therefore he says also in another psalm,
'Thou wilt not let thy Holy One see corruption.'
36 For David, after he had served the counsel of God in his own generation, fell asleep, and was laid with his fathers, and saw corruption; 37 but he whom God raised up saw no corruption. 38 Let it be known to you therefore, brethren, that through this man forgiveness of sins is proclaimed to you, 39 and by him every one that believes is freed from everything from which you could not be freed by the law of Moses. 40 Beware, therefore, lest there come upon you what is said in the prophets:
41 'Behold, you scoffers, and wonder, and perish;
for I do a deed in your days,
a deed you will never believe, if one declares it to you.' "

Paul's sermon is addressed to Jews and God-fearers, the Jews being approached in terms of their covenant name "Israel" (13: 16) and as "sons of the family of Abraham" (13: 26). Paul will give them no encouragement, however, to believe that any covenant has bound God to their nation or race, as was widely held by his Jewish contemporaries. Men of Israel and sons of Abraham can be rejected just as King Saul was removed (13: 22). The Gentiles are offered the same salvation, but they too can be rejected, as were the 'seven nations in the land of Canaan" (13: 19). All are called to decision leading to salvation or to judgment. The sermon falls into three parts: (1) God's preparation of a people and the Saviour (vs. 17-25), (2) the gospel message (vs. 26-37), and (3) the call to decision (vs. 38-41).

Paul used the historical approach in showing God's work in making ready a people and a Saviour. He stressed God's initiative in preparing a people for his salvation and his care for them (v. 17). The choice was not on their merit; in his patience "he bore with them," or "suffered their manners" (v. 18).[13] God made every provision for their preparation in giving them the "fathers," the judges, prophets like Samuel, David the king, John the herald, and finally Jesus the Saviour.[14] Paul passed over the giving of the law and stressed the promise, instead; this is one of the many affinities to Galatians. All this pointed to the true son of David, the Saviour, Jesus (v. 23).

In the second part of the sermon (vs. 26-37) are the basic elements in early apostolic preaching: the fulfillment of prophecy, the denial that his death by crucifixion carried the usual implication of guilt by showing the innocence of Jesus, the death as a part of the divine plan, the resurrection as his vindication, and his risen life as witnessed by many. The guilt was laid upon the Jewish rulers and the Romans, but their monstrous deed was done without a real understanding of what they did. Jesus was put to death though no capital charge could be established against him. The emphasis on the burial was twofold, to establish beyond any doubt the reality of the death and hence, of the resurrection of Jesus. The resurrection, adequately witnessed to by those who saw the risen Jesus, fully vindicated the death as triumph rather that defeat. Israel's true destiny was realized in Jesus, God's Son.

The closing part of the sermon (vs. 38-41) includes appeal and warning. Forgiveness of sins is offered to all through Jesus. "In this one" those believing are made righteous; the law of Moses was not able to do this (13: 38f.). Paul's great doctrine of

---

[13] This follows the best manuscripts in a disputed reading.
[14] Cf. Rackham, *op. cit.*, p. 214.

justification by faith, or righteousness by faith, is emphatic here. This includes both new standing and new quality of life. Paul's "in Christ" theme is present too; for "by him" should rather be translated "in this one" (13: 39). The vital union with Christ is what issues in the righteousness: new standing and new life. With the invitation to trust is the warning of judgment consequent upon rejection.

Response to Paul's sermon [13: 42-43]

42 As they went out, the people begged that these things might be told them the next sabbath. 43 And when the meeting of the synagogue broke up, many Jews and devout converts to Judaism followed Paul and Barnabas, who spoke to them and urged them to continue in the grace of God.

Paul could preach Jesus as the Son of God (13: 33) and man's Saviour (13: 23) in a Jewish synagogue and be invited back! This situation obtained more than fifteen years after the crucifixion of Jesus. This favorable response came from "Jews and devout converts to Judaism [proselytes]." These devout proselytes are not to be confused with the God-fearers of verses 16 and 26. The Greek words are different, and distinct groups are contemplated. Paul's audience included Jews (native-born), proselytes (Gentile converts to Judaism), and God-fearers (Gentile students of Judaism). The last group is not mentioned here, for Luke is concerned only to show that those actually within Judaism were favorable to Paul's message. The divisive issue did not appear until the sabbath following.

Turning to the Gentiles [13: 44-52]

44 The next sabbath almost the whole city gathered together to hear the word of God. 45 But when the Jews saw the multitudes, they were filled with jealousy, and contradicted what was spoken by Paul, and reviled him. 46 And Paul and Barnabas spoke out boldly, saying, "It was necesssary that the word of God should be spoken first to you. Since you thrust it from you, and judge yourselves unworthy of eternal life, behold, we turn to the Gentiles. 47 For so the Lord has commanded us, saying,
'I have set you to be a light for the Gentiles,
    that you may bring salvation to the uttermost parts of the earth.' "

> 48 And when the Gentiles heard this, they were glad and glorified the
> word of God; and as many as were ordained to eternal life be-
> lieved. 49 And the word of the Lord spread throughout all the
> region. 50 But the Jews incited the devout women of high stand-
> ing and the leading men of the city, and stirred up persecution
> against Paul and Barnabas, and drove them out of their district.
> 51 But they shook off the dust from their feet against them, and
> went to Iconium. 52 And the disciples were filled with joy and
> with the Holy Spirit.

On the sabbath following a fourth group appeared in the audience, and their presence made utterly unacceptable that which
had just been received with enthusiasm. The rank and file of
Gentiles, "the multitudes," unconditioned by Judaism, now
appeared "to hear the word of God"; and their presence was
too much for the Jews. These multitudes were by-passing Judaism
for this Jesus, and the Jews were made jealous. They tried to
discredit Paul and Barnabas and the gospel which they preached.

Choices and decisions were being made, with consequences
which were doubtless beyond the power of any of them fully
to measure. The Jews were not being by-passed; the word of God
was spoken first to them. Paul and Barnabas laid bare the issue
when they charged, "You thrust it from you, and judge yourselves unworthy of eternal life" (13: 46). This was the beginning
of the self-exclusion of the Jews. With this sad consequence was
its companion, "We turn to the Gentiles." This is now the last
group, the pagans unreached by Judaism.

Turning to the Gentiles was both happy and sad. It hastened
the conversion of the Gentiles, but made less probable the winning of the Jews. This weighed heavily with Paul through subsequent years (cf. Rom. 9-11). Paul's yearning for the Jews never
diminished; his desire was to minister to the two as one. But if
the issue was forced, *he would cast his lot with the excluded and
not with the excluders.* He came to see more clearly through the
years that God's purpose of the ages was to create out of Jews
and Gentiles one new humanity in Christ; the Ephesian letter
is his greatest statement of that ideal.[15] But even at this earlier

---

[15] Cf. W. O. Carver, *The Glory of God in the Christian Calling* (Nashville: Broadman Press, 1949) for the classic treatment of this epistle.

date, Paul could get no joy in being forced to turn from the synagogue. The proof is in the fact that he entered the next synagogue whose door was open to him.

Persecution drove the missionaries out of Antioch; and in leaving, they "shook the dust from their feet against them," as a Jew would do in asserting the uncleanness of Samaritan or Gentile. Those who are really "unclean" are those who "judge themselves unworthy of eternal life." Jews who found Gentile equality in Christ unacceptable proved to be the real "Gentiles." Later Paul will distinguish true "Israel" from national Israel, and show that in this distinction the Jew naturally may be virtually a "Gentile" (cf. Gal. 3: 7, 28f.; Rom. 9: 6ff.).

Iconium: more of the same [14: 1-7]

> 1 Now at Iconium they entered together into the Jewish synagogue, and so spoke that a great company believed, both of Jews and of Greeks. 2 But the unbelieving Jews stirred up the Gentiles and poisoned their minds against the brethren. 3 So they remained for a long time, speaking boldly for the Lord, who bore witness to the word of his grace, granting signs and wonders to be done by their hands. 4 But the people of the city were divided; some sided with the Jews, and some with the apostles. 5 When an attempt was made by both Gentiles and Jews, with their rulers, to molest them and to stone them, 6 they learned of it and fled to Lystra and Derbe, cities of Lycaonia, and to the surrounding country; 7 and there they preached the gospel.

The English word "together" translates three Greek words which literally say "according to the same" (14: 1). This seems to be an idiom meaning "in the same way" (cf. similar expression in Luke 6: 23, 26). Luke is saying that they entered Iconium as Antioch: they began with the synagogue and attempted to minister to Jews and Gentiles through that medium. The story was repeated; after initial success, Jewish opposition forced them out of the synagogue and finally out of the city.

Though there are textual difficulties which make the reconstruction of the story difficult, it seems that there was an initial success in the synagogue as Jews and Greeks (God-fearers) believed (14: 1). This precipitated Jewish opposition, and these unbelieving or disobedient (the Greek word can have either meaning) Jews aroused the Gentiles against the brethren (14:2). The next verse speaks of a long period of sufficient peace to enable them to speak boldly for the Lord and accomplish signs and wonders by his power (14: 3). Probably during this period they went directly to the Gentiles, having been driven out of the synagogue. [Some have suggested that verses 2 and 3 should be transposed, because they probably were shifted by some early scribe. This would make easier reading, thus indicating only one persecution; but there is no manuscript evidence for placing verse 3 ahead of verse 2. Some important manuscripts do have at the end of verse 2 the explanatory statement, "and the Lord quickly gave peace."]

Verse 4 describes a schism among the people of the city as some sided with the Jews and some with the apostles. Assuming that the apostles had first been driven out of the synagogue and that this was followed by a period of direct approach to the Gentiles, we may now see the further effort of the Jews to force them out of the city. Possibly no charges were found that could be legally established, so the Jews resorted to mob violence. They would have their usual reason for the action, and the Gentile rulers of the city would desire to restore peace to the city by ridding it of the disturbers. The apostles, getting wind of the plot, escaped to the other towns and the surrounding country (14: 6).

It is noteworthy that in this paragraph the word "apostles" is used (14: 4). Barnabas and Paul are the ones so designated (cf. 14: 14). Paul made explicit claim in his letters that he was an apostle. The word means "ones sent," and it may refer here to their function as missionaries. Philip, too, was sent on important missions, but he is not termed an apostle. Though there was a group in the New Testament recognized as "apostles," there is no explanation of the distinctiveness of the office. (But see discussion of 1: 15-26.)

An elaborate story relating to Iconium is contained in the *Acts of Paul and Thecla* (*ca.* A.D. 150).[16] According to Tertullian

---

[16] Cf. Sir W. M. Ramsay, *The Church in the Roman Empire*, pp. 375–428; Rackham, *op. cit.*, pp. 226f.

this story was compiled by a presbyter in Asia Minor who was deposed in the year 160 for writing it. It tells of the devotion of Thecla to Paul and of her renunciation of her engagement to an aristocratic young man named Thamyris. This disturbing of family life led to much conflict and persecution. Possibly there is no historical foundation at all for this story—many excellent scholars so conclude—but it is possible that it may reflect some actual history. The story is obviously a glorification of virginity, and that may account for the whole story as a fabrication. However, there are some touches in the story which seem to reflect the contemporary situation. If so, some light may be thrown on the "schism" at Iconium; the conversion of a pagan would seriously disturb family and community relationships because of issues religious and moral. To say no more, imagine the tension between a Christian wife and a pagan husband who worshipped idols and believed in infanticide! Something of this is reflected in First Corinthians, especially in chapter seven.

The story also offers a description of Paul as "a man small in size, with meeting eyebrows, with a rather large nose, baldheaded, bowlegged, strongly built, full of grace, for at times he looked like a man, and at times he had the face of an angel." [17] Ramsay observes, "This plain and unflattering account of the Apostle's personal appearance seems to embody a very early tradition." [18] Whether true or not, it has influenced our mental pictures of Paul to this day.

Lystra: fickle pagans and persistent Jews [14: 8-20a]

> 8 Now at Lystra there was a man sitting, who could not use his feet; he was a cripple from birth, who had never walked. 9 He listened to Paul speaking; and Paul, looking intently at him and seeing that he had faith to be made well, 10 said in a loud voice, "Stand upright on your feet." And he sprang up and walked. 11 And when the crowds saw what Paul had done, they lifted up their voices, saying in Lycaonian, "The gods have come down to us in the likeness of men!" 12 Barnabas they called Zeus, and Paul, because he was the chief speaker, they called Hermes. 13 And the priest of Zeus, whose temple was in front of the city, brought oxen

---

[17] *The Church in the Roman Empire,* pp. 31f.
[18] *Ibid.,* p. 32.

and garlands to the gates and wanted to offer sacrifice with the people. 14 But when the apostles Barnabas and Paul heard of it, they tore their garments and rushed out among the multitude, crying, 15 "Men, why are you doing this? We also are men, of like nature with you, and bring you good news, that you should turn from these vain things to a living God who made the heaven and the earth and the sea and all that is in them. 16 In past generations he allowed all the nations to walk in their own ways; 17 yet he did not leave himself without witness, for he did good and gave you from heaven rains and fruitful seasons, satisfying your hearts with food and gladness." 18 With these words they scarcely restrained the people from offering sacrifice to them.

19 But Jews came there from Antioch and Iconium; and having persuaded the people, they stoned Paul and dragged him out of the city, supposing that he was dead. 20 But when the disciples gathered about him, he rose up and entered the city;

The atmosphere at Lystra is strictly pagan. No mention is made of a Jewish synagogue, but the cult of Zeus is prominent (14: 13). The Lystrans evidently spoke a broken Greek,[19] but their native tongue was Lycaonian. When they saw the cripple healed, they concluded that the apostles were Zeus and Hermes, and they sought to offer sacrifice to them. In the excitement it was normal for them to revert to their native tongue. Paul was called "Hermes" because he was the chief speaker. Hermes was the god of speech or messenger (in Greek the word is angel) of the gods. This incident may be reflected in Paul's later reference to being received as an "angel" (cf. Gal. 1: 8 and 4: 14).

Paul's message to the Lystrans reflects the simple and pagan background of his hearers. As is true of all the speeches in Acts, it is thoroughly suited to the situation. The people were pointed to the living God who created all things and away from the worship of gods which they have created (14: 15). In the synagogues Paul naturally appealed to the witness of the Jewish scriptures, but here he must appeal to that which is within their own experience. In the benefactions of nature they were asked to see the hand of God and the witness to himself which he had given them (14: 17).

Some difficulty may be encountered in harmonizing the state-

---

[19] So inscriptions of a later date show, and Paul presumably addressed them in Greek.

ment, "in past generations he allowed all the nations to walk in their own ways" (14: 16), with the argument in Romans 1: 18-32, where Paul insisted that the pagans were without excuse and that their "blindness" is the result of their refusal to follow the light which God gave them in nature. The passages can be harmonized if the problems being dealt with are remembered. In the Roman letter, Paul's chief concern was to establish the fact that *God is righteous* in his dealings with Jew and Gentile; if either is lost, it is because he has not followed the light God has provided. At Lystra, Paul was not dealing with proud people who insist that God must save them or else be guilty of being untrue to his commitments (many Jews argued that God would be unrighteous if he should let his covenant people be lost), but he was dealing with simple, ignorant people who need encouragement to venture out in an enlightened faith. Furthermore, Paul was here urging upon them an accountability for the light which they had in nature and to which they now have access in the gospel.

But pagan simplicity was not the apostles' major problem; persistent Jews followed from Antioch and Iconium and, having persuaded the emotional and fickle crowds, they (the Jews) "stoned Paul and dragged him out of the city, supposing that he was dead" (14: 19). The English translations can easily leave the impression that the Lystrans stoned Paul, but that is not the case. The Greek participles are decisive in showing that the "Jews from Antioch and Iconium" were the ones who stoned Paul. Supposing him to be dead, they probably returned to their towns; and this would account for the fact that Paul could re-enter Lystra. The Lystrans may have been sufficiently persuaded by the Jews to permit the assault, but they took no initiative in the persecution.

Derbe and the return trip to Syrian Antioch [14: 20b-28]

[20b] and on the next day he went on with Barnabas to Derbe. 21 When they had preached the gospel to that city and had made many disciples, they returned to Lystra and to Iconium and to Antioch, 22 strengthening the souls of the disciples, exhorting them to continue in the faith, and saying that through many

tribulations we must enter the kingdom of God. [23] And when they had appointed elders for them in every church, with prayer and fasting, they committed them to the Lord in whom they believed. [24] Then they passed through Pisidia, and came to Pamphylia. [25] And when they had spoken the word in Perga, they went down to Attalia; [26] and from there they sailed to Antioch, where they had been commended to the grace of God for the work which they had fulfilled. [27] And when they arrived, they gathered the church together and declared all that God had done with them, and how he had opened a door of faith to the Gentiles. [28] And they remained no little time with the disciples.

Only a general report of a successful mission in Derbe is given. "Gaius of Derbe" (20: 4) may have been converted at this time. Lystra and Derbe may not have been included in the original plans, for they fled to these parts because of the persecution in Iconium (14: 6). Whether by plan or not, cherished converts were made in these towns, though Lois, Eunice, and Timothy, as well as Gaius, may not have been won until the next trip.

The return through the communities recently evangelized was important for the usual reasons pertaining to a new work but also because of persecution. It was necessary for these new converts to realize that the "cross" could be expected in the kingdom of God (14: 22). There was a further work in organizing, especially necessary where the church was separate from the synagogue and where it had a large constituency of Gentiles. The apostles "appointed elders" in each church and left them with the Lord (14: 23). The Greek word for "appoint" originally referred to election by the show of the hands, but it cannot be established that the term was so used when Luke wrote. As seen earlier, "elders" (presbyters) and "bishops" are often used interchangeably in the New Testament (cf. Acts 20: 17 with 20: 28 and Titus 1: 5 with 1: 7).

Attalia is mentioned on the return, though it was unmentioned when the missionaries sailed from Cyprus and "came to Perga" (13: 13). Again, it is said that the apostles spoke the word in Perga on the return (14: 25), but no mention is made of preaching there on the earlier visit. P. H. Anderson [20] offers the most plausible solution to these problems. He points out that Attalia was the landing place for Perga and neither place would offer much preaching opportunity—especially as a ship came into port, for the people living there would then be their busiest. Paul and his company therefore hastened on to Antioch of Pisidia. On the return, however, they had to wait for a boat to take them back to Syrian Antioch. Sailing vessels could not operate on rigid schedules, so these missionaries would simply have to wait at Perga until passage was available at Attalia. While waiting at Perga, they preached.

Back in Syrian Antioch, there were many things to report from the missionary travels: sailing; witnessing to a Roman proconsul; unmasking a magician; invitations to preach in a Jewish synagogue; conversions of Jews, God-fearers, and pagans; being mistaken for gods; threats; stoning; and doubtless many other experiences not related by Luke. The campaign may have lasted several years; no clue is given as to its duration. *But of all that was to be reported, the most important to Luke was the fact that God "had opened a door of faith to the Gentiles"* (14: 27).

Of course open doors had long been offered the Gentiles: circumcision, the law, becoming a proselyte. But this door—personal faith in Christ Jesus—had no necessary connection with synagogue or any of these things.

Gentile Liberty Debated at Antioch and Jerusalem [15: 1-35]

Salvation and fellowship.—The successful campaign which brought many Gentiles as well as Jews into the churches also brought on a crisis in which decisive issues were at stake. The conditions of salvation and of fellowship were debated at Antioch and Jerusalem. The claim that a Gentile could not be saved without circumcision and the keeping of the law of Moses (15: 1, 5) was rejected by both churches. The inevitable further problem concerned the conditions of fellowship between Jews (Christian and non-Christian) and Gentile converts.

The clear demonstrations of the Spirit in the conversions of uncircumcised Gentiles were conclusive for all except a stubborn party of believing Pharisees that salvation was not dependent upon circumcision or the Mosaic law. These, known later as Judaizers, did not accept the decision of the churches; but, with the help of unbelieving Jews, they pressed a bitter fight with Paul for some years to come in Galatia, Corinth, Ephesus, and elsewhere.

The decision about salvation did not settle for some the matter of fellowship (just as race today is not a problem in salvation but in fellowship). The *agape* or fellowship supper and the Lord's Supper would provide the occasions for forcing that issue. Jewish scruples were expressed by some in their refusal to eat with Gentile Christians and in their denial of that right to others. The problem was made more acute for Jewish Christians who wanted to continue fellowship with non-Christian Jews; "defiling" contact with uncircumcised Christians would deny the Christian Jews the desired fellowship with non-Christian Jews.

It is highly probable that this issue of fellowship was a factor in the tension between Barnabas and Paul, as it certainly was between Peter and Paul (Gal 2: 11ff.). Paul and Barnabas separated over John Mark; but as stated previously, the underlying issue was most likely one of policy and not simply of personalities. Possibly Barnabas was more cautious about forcing Jewish prejudice to give way to a Christian brotherhood which stood for equality of Jew and uncircumcised Gentile. Paul, on the other hand, would tolerate no policy of first and second class Christians. To him, to refuse fellowship with uncircumcised Christians was to discredit their salvation; what he said to Peter at Antioch was tantamount to this (Gal. 2: 11ff.).

Exegetical problems.—No chapter in the New Testament is more difficult for the exegete than Acts 15. The text itself is uncertain at many points, due to differences in the manuscripts; [21] and there are major problems when Acts 15 is compared with Galatians 1: 11 to 2: 10. Kirsopp Lake is not far from the truth in saying: "The general problem of Acts 15 is so complicated

---

[21] This problem will be discussed in the exegesis of the chapter.

that it can only be stated—it cannot be solved—by a process of analysis into smaller ones." [22] Does the visit of Galatians 2: 1-10 parallel the visit of Acts 15, or of Acts 11: 30 and 12: 25? Were the provisions of the letter (Acts 15: 29) ritual or moral? Was Titus (not mentioned in Acts) circumcised (Gal. 2: 3)? Was the conference before or after the campaign of Barnabas and Saul? These are some of the questions debated at length in all critical commentaries.

Visits to Jerusalem.—Traditionally the conference of Acts 15 has been viewed as the parallel of the one of Galatians 2. Many, however, contend that tne visit mentioned in Acts 11: 30 and 12: 25 is the parallel to Galatians 2. In Galatians, Paul takes oath that he is telling the truth, as he contends that his apostleship was never derived from the twelve or dependent upon them. He tells of two visits to Jerusalem: one visit came three years after his conversion, at which time he spent fifteen days with Peter and saw James (Gal. 1: 18-19); then after fourteen years he went up to Jerusalem, "by revelation," with Barnabas and Titus and disputed privately with James, Cephas, John, and others over the question of circumcision (Gal. 2: 1-10). In Acts the second visit of Paul as a Christian to Jerusalem is that mentioned in 11: 30 and 12: 25; the visit of Acts 15 is the third mentioned. This, with other considerations, is decisive for many that the visit of Acts 11: 30 and 12: 25 is the parallel to Galatians 2: 1-10. Others hold that the passages refer to one visit and that Luke confused his sources, representing the one visit as two.

This writer would not want the task of "proving" that Luke was in such confusion that he treated one visit as though it were two; the evidences for Luke's trustworthiness are too strong for that. Moreover, for all the finality with which some write today, it is far from established that the visit of 11: 30 and 12: 25 is the parallel of Galatians 2: 1-10.

Theory that Acts 11:30 parallels Acts 15.—Lake presents at its strongest the position that the visit of Acts 11: 30 and 12: 25 was

---

[22] Kirsopp Lake and Henry J. Cadbury, editors, *Additional Notes*, Vol. V, *The Beginnings of Christianity* (London: Macmillan and Co., 1933), p. 195.

the occasion of the conference and that Acts 15 is but a confusion of the same visit.[23] He argues to this effect: "According to Galatians Paul went to Jerusalem by revelation, not because of any controversy in the church, and he hints that the visit was concerned with the care of the poor." [24] It is true that Paul went by "revelation," but that does not rule out a controversy as the occasion for the trip. The Galatians would know about the controversy and possibly had chided him about being forced to go to Jerusalem to be judged by the apostles. Paul is insisting that his action in going was not to answer a summons of the Apostles but because of a divine directive.

This in no way rules out the Acts 15 visit as the one Paul made "by revelation." The care of the poor was *not* the occasion for the visit mentioned in Galatians, and hence does not correspond to the visit of Acts 11. Had this been true, the plea as they parted that Paul "remember the poor" (Gal. 2: 10) would be superfluous. It is understandable that Paul and his friends be asked to remember the poor following the conference of Acts 15; but it would be strange indeed if this request came at the close of the Acts 11 visit, when that was precisely what Paul and Barnabas were doing. Applied to Acts 11 the plea would be: "By all means, please do not forget to do what you have just done."

It is further argued that Acts 15 cannot be anything but a confused account, for (so it is argued) the solution does not fit the problem.[25] The problem, according to Acts 15 and Galatians 2: 1-10, was about circumcision and the conditions of salvation, but the settlement in Acts 15 involved three (or four) requirements having to do with fellowship. It is argued that this inconsistency is fatal to Acts 15 as a trustworthy account. This simply does not follow, and the conclusive evidence is to be found in Galatians. It is not valid to impose upon the situation in Acts 15 a mechanical logic; it was normal for these leaders to turn from the problem of the conditions of salvation to the problem of fellowship. The two problems are inseparable; either leads to the other.

---

[23] *Additional Notes,* p. 201. For his full treatment, see pages 195–212.
[24] *Ibid.,* p. 202.
[25] Cf. *ibid.,* pp. 202f.

Paul himself, in Galatians 2: 11 and following, goes from the problem of fellowship to that of salvation. When Peter, and even Barnabas, backed off from eating with Gentiles because of the coming of some "from James," the problem was fellowship; but Paul turned to the issue of the conditions of salvation. When he said to Cephas, "If you, though a Jew, live like a Gentile and not like a Jew, how can you compel the Gentiles to live like Jews?" he was in a sense "jumping the track," that is, if the mechanical consistency demanded of Acts 15 were also demanded here. In reality, Peter was not trying to get the Gentiles to live like Jews; he was, as a Jew, refusing to live like a Gentile. But to impose this mechanical logic upon Paul is unfair. Yet more important, Paul's strong argument which followed had to do with the *conditions of salvation* (Gal. 2: 15ff.) and not with the conditions of fellowship. If Lake's logic be applied to Galatians, as it is applied to Acts 15, then it must follow that Paul's argument (conditions of salvation) is not related to his problem (conditions of fellowship). To demand this mechanical consistency of Acts 15 or Galatians 2: 11 and following is absurd.

The argument cannot stand that Acts 15 is unreliable because problem and solution are unrelated. The problems of salvation and fellowship are inseparable. So soon as it was concluded that a Gentile could be saved without circumcision, it was obvious that practical problems of fellowship would follow; these are anticipated by the letter of Acts 15. When fellowship was broken at Antioch by the refusal of some to eat with Gentiles, this reflected on the validity of the Gentiles' salvation, and Paul was quick to point out that fact (Gal. 2: 11ff.).

Theory that Galatians 2 :1-10 parallels Acts 11 :30.—To the argument that the second visit of Paul to Jerusalem was the one of Acts 11 rather than Acts 15, it was long ago pointed out that Paul, in Galatians, was not presuming to tell of each trip to Jerusalem but of his dealings with the twelve. The problem in Galatians concerned his apostleship and his relation to the twelve, not his trips to Jerusalem. In truth, the Antioch scene was as important as the Jerusalem ones for Paul's contention that his apostleship was not derived from the twelve or subordinate to the twelve. It is not implausible that, as many have suggested, Paul left the Acts 11 visit unmentioned because it was not germane to the problem. Much is made of Paul's oath that he is telling the truth (Gal. 1: 20), but he says nothing about listing each journey to Jerusalem; the oath concerns the truth about seeing none of the apostles except Peter and James. To read some of the comments today, one would conclude that Paul said, "Before God, I do not lie, these are the only trips I made to Jerusalem." Fortunately we still have Galatians by which to check its exegetes.

To identify the conference of Galatians 2: 1-10 with the visit of Acts 11 is to place it in an atmosphere less congenial than that of Acts 15. When Peter speaks of the choice that by him the Gentiles would hear the gospel, the obvious reference is to the Cornelius experience; and this experience is spoken of as something that is now little more than a memory. The Jerusalem Christians had not followed up its implications, else the controversy over circumcision would not have arisen in Antioch. The conference about circumcision certainly did not follow soon after Peter had been challenged at Jerusalem for eating with uncircumcised people at the home of Cornelius.

Lake [26] suggests that the missionary journey of Barnabas and Saul *followed* the council and the quarrel of Paul against Peter and Barnabas. This is almost inconceivable in the light of the campaign itself. If, however, the council followed the campaign, and the clash at Antioch followed the conference, light is thrown on the tension which led to the separation of Barnabas and Paul. The issue concerned policy, not merely personalities.

A further discussion of this problem will be found in the Appendix.

Issue of circumcision pressed by Pharisaic believers [15: 1-5]

1 But some men came down from Judea and were teaching the brethren, "Unless you are circumcised according to the custom of Moses, you cannot be saved." 2 And when Paul and Barnabas had no small dissension and debate with them, Paul and Barnabas and

---

[26] *Additional Notes*, pp. 203f.

158 THE BOOK OF ACTS

some of the others were appointed to go up to Jerusalem to the apostles and the elders about this question. 3 So, being sent on their way by the church, they passed through both Phoenicia and Samaria, reporting the conversion of the Gentiles, and they gave great joy to all the brethren. 4 When they came to Jerusalem, they were welcomed by the church and the apostles and the elders, and they declared all that God had done with them. 5 But some believers who belonged to the party of the Pharisees rose up, and said, "It is necessary to circumcise them, and to charge them to keep the law of Moses."

Paul and Barnabas had "risked [devoted] their lives for the sake of our Lord Jesus Christ" (15: 26), but here were men who would scuttle the whole mission for circumcision and the law of Moses (15: 1, 5). Their concern was for the institutions which would supposedly save a chosen people, not for a human brotherhood in Christ. Their presence stirred discord and debate, and made advisable a conference in Jerusalem.

The Greek is ambiguous in verse 2; it is not clear who "appointed" Paul and Barnabas and the others to go up to Jerusalem. Manuscripts containing what is known as the Western text have it that "those who had come from Jerusalem charged Paul and Barnabas and certain others to go up to the apostles and elders in Jerusalem in order that they be judged by them concerning this debate." It is hardly conceivable that Paul would have respected a command from these men; his Galatian letter is the strongest possible statement that he did not acknowledge the jurisdiction of those at Jerusalem over him; and it is strong evidence that the Western text is not to be trusted at many points. The appointment was probably by the church at Antioch.

There is nothing to suggest that the church at Antioch was under necessity to appeal to the church at Jerusalem, and there is nothing to suggest that the church at Jerusalem considered itself in position to give a directive. The whole experience was in the spirit of conference and advice. Paul's claim in Galatians (2: 1) that he went up by revelation need not be in conflict with the development as Acts has it; Paul experienced a sense of divine guidance, and in that he found his reason for a conference rather than a curt answer.

The reports of the conversion of the Gentiles brought joy to

Phoenicia (an untraced mission) and Samaria, and the church at Jerusalem welcomed those from Antioch. The sour note was struck by "believers who belonged to the party of the Pharisees" who contended that circumcision and the law of Moses were necessary. Evidently such disorder followed that the meeting was adjourned in favor of a private meeting—the private conference referred to in Galatians 2: 1-10.

Peter's recognition of no distinction in salvation [15: 6-11]

> 6 The apostles and the elders were gathered together to consider this matter. 7 And after there had been much debate, Peter rose and said to them, "Brethren, you know that in the early days God made choice among you, that by my mouth the Gentiles should hear the word of the gospel and believe. 8 And God who knows the heart bore witness to them, giving them the Holy Spirit just as he did to us; 9 and he made no distinction between us and them, but cleansed their hearts by faith. 10 Now therefore why do you make trial of God by putting a yoke upon the neck of the disciples which neither our fathers nor we have been able to bear? 11 But we believe that we shall be saved through the grace of the Lord Jesus, just as they will."

Because Galatians 2: 2 speaks of a private conference with the apostles, it has appealed to many that Acts 15: 6 reflects such a meeting. Reading between the lines, many scholars have concluded that the private conference came between two open meetings of the church. This is not explicit, but may be implied.

Peter, speaking apparently in open meeting to the church, reminds them of how God used him in reaching the Gentiles. Though the reference need not be limited to the Cornelius experience, it must certainly have included it as the focal point. Peter speaks of it as belonging to the distant past, "in the early days," and it is little more than a memory. Evidently its implications had not been followed by the Jerusalem disciples.

The emphasis given by Peter is important: God made "no distinction" between Jew and non-Jew (15: 9), the hearts of the Gentiles were cleansed by faith (15: 9), and *Jews were saved by faith just as Gentiles were* (15: 11). Peter was not only affirming that Gentiles were saved by faith, but that Jews were saved in the way Gentiles were. We might have expected him to say that

Gentiles are saved as Jews are saved, but it is pleasing to see that he gave it the other stress. To challenge the validity of the salvation of these uncircumcised believers would be to "make trial of" or challenge God (15: 10). If God made no distinction, why should men do so? If God called an uncircumcised believer "clean," why should men call him "unclean"?

The future idea in the statement about salvation (15: 11) is not fair to the Greek, which doubtless means "we believe (so as) to be saved," the infinitive being epexegetical and denoting purpose or result.[27]

The silenced assembly hears Barnabas and Paul [15: 12]

12 And all the assembly kept silence; and they listened to Barnabas and Paul as they related what signs and wonders God had done through them among the Gentiles.

The testimony of Peter quieted the assembly, and then Barnabas and Paul submitted recent evidence to substantiate the position affirmed by Peter. The Cornelius experience was not exceptional or isolated; it had been repeated wherever the gospel was preached to the Gentiles. The validity of these conversions had been confirmed by signs and wonders.

The proposal of James [15: 13-21]

13 After they finished speaking, James replied, "Brethren, listen to me. 14 Symeon has related how God first visited the Gentiles, to take out of them a people for his name. 15 And with this the words of the prophets agree, as it is written,
16 'After this I will return,
    and I will rebuild the dwelling of David, which has fallen;
    I will rebuild its ruins,
    and I will set it up,
17 that the rest of men may seek the Lord,
    and all the Gentiles who are called by my name,
18 says the Lord, who has made these things known from of old.'
19 Therefore my judgment is that we should not trouble those of the Gentiles who turn to God, 20 but should write to them to abstain from the polutions of idols and from unchastity and from what is strangled and from blood. 21 For from early generations Moses has had in every city those who preach him, for he is read every sabbath in the synagogues."

---

[27] Cf. Lake and Cadbury, *Commentary*, p. 174; Bruce, *op. cit.*, pp. 294f.

James was apparently the most influencial one among the Hebrew Christians, and his acquiescence would virtually assure the outcome of the conference. He betrays at every point the fact that he is still a Jew. "Symeon" is Peter's Jewish name in its Hebrew form (15: 14). The importance of Jewish scruples (15: 20) and the normalcy of the synagogue and Sabbath services (15: 21) reflect his perspective.

The quotation from Amos 9: 11-12 comes from the Greek Septuagint, not from the Hebrew. The point that James is making is dependent upon the Greek translation. The Hebrew pictures Israel as possessing what remains of Edom and the other nations; the Septuagint pictures a restored "tent of David" in which Jews and Gentiles may be united. The further point, that this uniting of the two into one the Lord had "made known from of old," is possibly from Isaiah 45: 21, but it is not from Amos. These two ideas are the very ones which are given their classic statement in Ephesians: that Jew and Gentile are to be made one new humanity in Christ, and that this has been the purpose of God through the ages.

No satisfactory explanation has been given for James' use of the Septuagint rather than the Hebrew Bible. Of course the Septuagint has the statement most helpful for the problem at hand, but James would naturally be expected to use the Hebrew. One is tempted to suggest, with misgivings, that as a Galillean he would speak Aramaic, as well as Greek, but would not read Hebrew.

James took his stand for a clear-cut decision about salvation: circumcision was not required, and they should no longer be annoyed by that subject (15: 19). Recognizing the problems in fellowship between Jews and Gentiles, he advised that Gentile believers respect certain Jewish customs and standards. This was not so much a compromise as an adjustment designed to facilitate the fellowship of two groups whose backgrounds were so different.

The textual problem in the apostolic letter is so difficult that two points are inconclusive: were there three or four proposed restrictions? Were the restrictions all moral or both moral and ritual? The very ancient text known as the Western, surviving in a fifth century manuscript and in the quotations of Irenaeus, Tertullian, Cyprian, and others, omits the words, "and from what is strangled" (15: 20, 29). Many scholars, following the Western text, not only omit "things strangled" but understand "blood" to refer to murder; this seems to have been the position of Tertullian. This would make all the restrictions moral, having to do with idolatry, fornication, and murder.

Though the Western text would be easier to harmonize with Paul's unwillingness to compromise (see Galatians), it is probably to be rejected. It is true that these were sins of the Gentiles from which some would turn with difficulty, but that is hardly the extent of the concern at this point. The Jewish abhorrence of flesh with the blood in it would have to be reckoned with. Paul would certainly not consider it undue compromise to ask Gentile believers to respect kosher laws of their Jewish brothers.

Letter to Gentiles in Antioch, Syria, and Cilicia [15: 22-35]

22 Then it seemed good to the apostles and the elders, with the whole church, to choose men from among them and send them to Antioch with Paul and Barnabas. They sent Judas called Barsabbas, and Silas, leading men among the brethren, 23 with the following letter: "The brethren, both the apostles and the elders, to the brethren who are of the Gentiles in Antioch and Syria and Cilicia, greeting. 24 Since we have heard that some persons from us have troubled you with words, unsettling your minds, although we gave them no instructions, 25 it has seemed good to us in assembly to choose men and send them to you with our beloved Barnabas and Paul, 26 men who have risked their lives for the sake of our Lord Jesus Christ. 27 We have therefore sent Judas and Silas, who themselves will tell you the same things by word of mouth. 28 For it has seemed good to the Holy Spirit and to us to lay upon you no greater burden than these necessary things: 29 that you abstain from what has been sacrificed to idols and from blood and from what is strangled and from unchastity. If you keep yourselves from these, you will do well. Farewell."

30 So when they were sent off, they went down to Antioch; and having gathered the congregation together, they delivered the letter. 31 And when they read it, they rejoiced at the exhortation. 32 And Judas and Silas, who were themselves prophets, exhorted the brethren with many words and strengthened them. 33 And after

they had spent some time, they were sent off in peace by the
brethren to those who had sent them. 35 But Paul and Barnabas
remained in Antioch, teaching and preaching the word of the
Lord, with many others also.

The whole church shared in the position assumed in the letter;
this of course does not mean that each individual was in agreement with it, for the Judaizers were at work for some years after
this, seeking to force circumcision on the Gentiles. The letter was
sent to Gentiles of Antioch, Syria, and Cilicia, where the trouble
had been caused by those claiming to speak for the Jerusalem
church. This Antioch was a city in Syria, and Cilicia was united
with Syria. The Judaizers may not yet have molested the churches
beyond Derbe and Lystra; the letter is not mentioned after
Paul, on his next journey, got beyond those towns.

The Jerusalem church sent two of its leading members, Judas
and Silas, to convey additional assurance of the good will of
the Jerusalem brethren. Judas, called Barsabbas, was evidently
a Hebrew, as his name would suggest; and Silas was probably a
Hellenist, as is suggested by his name and by the fact that he
became so close a companion to Paul.

The letter and the messages of Judas and Silas brought peace
into the community at Antioch. Silas, it seems, went back to
Jerusalem with Judas; but, if so, he soon returned to Antioch.

Separation of Paul and Barnabas [15: 36-41]

36 And after some days Paul said to Barnabas, "Come, let us return
and visit the brethren in every city where we proclaimed the word
of the Lord, and see how they are." 37 And Barnabas wanted to
take with them John called Mark. 38 But Paul thought best not to
take with them one who had withdrawn from them in Pamphylia,
and had not gone with them to the work. 39 And there arose a
sharp contention, so that they separated from each other; Barnabas took Mark with him and sailed away to Cyprus, 40 but Paul
chose Silas and departed, being commended by the brethren to the
grace of the Lord. 41 And he went through Syria and Cilicia,
strengthening the churches.

The separation of Paul and Barnabas has been given some
consideration already. John Mark figured prominently in the
separation, but doubtless much that Luke passes over is involved.

It was suggested earlier that probably policy, and not merely personalities, was the divisive issue. From Galatians 2: 13 it is learned that at Antioch Barnabas joined those who separated themselves from the uncircumcised believers, refusing to eat with them. Barnabas perhaps was not as liberal as Paul on the race question, and that probably accounts for some of Paul's sensitiveness when the case of John Mark came up.

There was some salvage value from the painful separation: two mission parties were formed, and Paul doubtless found greater freedom in the Gentile mission. The curtain was dropped on Barnabas and Mark as they left for Cyprus. Luke's concern was not with geography, but with the freedom of the gospel.

Galatian Churches Revisited [16: 1-5]

1 And he came also to Derbe and to Lystra. A disciple was there, named Timothy, the son of a Jewish woman who was a believer; but his father was a Greek. 2 He was well spoken of by the brethren at Lystra and Iconium. 3 Paul wanted Timothy to accompany him; and he took him and circumcised him because of the Jews that were in those places, for they all knew that his father was a Greek. 4 As they went on their way through the cities, they delivered to them for observance the decisions which had been reached by the apostles and elders who were at Jerusalem. 5 So the churches were strengthened in the faith, and they increased in numbers daily.

This section marks the close of a great mission; it marks, too, the end of a major division of the book. One of Luke's summary statements appears in verse 5, as in 2: 47, 4: 4, 6: 7, and 12: 24. The atmosphere has been Oriental to this point, but it changes after this section.

The circumcision of Timothy is the major problem of this paragraph. It is difficult to reconcile Paul's action here with his bold statements in Galatians (cf. chap. 5). It is easier to understand his actions, however, if Timothy was circumcised before Galatians was written, for some consistent pattern may thus be seen. At the Jerusalem conference (Acts 15) and in circumcising Timothy, Paul went far in the interest of expediency and harmony. Certainly he did not feel that he was compromising the truth in so doing. Later, as the issues were pressed and as his visit to Jerusalem and his circumcising of Timothy came in for criticism, Paul adopted the sterner policy reflected in Galatians. When Galatians was written, Paul had doubtless circumcised someone; it is known that he circumcised Timothy, but it is doubtful that he circumcised Titus.

Paul went beyond the proposal of the Jerusalem church as he read the letter of the conference to churches in Galatia (16: 4); the letter was addressed only to Syria-Cilicia. It is incredible that Paul would have made a trip to Jerusalem and then have accepted the terms of the council's letter and read it to the Galatian churches *after* the things he wrote in the Galatian letter. The most plausible conclusion is that a situation later and far more critical drew from him this brutally plain letter.

Was Timothy from Lystra or Derbe? The text is not clear, but he is usually connected with Lystra. Acts 20: 4 seems to assign Timothy to Derbe, and a very early tradition is of that position. The point is of interest but of little value. Timothy's father was probably dead; the Greek is not conclusive, but it is favorable to that conclusion. The fact that his mother had married a Greek indicates that the family, if not the community, was little influenced by the narrow exclusiveness of the Pharisees. Timothy seems already to have been converted, with Lois and Eunice, probably on Paul's first mission there.

JEWS AND GENTILES APPROACHED CHIEFLY APART FROM SYNAGOGUES: INCREASING SELF-EXCLUSION OF THE JEWS [16: 6 to 19: 20]

AFTER THE SEPARATION from Barnabas and the delivery of the Jerusalem letter to the churches concerned, Paul with new companions launched into a second major campaign which took him into the great Greco-Roman cultural center on the shores of the Aegean Sea, including the Roman provinces of Macedonia, Achaia, and Asia. Rackham is correct in the suggestion that the division of Paul's work into three "missionary journeys" is misleading.[28] He was engaged in one great campaign with Barnabas

---

[28] *Op. cit.,* p. 271.

and in another great campaign (commonly termed the second and third missionary journeys) after separating from Barnabas. These campaigns involved extended work in and around great cities: eighteen months in Corinth, over two years in Ephesus, and briefer periods in other centers. The hurried trip to Palestine after the Corinthian campaign (18: 22f.) was only an interruption in the great campaign in Ephesus.[29]

What is new in this second campaign? Luke is *not* informing us about how the gospel reached Europe (see below). He shows, in this section how pagans were converted apart from any connection with Judaism. He shows how, as the work progressed among the pagans, the Jews found increasing conflicts between this gospel and what they understood to be their national interests. He shows how Paul and the churches were gradually driven out of the synagogues. He shows how the inclusion of the pagans, won apart from the synagogues, led to the self-exclusion of the Jews from Christianity.

With this development, there were many problems rising out of the pagan world to be wrestled with: mercenary interests, Greek philosophy, pagan religions, and the many forces and factors which emerged when Greek, Roman, and Oriental cultures met.

The Call to Macedonia and a New Campaign [16: 6-10]

6 And they went through the region of Phrygia and Galatia, having been forbidden by the Holy Spirit to speak the word in Asia. 7 And when they had come opposite Mysia, they attempted to go into Bithynia, but the Spirit of Jesus did not allow them; 8 so, passing by Mysia, they went down to Troas. 9 And a vision appeared to Paul in the night: a man of Macedonia was standing beseeching him and saying, "Come over to Macedonia and help us." 10 And when he had seen the vision, immediately we sought to go on into Macedonia, concluding that God had called us to preach the gospel to them.

Paul had fulfilled his purpose to revisit the brethren won on the first campaign (15: 36), and now a new departure is made as a new campaign is entered. This campaign is under the guidance of the Holy Spirit, just as the previous one had been (13: 2). With-

[29] Cf. Rackham, *op. cit.,* p. 271.

out explanation or the use of the term "Trinity," Luke refers to the Triune God in this paragraph. He speaks of the "Holy Spirit" (16: 6); next, with no apparent change of subject, he speaks of the "Spirit of Jesus" (16: 7); and finally, he refers to this as the direction of "God," evidently the Father (16: 10).

Paul's heart for some years had seemingly been set on going to Ephesus in Asia; probably it was there that he desired to go when forced to turn to the Galatians because of a "bodily ailment" (Gal. 4: 13). That probably accounts for "Asia" being mentioned first in this paragraph (16: 6). The Greek of verse 6 is difficult, but possibly Luke means that Paul contemplated the journey to Asia before leaving the Derbe-Lystra (Pisidian Antioch?) area, and that after being prevented from carrying out this desire, he traveled through the region of Phrygia and Galatia. Of course, he was in the Galatian-Phrygian region when frustrated in his purpose to visit Asia. He then sought an alternate course and was finally guided to Macedonia.

There have been many naïve ideas expressed about the Macedonian call. It has been said countless times that it was here that the gospel was carried to Europe. Many, apparently oblivious to the difference between the Roman province of Asia and the great continent of Asia, have spun fancy tales about how, except for the Macedonian call, Paul would have gone to India and China! *No one has the evidence to say that Paul was the first to take the gospel to Europe or that Lydia was the first convert in Europe.* The evidences are strong to the effect that Christianity reached Rome at a very early date. Furthermore, modern ideas of "Asia" and "Europe" are foreign to the situation in Acts. The Roman provinces of Asia, Macedonia, and Achaia constituted a great Greco-Roman cultural center on the shores of the Aegean Sea. They were not divided into "Asia" and "Europe" or into "East" and "West." Rackham aptly states it in saying, "The Macedonian did not say, 'Come over into Europe,' but 'Come over into Macedonia.' " [30] The divide between East and West was not the Bosporus or Dardanelles, but the Taurus mountains.[31]

---

[30] *Op. cit.*, p. 272.
[31] *Loc. cit.*

Luke's concern is not primarily with geography but with the conditions of salvation, the liberty of the gospel, and the meaning of this (when seen) for Jews and Gentiles.

In verse 10 is the first undisputed "we section." The author turns to the first person, identifying himself with the group, and claiming a share in the decision. The fact that he seems to have had such a prominent part in the decision would suggest that he was neither a new convert nor a recent acquaintance. It is not known, however, when he joined the company of Paul. He does not even give his own name, but he is assumed to be "Luke, the beloved physician" (Col. 4: 14).

Work Established in Philippi [16: 11-15]

11 Setting sail therefore from Troas, we made a direct voyage to Samothrace, and the following day to Neapolis, 12 and from there to Philippi, which is the leading city of the district of Macedonia, and a Roman colony. We remained in this city some days; 13 and on the sabbath day we went outside the gate to the riverside, where we supposed there was a place of prayer; and we sat down and spoke to the women who had come together. 14 One who heard us was a woman named Lydia, from the city of Thyatira, a seller of purple goods, who was a worshiper of God. The Lord opened her heart to give heed to what was said by Paul. 15 And when she was baptized, with her household, she besought us, saying, "If you have judged me to be faithful to the Lord, come to my house and stay." And she prevailed upon us.

Philippi was first famous for its gold and silver mines and bore the name Krenides until taken over about 360 B.C. from the Thasians by Philip of Macedon, who changed its name to honor himself.[32] Philip fortified the town to guard the great east-west highway which at this point ran between the mountains and marshes. Its importance grew when the Roman republic under Brutus and Cassius made its last stand there, falling before Mark Anthony and Octavian in 42 B.C. It was again prominent when at the battle of Actium, 31 B.C., Octavian defeated Antony and Cleopatra and went on to become emperor. After the battle of 42 B.C., Philippi was made a Roman colony. A number of the towns mentioned in Acts were colonies (Pisidian Antioch, Lystra,

---

[32] Cf. Lake and Cadbury, *Commentary*, p. 187.

Troas, Ptolemais, Corinth, Syracuse, and Puteoli), but Philippi is the only one so designated. A Roman colony was given the right to self-government, land ownership, and sometimes freedom from tribute and taxation.[33] A Roman colony was a part of Italy, or Rome, in a foreign land. Two passages in Philippians, usually obscured in translation, can be understood only if it is remembered that Philippi was a colony (cf. Phil. 1: 27; 3: 20).

Luke's description of Philippi as "the leading city of the district of Macedonia" (16: 12) is puzzling. Thessalonica was the capital of Macedonia, and, of the district to which Philippi belonged (one of four into which Macedonia had been divided by the Romans), Amphipolis was the chief town. Possibly under one of the administrative changes known to Luke, Philippi was given official rank over Amphipolis,[34] but probably the term used by Luke means only "a leading city." [35]

The missionaries seem to be strangers to Philippi; they have no certain knowledge of the meeting place of the Jewish people, and they find lodging with Lydia, unknown to them before their arrival. The view made prominent by Ramsay,[36] that Philippi was the home of Luke, has been abandoned for these and other reasons. Luke's special interest in Philippi is best explained by his stay there as a missionary; he may have been there for some years after the work was started, for he drops out of the narrative at this point and does not re-enter it until Paul passes through Philippi on his last mentioned journey to Jerusalem (20: 6).

The "place of prayer" (16: 13) may have been a synagogue, but this is not likely. The seeming absence of men, without whom there could be no synagogue, and the difficulty in locating the worshippers would indicate that it was simply a place of prayer. Philippi was not the sort of town to attract Jews, and few were there. Ten men were the minimum for a synagogue, and apparently Philippi had no synagogue.

Lydia was named for her native country, which indicates that she was not of the nobility, even though apparently a person of

---

[33] Cf. *Ibid.*, p. 190.
[34] Cf. Rackham, *op. cit.*, p. 280.
[35] Lake and Cadbury, *Commentary*, p. 188.
[36] Sir William M. Ramsay, *St. Paul the Traveler and the Roman Citizen*, pp. 200ff.

some wealth. Her house seems to have been the earliest home for one of the choicest of all Paul's churches (16: 40). As is universally true in Acts, baptism *followed* conversion. Those who see infant baptism in the reference to her "household" (v. 15) are desperate for a "proof text" in support of an inherently weak doctrine. Later practices are not to be read back into primitive stories. Lydia was probably a widow or unmarried, and those of her household would include servants or associates.

Pagan Resistance over Matter of Money [16: 16-24]

16 As we were going to the place of prayer, we were met by a slave girl who had a spirit of divination and brought her owners much gain by soothsaying. 17 She followed Paul and us, crying, "These men are servants of the Most High God, who proclaim to you the way of salvation." 18 And this she did for many days. But Paul was annoyed, and turned and said to the spirit, "I charge you in the name of Jesus Christ to come out of her." And it came out that very hour.

19 But when her owners saw that their hope of gain was gone, they seized Paul and Silas and dragged them into the market place before the rulers; 20 and when they had brought them to the magistrates they said, "These men are Jews and they are disturbing our city. 21 They advocate customs which it is not lawful for us Romans to accept or practice." 22 The crowd joined in attacking them; and the magistrates tore the garments off them and gave orders to beat them with rods. 23 And when they had inflicted many blows upon them, they threw them into prison, charging the jailer to keep them safely. 24 Having received this charge, he put them into the inner prison and fastened their feet in the stocks.

This is the first recorded conflict with paganism apart from Jewish instigation. The issue was not doctrine but money; when her masters could no longer exploit the poor slave girl, they sought to destroy those who interfered with their source of gain. Of course, they could not state the true reason for their action, so they charged that the missionaries were disturbing the peace and teaching customs unlawful for Romans (v. 21). Appeal was made to prejudice against the Jews—the counterpart of Jewish prejudice against the Gentiles. The prejudice angle was played up to its maximum in the contrast made emphatic by the Greek: "These men are troubling our city, *being Jews;* and they are proclaiming customs which are neither lawful for us to receive nor to practice, *being Romans*" (vs. 20, 21). Doubtless there was strong prejudice against the few Jews in Philippi, and little concern was had for an investigation of the charges. Though Judaism was tolerated in the Roman Empire, the Jews were not permitted to make proselytes of Romans. The charge may have been that of illegal proselytism.[37]

The slave girl, according to the Greek text, had "a spirit, a python" and practiced "divination" (v. 16). This girl may have been a ventriloquist, but probably was one who thought that a god spoke through her. In ancient belief, "Python" was the snake at Delphi which embodied a god. One in whom the python dwelt would have the power of inspired speech, sometimes called ventriloquism. The girl lost this power of speech when the spirit came out of her. Whether or not Luke means that she was converted is not clear.

The terms "rulers" and "magistrates" (vs. 19, 20) were probably used for the same people; and perhaps the term "magistrates" was the popular or local term for what in the Roman system would be the *duoviri*, the "two-men." Paul and Silas were beaten with rods and placed in stocks. The "stocks" were instruments of torture, so constructed as to force the legs widely apart and cause terrible pain.

Conditions for a Pagan's Salvation [16: 25-34]

25 But about midnight Paul and Silas were praying and singing hymns to God, and the prisoners were listening to them, 26 and suddenly there was a great earthquake, so that the foundations of the prison were shaken; and immediately all the doors were opened and every one's fetters were unfastened. 27 When the jailer woke and saw that the prison doors were open, he drew his sword and was about to kill himself, supposing that the prisoners had escaped. 28 But Paul cried with a loud voice, "Do not harm yourself, for we are all here." 29 And he called for lights and rushed in, and trembling with fear he fell down before Paul and Silas, 30 and brought them out and said, "Men, what must I do to be saved?" 31 And they said, "Believe in the Lord Jesus, and you will be saved, you and your household," 32 And they spoke the word of the Lord to him and to all that were in the house. 33 And he took

---

[37] Cf. Lake and Cadbury, *Commentary*, p. 195.

> them the same hour of the night, and washed their wounds and
> he was baptized at once, with all his family. 34 Then he brought
> them up into his house, and set food before them; and he rejoiced
> with all his household that he had believed in God.

This is a climax and one of the key passages of the whole book of
Acts! How can a pagan be saved? Surely this Philippian jailer
had no conditioning in Judaism. Only a few women met for
prayer, and there is no evidence of a synagogue in the town. Jews
were despised by the very people who had Paul and Silas arrested
and by those who subjected them to torture. This is the first
clear case of a Gentile's conversion out of paganism and apart
from Jewish influence.

The Samaritans were Israelites and cherished the Torah; the
proselyte converts had fully embraced Judaism; the Ethiopian
eunuch and Cornelius were God-fearers who had been students
of Judaism, as were many others won to Christianity through
the synagogues. But here is a pagan whose salvation is through
faith in the Lord Jesus, and without the influence of circumcision
or synagogue. The last group has now been reached.

When the jailer saw the prison doors open, he naturally concluded that the prisoners had escaped. Though Roman law was
strict about responsibility for a prisoner's escape, this jailer would
have had a strong defense in view of the earthquake. Possibly
his attempted suicide was simply in keeping with a code of honor
which as a military man he would observe voluntarily.

The jailer's question was to the point, "What must I do to be
saved?" (16: 30). The answer, "Believe on the Lord Jesus, and
you will be saved" (16: 31), if valid for this man, would be valid
for *anyone*. The parallel to the case of Philip and the conversation
of the Ethiopian is striking. "What is to prevent my being
baptized?" asked the Ethiopian (8: 36); he had been prevented
from becoming a Jew because of his mutilation, but he was
"unhindered" in becoming a Christian. As was true for the God-
fearing eunuch, so for this pagan jailer, there was no barrier except it be in his failure to trust himself to the Lord Jesus.

Roman Citizenship and Release [16: 35-40]

35 But when it was day, the magistrates sent the police, saying, "Let those men go." 36 And the jailer reported the words to Paul, saying, "The magistrates have sent to let you go; now therefore come out and go in peace." 37 But Paul said to them, "They have beaten us publicly, uncondemned, men who are Roman citizens, and have thrown us into prison; and do they now cast us out secretly? No! let them come themselves and take us out." 38 The police reported these words to the magistrates, and they were afraid when they heard that they were Roman citizens; 39 so they came and apologized to them. And they took them out and asked them to leave the city. 40 So they went out of the prison, and visited Lydia; and when they had seen the brethren, they exhorted them and departed.

The magistrates may have connected the earthquake with powers commanded by Paul and Silas, and thus in fear they may have ordered their release. Again, they may have been simply following a routine pattern in ordering the release, considering the public flogging and night in jail sufficient punishment. Paul, however, was unwilling to be cast out secretly after the public beating. His reasons are not clear, but it is likely that he was seeking greater respect and protection for the saints in the days ahead.

By the Valerian and Porcian laws (passed between 509 and 195 b.c.), Roman citizens were protected against degrading forms of punishment, including flogging and crucifixion; and any official or community was in jeopardy should these laws be violated.[38] There were violations of these laws, but there were also severe reprisals on some who were guilty; Rhodes was deprived of its freedom by Claudius for crucifying Roman citizens (Suetonius, *Claudius*, xxv). Why Paul (and Silas, who seems also to have been a Roman citizen) did not assert his Roman citizenship before the flogging is not clear; probably in the brutal affair there was no opportunity for it. Later at Jerusalem (22: 25) Paul escaped a beating by the Roman soldiers by affirming his Roman citizenship. Paul himself tells us of three beatings with rods (Roman) and five scourgings by the Jews (2 Cor. 11:24f.); the

---

[38] Cf. Bruce, *op. cit.*, p. 322.

Jewish scourging was not as brutal as the Roman, which could easily end in death.

The narrative seems to indicate that Luke remained in Philippi as the rest of the party went on to other fields. The magistrates would be especially anxious for Paul and Silas, the Roman citizens, to leave their town, for they did not want the responsibility of protecting them against angry mobs. Those who remained had occasion to suffer for Christ (Phil. 1: 29). The church itself suffered from tension or division within, but it proved to be one of the finest of the churches in its sharing with Paul and in the spread of the gospel. When the church was but a few weeks or months old, it sent help more than once to Paul in Thessalonica (Phil. 4: 14ff.) and again sent help through Epaphroditus when later Paul was in prison (Phil. 2: 25ff. and 4: 10ff.). It is probable that it was this Macedonian church that sent to Paul's needs while he was in Corinth (cf. 2 Cor. 11: 9; Phil. 4: 15).

Thessalonica: Another King, Jesus [17: 1-9]

1 Now when they had passed through Amphipolis and Apollonia, they came to Thessalonica, where there was a synagogue of the Jews. 2 And Paul went in, as was his custom, and for three weeks he argued with them from the scriptures, 3 explaining and proving that it was necessary for the Christ to suffer and to rise from the dead, and saying, "This Jesus, whom I proclaim to you, is the Christ." 4 And some of them were persuaded, and joined Paul and Silas; as did a great many of the devout Greeks and not a few of the leading women. 5 But the Jews were jealous, and taking some wicked fellows of the rabble, they gathered a crowd, set the city in an uproar, and attacked the house of Jason, seeking to bring them out to the people. 6 And when they could not find them, they dragged Jason and some of the brethren before the city authorities, crying, "These men who have turned the world upside down have come here also, 7 and Jason has received them; and they are all acting against the decrees of Caesar, saying that there is another king, Jesus." 8 And the people and the city authorities were disturbed when they heard this. 9 And when they had taken security from Jason and the rest, they let them go.

Thessalonica, the capital of Macedonia, was a thriving commercial city whose harbor attracted much of the commerce of the province. Its position on the great Egnatian Way added to its commercial advantage. Known originally as Therme, its name was changed by Cassander to Thessalonica in honor of his wife, a sister to Alexander the Great. Since 42 B.C. it had been a free city, and accordingly it was governed by "the people," or demos (from which is derived "democracy"), as seen in verse 5. Its "authorities" or politarchs (vs. 6 and 8) were the city rulers; the accuracy of Luke's title has long since been established by inscriptions recovered at Thessalonica and elsewhere in Macedonia. Thessalonica was about a hundred miles from Philippi; and the towns cited, Amphipolis and Apollonia, would divide the distance into almost equal parts (33, 30, and 37 miles, respectively, between the towns). Whether traveled in three days or more, or whether traveled on foot or horseback, is not known.

The presence of a synagogue in Thessalonica is not surprising, for its commerce would attract a Jewish colony. Paul spent three sabbaths (this translation rather than "weeks" seems correct) in the synagogue, a period of at least fifteen days. Possibly he spent a longer time apart from the synagogue, but this is not suggested in Acts. The Thessalonian letters may reflect a longer period than "three sabbaths," but not even they require this inference. Paul employed the familiar synagogue method of "arguing" (the Greek term has given us the word "dialectic" or "reasoning"), teaching by discussion involving questions and answers.

Paul, according to Luke, developed two major points: (1) the Christ (Messiah) must suffer and arise from the dead and (2) the Christ (Messiah) is Jesus (17: 3). It was difficult for the Jews under foreign oppression to accept the picture of a suffering Messiah; to them Messiah would put an end to suffering for his people and inaugurate a triumphant reign. For this reason the cross was a "scandal" (stumbling block) to the Jews, and only the fact of the resurrection could enable any of them to re-examine the cross in the light of the scriptures (17: 2f.). Paul's next point would be that this Messiah is Jesus, whose death and risen life he proclaims.

Many converts were made among the "devout Greeks," that is, the God-fearers—Gentiles who were attached to the synagogues.

With them were "not a few of the leading women" or "wives of the leading men" (the text in v. 4 can mean either). Luke makes the strange statement that "some of them [Jews] were persuaded, and *joined* Paul and Silas; as did a great many of the devout Greeks and not a few of the leading women" (17: 4). The word "joined" means "to allot" or "to assign." Moulton and Milligan[39] suggest the translation, "were allotted to"; Liddell and Scott suggest "to be attached to."[40] Whatever the best translation, what is obvious is that both Jews and God-fearing Gentiles were forming a group in the synagogue around Paul and Silas. From previous experience, it is certain that Paul made no requirement of circumcision or ritual compliance of these Gentiles. Not only were Paul and Silas making inroads into a group of prospective proselytes to Judaism, but they were destroying the middle wall of separation between Jew and Gentile. In their jealousy the Jews are reported to have enlisted some of the "rabble" (17: 5) in creating a mob scene. (The term "rabble" for the "lower class," if a correct translation, may reflect Luke's distinction between the "wellborn" or "refined" as against the "ill-bred" or "uneducated," or it may simply reflect local terminology which he employs; in Luke's favor it may be said that in the Gospel he shows a keen sympathy for the poor and downtrodden.)

The Christians were charged with disturbing the peace, locally and throughout the world. Of course it was an exaggeration to say that they had "turned the world upside down," but it serves as some indication of the amazing impact this young movement was making throughout the empire. The major charge was that of treason, "saying that there is another king, Jesus" (17: 7). Probably the title "emperor" would more fairly represent the term used in the charge, for Jesus was represented as the rival to Caesar.

There can be no doubt that Paul did preach Jesus as Messiah (God's anointed) or that he did preach a kingdom. The fact that in both of his Thessalonian letters he was compelled to correct

[39] James Hope Moulton and George Milligan, *The Vocabulary of the Greek Testament* (London: Hodder and Stoughton, Ltd., 1949), p. 549.
[40] Henry George Liddell and Robert Scott, *A Greek-English Lexicon* (a new edition by Henry Stewart Jones; Oxford: at the Clarendon Press, 1939), II, 1517.

them on what he had said about the return of Jesus is evidence that he had dwelt on that theme in his preaching. The charge of disturbing the peace would have some truth to it, too, for the Thessalonian letters mention "idlers" who had ceased work and were merely busybodies, sponging on their fellow Christians and inviting the contempt of outsiders.

Two factors in the historical situation gave the Thessalonians cause for anxiety (if sincere) or excuse for persecution (if that was what they sought). Thessalonica was a free city, and it would be very sensitive toward anything that had the appearance of sedition. Rome would readily revoke her status as a free city if she tolerated treason. Then, too, there had been a recent expulsion of Jews from Rome by the edict of Claudius (A.D. 49) because of a tumult which concerned "Chrestus." This datum comes from Suetonius, and it is not clear whether or not "Chrestus" is a mispelling of Christ. If so, as many hold, then this would be a strong reason for more than usual tenseness in Thessalonica over a sedition charge. It follows, then, that Acts, the Thessalonian letters, and the life situation at Thessalonica and at Rome all contribute to our understanding of a situation in which the preaching of Jesus as God's anointed would be explosive.

The politarchs took "security" from Jason (17: 9) when they were unable to locate the men he was charged with concealing. This "security" was probably a bond which he would forfeit should it be established that he actually was protecting the accused men. This may account for the hasty and secret departure of Paul and Silas.

Beroea: Open Minds; Outside Interference [17: 10-15]

10 The brethren immediately sent Paul and Silas away by night to Beroea; and when they arrived they went into the Jewish synagogue. 11 Now these Jews were more noble than those in Thessalonica, for they received the word with all eagerness, examining the scriptures daily to see if these things were so. 12 Many of them therefore believed, with not a few Greek women of high standing as well as men. 13 But when the Jews of Thessalonica learned that the word of God was proclaimed by Paul at Beroea also, they came there too, stirring up and inciting the crowds. 14 Then the

brethren immediately sent Paul off on his way to the sea, but
Silas and Timothy remained there. [15] Those who conducted Paul
brought him as far as Athens; and receiving a command for Silas
and Timothy to come to him as soon as possible, they departed.

Beroea was off the Egnatian Way but on the course to Achaia.
It is not known whether or not Paul had intended to campaign in
Achaia after his work in Macedonia. Whatever his ultimate plans,
he certainly must not have planned so early a departure from
Macedonia; he was driven out by blind prejudice. Ironically
enough, it was in Beroea where open minds were found that
the heresy hounds from Thessalonica were able finally to over-
take him and drive him from their country. Though his Macedonian ministry was cut short, his work was established. Did a
work survive in Beroea? The fact that we have no Beroean correspondence proves nothing. After all, most of Paul's letters
were written in response to church problems; if a church survived
at Beroea, it may have worked out its problems in that generous
spirit by which Luke characterizes the people there. This is but
speculation and is futile to pursue.

The word "noble" probably does justice to the Greek word
which it translates. The word originally meant "well born" and
then had come to describe the disposition expected of one so
born. The idea could be expressed in words like "liberal,"
"generous," "open-minded."

The journey to Athens may have been made in part by sea,
but this is not likely, since Luke's fondness for the sea usually led
him to mention it whenever it was involved. At least a part of
the escort continued with Paul all the way to Athens. It is
difficult, but not impossible, to harmonize Acts 17: 14-15 with
1 Thessalonians 3: 1 and following. From Acts it appears that
Silas and Timothy remained in Beroea until Paul reached Athens
and that from there Paul sent for them. From 1 Thessalonians it
appears that Paul sent Timothy from Athens to Thessalonica
(and Silas elsewhere in Macedonia). Later both joined him in
Corinth (Acts 18: 5; 1 Thess. 1: 1; 3: 6). The matter admittedly
is not clear, but there is not necessarily a conflict between Paul
and Acts.

Athens: Dilettanti in Thought and Religion [17: 16-21]

16 Now while Paul was waiting for them at Athens, his spirit was provoked within him as he saw that the city was full of idols. 17 So he argued in the synagogue with the Jews and the devout persons, and in the market place every day with those who chanced to be there. 18 Some also of the Epicurean and Stoic philosophers met him. And some said, "What would this babbler say?" Others said, "He seems to be a preacher of foreign divinities"—because he preached Jesus and the resurrection. 19 And they took hold of him and brought him to the Areopagus, saying, "May we know what this new teaching is which you present? 20 For you bring some strange things to our ears; we wish to know therefore what these things mean." 21 Now all the Athenians and the foreigners who lived there spent their time in nothing except telling or hearing something new.

Though her greatest creative age was in the past, Athens continued to hold her place as the "intellectual and artistic capital of the world." [41] The Romans followed the pattern of earlier conquerors when they made Greece a Roman territory (146 B.C.). In deference to her glorious past, they granted Athens the status of a free and federated city. The authority, however, did not rest with the demos (people) as at Thessalonica and Ephesus, but with the council known as the Areopagus. Evidently the reference in verse 19 is to the Areopagus as a council rather than as a place, and it seems to have had some control over what was taught in Athens. [42] The agora (the "market place" of v. 17) was an open space in the heart of the city. It was a center for business and civic activity and also for propaganda and informal exchange of news and ideas.

Paul's irritation over the idols in Athens (17: 16) has been questioned because of his familiarity with them in all pagan cities, [43] but his reaction is understandable. Athens was famed as the intellectual capital of the world; when Paul saw that it differed nothing in respect to idols from ordinary towns, it irked him. Monstrous was the absurdity that in the home of

[41] Rackham, op. cit., p. 301.
[42] Cf. Lake and Cadbury, Commentary, pp. 212f.
[43] Cf. Foakes-Jackson, The Acts of the Apostles, pp. 163f.

philosophy men should worship things made with their own hands!

In Athens Paul reasoned in the synagogue with Jews and God-fearers but also made a direct approach to the pagans of the city through the agora or market place (17: 17). This is the first instance where Paul undoubtedly took the initiative in seeking out pagans *apart from* the synagogue. At Lystra this may have been done, but the situation is somewhat obscure at that point. In Thessalonica he may have spent some time in such campaigning after being driven out of the synagogue, but it is simply not known whether his departure followed immediately after the expulsion from the synagogue or after an interval. Later, in Corinth and in Ephesus, his major work was done in a direct approach to the pagans, *after* being driven out of the synagogues. The pattern is clear: gradually the exponents of a gospel providing for equality of Jew and Gentile in the kingdom of God are being driven out of the synagogues. The ultimate, beyond the period of Acts but rapidly approaching, was the separation of the synagogue and the church into two distinct movements—the terrible price for the indispensable victory of an unhindered gospel.

Paul encountered some of the Epicurean and Stoic philosophers along with the common people in the agora. Lake and Cadbury hold that the reference to these philosophers was incidental, that the challenge came from the Athenians in general, and that reference to the Epicureans and Stoics has unduly influenced the interpretation of this passage.[44] No doubt this is a needed caution, but one can hardly escape seeing reflections of Epicurean and Stoic thought in Paul's speech.

The Epicurean school was founded by Epicurus (342?-270? B.C.); it was based on the atomic theory of Democritus, according to which the universe consists of eternal atoms, without beginning or end, constantly forming new combinations (a fortuitous concourse of atoms).[45] These atoms, contrary to the modern view, were material in nature. Though the atoms were viewed as indestructible, the resultant combinations were temporal. Con-

---

[44] *Commentary*, p. 211.
[45] *Ibid.*, pp. 210f.

sequently the idea of personal immortality was rejected, it being
held that at the body's death the soul (personality) ceased to
exist, reverting to the impersonal atoms which in turn might
regroup into new formations.[46]

This position in one important respect (one only) is in
agreement with the Biblical view in that it sees man as a
whole and rejects the idea of a "soul" as some separate entity
which may be isolated from the self. The Biblical view is
not that man *has a soul* but rather that *he is a soul*. A soul
is a person. This is clear in the creation story: ". . . then the
Lord God formed man of the dust from the ground, and
breathed into his nostrils the breath of life; and man *became a
living being*" (Gen. 2: 7). In seeing man as a whole and in rejecting the idea of a soul isolated from body, the Epicureans (on
this one point) were closer to the Biblical view than are many who
speak about an "immortal soul" as though it were something
imprisoned in the body.[47] H. Wheeler Robinson sums it up
neatly: "The Hebrew idea of the personality is an animated body,
and not an incarnated soul" (*The People and the Book*, 362).[48]
But the Epicureans differed radically from Paul at an all-
important point. They held that the self ends when the body
dies. Paul argued (1 Cor. 15) that the body (*sōma*) does survive
death, insisting that "flesh [*sarks*] and blood [*haima*] cannot inherit the kingdom of God" (15: 50) but that the body may do so.
He distinguished between "physical body" (*sōma psychikon*) and
"spiritual body" (*sōma pneumatikon*), thus preserving the Hebrew idea of the wholeness of man and rejecting the Greek idea
of a "naked soul."

The Epicureans believed in gods, but held them to be com-

---

[46] The view propounded by Corliss Lamont, who holds that the "soul," or "personality," is but the functioning of the body and hence coextensive with the body,
is similar to that of the Epicurean, having the same element of truth and error. Cf.
Corliss Lamont, *The Illusion of Immortality* (second edition; New York: Philosophical Library, 1950).
[47] W. G. Kümmel, *Das Bild des Menschen im Neuen Testament* (Zürich: Zwingli-
Verlag, 1948), pp. 16–20, finds in the teaching of Jesus this view of the wholeness
of man as a person before God, rejecting the idea of a schism (*Zwiespalt*) in man.
Commenting on apparent exceptions to this, he says on Matt. 6: 25: "The warning
. . . turns out only as an apparent contrast between soul and body; . . . life and
body are both designations for the earthly being of man, for whose support God,
not man, is to care" (p. 17).
[48] Cited by John A. T. Robinson, *The Body, a Study in Pauline Theology* (Chicago: Henry Regnery Co., 1952), p. 14.

pletely transcendent and unconcerned with human affairs. The object of life for the Epicurean would more fairly be described as "happiness" than "pleasure." The popular idea that the Epicurean stood for sensual dissipation is incorrect; the Epicurean might forego many pleasures for greater enjoyment. The obvious indictment is that he was egocentric.

Stoicism was founded by Zeno (ca. 336–ca. 264 b.c.), a native of Cyprus, and it derived its name from the fact that Zeno frequently taught in the Stoa Poikile (painted portico) in Athens. Like the Epicureans, the Stoics were materialists for all their belief in the divine and in the reality of spirit; to them spirit was but refined (living) matter. They were pantheists, holding that a universal reason, of which we partake, pervades the universe. They believed in a modified immortality, holding a cyclic view of creation in which there would be a periodic cosmic conflagration reabsorbing all existence into the fire of the divine spirit.[49] The Stoic ideal was to live "according to nature" and to attain to a self-sufficiency by which one might live above circumstances.

Though the Stoic made much of "brotherhood," he virtually repudiated it by his exclusiveness and proud contempt for the "vulgar" or common man, from whom he distinguished himself as a philosopher. Stoic apathy, a steeling of one's nerves against the sufferings of humanity, also allowed an outward show of sympathy but rejected inward compassion. It was a betrayal of brotherhood and stood in sharp contrast to Christian love. It may be true that in this "apathy" the Stoic was not indifferent to human need, but his refusal to be identified with the sufferer sets him off in sharp contrast with one who shares in the Cross. Like the Epicurean, he was egocentric. All of us are self-centered; but what the Christian acknowledges with shame as the core of his depravity, the Stoic and Epicurean proudly glorified as virtue.

"Seedpicker" is the literal translation of the Athenian slang used in speaking disparagingly of Paul (17: 18).[50] It seems that this was Attic slang to describe one who, like a sparrow picking up grain, lived on what he could salvage in the market place.

---

[49] Cf. Rackham, op. cit., p. 304.
[50] Ibid., 310. Martin Dibelius gives "catch-word hunter" (Schlagwortjäger) as an interesting German translation; cf. Aufsätze, p. 114.

Next, it was probably applied to one who picked up odds and ends of knowledge. Possibly there was the further implication of a plagiarism by one who was incapable of using his borrowed knowledge.[51] Whatever its particular history or meaning, it was used condescendingly.

Paul was charged with being a "preacher of foreign divinities" because "he preached Jesus and the resurrection" (17: 18). The theory, suggested by many and rejected by others, that they understood Jesus and the resurrection (*anastasis*) to be a god and a goddess, is not improbable. A people who had deified mercy, shame, rumor, and the moods and emotions would have no difficulty in thinking of "resurrection" as a god or goddess (the gender in Greek is feminine). Because of the importance of the gods to the well-being of the city or state, the rulers exercised some care over the introduction of new dieties to the worship of a community.

Paul's Sermon at the Areopagus [17: 22-34]

22 So Paul, standing in the middle of the Areopagus, said: "Men of Athens, I perceive that in every way you are very religious. 23 For as I passed along, and observed the objects of your worship, I found also an altar with this inscription, 'To an unknown god.' What therefore you worship as unknown, this I proclaim to you. 24 The God who made the world and everything in it, being Lord of heaven and earth, does not live in shrines made by man, 25 nor is he served by human hands, as though he needed anything, since he himself gives to all men life and breath and everything. 26 And he made from one every nation of men to live on all the face of the earth, having determined allotted periods and the boundaries of their habitation, 27 that they should seek God, in the hope that they might feel after him and find him. Yet he is not far from each one of us, 28 for

'In him we live and move and have our being':

as even some of your poets have said,

'For we are indeed his offspring.'

29 Being then God's offspring, we ought not to think that the Deity is like gold, or silver, or stone, a representation by the art and imagination of man. 30 The times of ignorance God overlooked, but now he commands all men everywhere to repent, 31 because he has fixed a day on which he will judge the world in

---

[51] Cf. Ramsay, *St. Paul the Traveller*, pp. 242ff.

righteousness by a man whom he has appointed, and of this he has given assurance to all men by raising him from the dead."
32 Now when they heard of the resurrection of the dead, some mocked; but others said, "We will hear you again about this." 33 So Paul went out from among them. 34 But some men joined him and believed, among them Dionysius the Areopagite and a woman named Damaris and others with them.

Paul has been taken to task through pen and pulpit by those who continue to echo an old but erroneous opinion. He is accused of trying out the wisdom of the world only to find it wanting. At Corinth, so declare the sermon notes, yellow with age, Paul repudiated his Athenian experiment and determined to know nothing but Jesus Christ and him crucified (cf. 1 Cor. 2: 1f.). But did Paul fail at Athens? Did he use the wrong strategy? There were conversions, including a member of the council of the Areopagus. Do Paul's critics deem their sermons failures when in a pioneer field city officials are converted? Lazy preachers may find easy excuse for neglect of study and the disparagement of learning, but they do so by perpetuating an interpretation which reflects blind exegesis and faulty logic. Pious platitudes preached with no adjustment to the thought patterns and intellectual and cultural background of the audience are not encouraged by Paul at Athens *or* Corinth. In 1 Corinthians 2: 1-2, Paul was not contrasting his *Corinthian* preaching with that at *Athens;* he was contrasting *his* Corinthian preaching with that of the *pseudowisdom group* at Corinth.

In Athens, as in Pisidian Antioch before Jews or in Lystra before simple village folk, Paul met his audience on its own ground and then took a straight course to Jesus. He met the charges about "Jesus and the resurrection"; he acknowledged the truth and exposed the error of Stoic and Epicurean tenets; he pointed out further deductions from the Athenians' own basic beliefs; he led up to and preached the gospel, presenting God as Spirit, Creator, Father, and as present in human affairs; he pictured man as of common origin, created for God, and responsible to God; he preached salvation in terms of conversion; he reached a climax in confronting them with the risen Man in whom they must reckon with God!

Paul's audience, or much of it, left him when he came to the resurrection. Suppose he had abruptly started with the death and resurrection of Jesus—would he have held anyone at all?

Paul's reference to the altar "to an unknown god" (17: 23) served a double purpose: (1) it answered the charge about "foreign divinities" (17: 18); he was introducing these people to the God whose existence their altar acknowledged; (2) it thereby made a point of contact with his audience. Paul of course did not call them "superstitious" (v. 22) and "ignorant" (v. 23) as the King James Version has it; the above translation is much closer to Paul's meaning.

The Stoics would not quarrel with Paul's claim that God made the world (v. 24), but the Epicureans would disagree, holding to the eternity of material atoms. Paul discredited images and idols in saying that the Creator does not dwell in "handmade temples" (v. 24) nor does he need to be fed with their sacrifices (v. 25). (Jews, too, needed frequent reminder that God is not enshrined in their temple, and Christians today need to remember that "mental images" can be as fatal as "handmade" ones.) [52] The Stoic belief in pantheism and the practice of idolatry were challenged by reference to their own poets who said, "We are indeed his offspring" (v. 28); [53] God is distinct from his creatures, and since we are his offspring, it follows that the divine nature (*to theion*) is of our genus (*kind*) and not that of gold, silver, or stone (v. 29). He corrected the Epicurean doctrine that God (the gods to them) is completely transcendent and indifferent to human affairs by asserting that he not only created all that is (v. 24)

---

[52] Cf. Lake and Cadbury, Commentary, p. 218.

[53] Many point out that the Stoic world-view is reflected here, since the Hebrew conception is that natural man was *made* rather than *begotten*. For full discussions of difficulties, cf. Albert Schweitzer, *The Mysticism of Paul the Apostle*, tr. by Wm. Montgomery (London: A. & C. Black, 1931), pp. 6ff.; M. Dibelius, "Paulus auf dem Areopag," *op. cit.*, pp. 29-70; Werner Georg Kümmel, *op. cit.*, pp. 48-56; *et al.* This reflection of Stoic thought is to be acknowledged, but the obvious should also be acknowledged, that the text itself ascribes the view to Stoicism. If, as Luke represents it, the address is Paul's, it is understandable as a meeting of the Stoics on their own ground; even by their own world-view, idolatry is condemned. The discussion does not concern the problem of whether man is "made" or "begotten" of God; whichever view is held, Hebrew or Stoic, the same conclusion is reached: he cannot be represented by material images. That Paul himself could have thought of natural man as begotten of God is possibly, though probably not, supported by Rom. 11: 36.

but sustains (v. 25) and directs (v. 26) all men and purposes that they should seek him out, for he is not far from each one of us (v. 27).

Local pride, which boasted that Athenians sprang from their own soil as a separate people, was rebuked by Paul as he declared that all the nations were "made from one" (v. 26). No word, such as "blood" or "flesh," is needed to complete Paul's statement; we are *one people* for all the differences of race and nationality. Athenian pride in dividing humanity into "Greeks and barbarians" was as depraved as Jewish pride in dividing humanity into "clean" Jew and "unclean" Gentile. Less excusable was the Jew; more was to be expected of him, for he had been warned by his own prophets against the self-deception of such particularism. More serious than this was the fact that the Jew sought to give divine sanction to his own bigotry.

In thus castigating the Jew of the first century, it is not to be forgotten that the very nation which produced this bigotry also produced the greatest exponents of the view that all people are equally the objects of God's love and that he purposes the remaking of all into one. This but serves to bear out the point that there are no "chosen" nations or races. Prophets and bigots can come from the Jews, the Greeks, or any other people. It is to be further observed that Christendom, too, has always had its prophets and bigots, the latter reflected in its sectarian antagonisms, its persecutions in the interest of "truth," and its racial prejudices and discriminations. Inquisitions and modern denials of basic liberties are practiced in the name of Jesus! Others, spurning violence, assert egocentric pride in naïve claims to membership in some exclusive group of the "elect."

Paul acknowledged the obvious fact that there are such things as nations and that God does place them and work through them in the successive "seasons" of man's development (v. 26), but his manifold working is to the end that all might be reunited in God.

Paul's climax was reached in the portrayal of "a man" whom God has marked out and in whom on an appointed day the inhabited world is to be judged in righteousness (v. 31). Possibly

Paul was referring to Jesus as the "Son of man"; the conception is from Daniel, but the Athenians would not know that title. The term "repent" (v. 30) carries also the idea of "turn." Some did, and their conversion stands in sharp contrast with the smug complacency of those who in their intellectual pride simply mocked at the mention of the "resurrection" (v. 31). What for some was good for one laugh was for Paul—and for countless others—the deepest reality of life.

Corinth: Break with the Synagogue [18: 1-11]

1 After this he left Athens and went to Corinth. 2 And he found a Jew named Aquila, a native of Pontus, lately come from Italy with his wife Priscilla, because Claudius had commanded all the Jews to leave Rome. And he went to see them; 3 and because he was of the same trade he stayed with them, and they worked, for by trade they were tentmakers. 4 And he argued in the synagogue every sabbath, and persuaded Jews and Greeks.

5 When Silas and Timothy arrived from Macedonia, Paul was occupied with preaching, testifying to the Jews that the Christ was Jesus. 6 And when they opposed and reviled him, he shook out his garments and said to them, "Your blood be upon your heads! I am innocent. From now on I will go to the Gentiles." 7 And he left there and went to the house of a man named Titius Justus, a worshiper of God; his house was next door to the synagogue. 8 Crispus, the ruler of the synagogue, believed in the Lord, together with all his household; and many of the Corinthians hearing Paul believed and were baptized. 9 And the Lord said to Paul one night in a vision, "Do not be afraid, but speak and do not be silent; 10 for I am with you, and no man shall attack you to harm you; for I have many people in this city." 11 And he stayed a year and six months, teaching the word of God among them.

From Paul's extensive correspondence we know more about the Corinthian church than any other, yet Luke's concern is primarily with two things: the setting up of a church distinct from the synagogue and the refusal of Gallio, the Roman proconsul, to consider the case of the synagogue against the church. From Paul's letters it is known that from Corinth the work was developed throughout Achaia (2 Cor. 1: 1) and that it was a most vigorous (and disorderly) community of believers. Luke shows no interest in this expansion or in these problems. This should leave little doubt about Luke's purpose.

Corinth was destroyed in 146 B.C. and rebuilt by Julius Caesar in 46 B.C. It was a thriving commercial center, controlling the isthmus of Corinth; ships were hauled across the narrow isthmus and thus avoided the dangerous voyage around the Peloponnesus. The city was cosmopolitan and notorious for its immorality. The presence of a thousand priestess-prostitutes in the temple of Aphrodite is evidence that sexual lust was "sanctified" by religion. This in part accounts for the fact that members of the Corinthian church were *proud* of a case of incest in the church (1 Cor. 5: 1f.).

In Aquila and Priscilla Paul made lifelong friends, and they were among his most intimate. Whether or not they were Christians when Paul met them is not known. All that is stated is that they were brought together by a common trade. The fact that no reference is made to their conversion would seem to imply that they were already believers. If so, this is evidence for a Christian group in Rome at an early date. Luke states that they had come recently from Italy because Claudius had commanded the Jews to leave Rome (18: 2). Suetonius (*Life of Claudius,* xxv, 4) states that the expulsion was due to constant tumults among the Jews instigated by one "Chrestus." The majority of scholars understand this to be a reference to Christ, with the usual mispelling of the name by Roman writers; this is probably true, but cannot be established. Orosius, an early fifth century writer, in his *Historia Contra Paganos,* vii, 6, 15, locates the expulsion edict in the ninth year of Claudius, which would be January 25, A.D. 49, to January 24, 50; this is generally accepted as trustworthy, but is challenged by some.[54]

Another valuable datum in approximating chronology in Acts is the reference to Gallio, the proconsul of Achaia (18: 12). An inscription at Delphi preserves a greeting by Claudius made in the twelfth year of his tribunicial power, at which time he had been acclaimed emperor for the twenty-sixth time, and in which he made reference to Gallio, his friend and proconsul of Achaia.[55] Though an emperor reigned for life, he was acclaimed frequently

---

[54] Cf. Lake and Cadbury, *Additional Notes,* p. 459.
[55] Cf. *Ibid.,* p. 461.

and at irregular intervals. The twelfth year of Claudius was from January 25, A.D. 52, to January 24, 53, and in this year Gallio was proconsul. Since the twenty-seventh acclamation also came in 52, it is probable that Gallio was proconsul early in 52. A proconsul usually took office July 1, so it is likely that it was July 1, 51, that Gallio became proconsul. A proconsul usually served for one year only, but some served for two years. This leaves some uncertainty about the time of Gallio's appointment. What is reasonably certain is that he was proconsul in 52; if so, Paul was in Corinth during 52. Allowing for a possible two year proconsulship and for the fact that 52 could be at any point of his possible two years in office, Gallio could have been proconsul for two years between 50 and 54. Furthermore, Paul's eighteen months could have intersected this period at any point. The implication seems to be that Gallio had just arrived in Corinth when the Jews brought Paul before him (18: 12). The likelihood is that Gallio served for only one year and that that year began July 1, 51. If these assumptions are correct, Paul's Corinthian ministry was from the fall of 50 until the spring of 52.

The common trade which brought Paul and Aquila together is usually held to have been that of tentmaker. The Greek word means exactly that etymologically, but early writers refer the term to leather-workers. This latter is not a likely trade for a Jew, because of the "defiling" force of skins; and cloth made of goat hair would have offered Paul a ready trade, since it was the special product of Cilicia. Again the reader is faced with inconclusive evidence and in honesty must plead ignorance. In view of the uncertainty of the evidence, there is little reason for departing from the traditional view that Paul was a tentmaker.

Verse 5 seems to indicate that at the coming of Silas and Timothy from Macedonia, Paul's preaching suddenly took on new power: "Paul was being constrained by the word." It is suggested that his friends brought him money from Macedonia (cf. 2 Cor. 11: 9, Phil. 4: 15) and that this enabled him to give full time to preaching. This may be true, but it probably does not touch the major reason for the new note in Paul's preaching. The good news that the churches in Macedonia were continuing in faith and love is what gave him new life: "for now we live, if you stand fast in the Lord!" (1 Thess. 3: 8). After being driven out from Macedonia and after the smug complacency of the Athenians, Paul suffered deep emotional depression upon reaching Corinth (cf. 1 Thess. 3: 1-5), but the coming of Timothy and Silas gave him new life (Acts 18: 5 and 1 Thess. 3: 6-10). It was at this point that he wrote 1 Thessalonians.

Once Paul had regained his old zeal, it was not long before the usual opposition arose. He preached in the synagogue that "the Christ was Jesus" (v. 5). These Jews believed in Messiah, but Paul affirmed that the Christ was to be identified with Jesus. Luke gives almost no details of the Corinthian experience, merely indicating that Paul left the synagogue where he was opposed in order to go directly to the Gentiles. It was a daring decision to set up a work apart from and next to the synagogue. Paul may have left the synagogue before being actually driven out; if so, this marked an epoch in Christian history. Its far-reaching significance would be in that it represented a further step toward the eventual complete separation between synagogue and church. The fact that meetings were held next door to the synagogue would indicate that there was no actual persecution at this time. Paul evidently exercised some choice in leaving the synagogue. That would be a most painful choice for him to make. The vision (v. 9) was God's authentication of this mission to the Gentiles. The Greek may be translated: "Stop being afraid, but keep on speaking, and do not begin to be silent" (v. 9).

Abortive Attempt to Have Christianity Ruled Illegal [18: 12-17]

12 But when Gallio was proconsul of Achaia, the Jews made a united attack upon Paul and brought him before the tribunal, 13 saying, "This man is persuading men to worship God contrary to the law." 14 But when Paul was about to open his mouth, Gallio said to the Jews, "If it were a matter of wrongdoing or vicious crime, I should have reason to bear with you, O Jews; 15 but since it is a matter of questions about words and names and your own law, see to it yourselves; I refuse to be a judge of these things." 16 And he drove them from the tribunal. 17 And they all seized Sosthenes, the ruler of the synagogue, and beat him in front of the tribunal. But Gallio paid no attention to this.

The Jews charged Paul with "persuading men to worship contrary to the law" (v. 13). The reference could be to Jewish or to Roman law, but Gallio's remark seems to imply the Jewish law. However, the reference could easily be to *both* laws. Judaism was a "lawful religion," and the Christians were protected by Rome only because they were not distinguished from the Jews in Roman eyes. These Jews could deprive Paul of license to preach should they be able to get Gallio to declare Christianity to be a new religion, distinct from Judaism. These Jews certainly held Paul's preaching to be contrary to Jewish law; and if it could be declared outside Judaism, it would be as an "unlawful religion," against Roman law. Gallio refused to accept the responsibility for deciding whether the religion Paul advocated was within or without the pale of Judaism; this indecision left the situation unchanged. Christianity was not given status in its own name, but for all practical purposes it had it, since it was not distinguished from Judaism.

Sosthenes was beaten, for certain, but by whom? Lake and Cadbury say, "Possibly Sosthenes was beaten by both parties— by the Jews for mismanaging the case, and by the Greeks on general principles." [56] Luke seems to represent Gallio as having little patience with the Jews; his "O you Jews" protest in verse 14 seems to express weariness, real or affected. The beating Sosthenes received was probably at the hands of "Jew-hating" Greeks who took advantage of their rebuff to assert further their anti-Semitism. "Sweet Gallio," as his brother Seneca termed him, either shared in the bigoted prejudice, or showed his indifference by ignoring the outburst.

Ephesus and Syria [18: 18-23]

18 After this Paul stayed many days longer, and then took leave of the brethren and sailed for Syria, and with him Priscilla and Aquila. At Cenchreae he cut his hair, for he had a vow. ¹⁹ And they came to Ephesus, and he left them there; but he himself went into the synagogue and argued with the Jews. ²⁰ When they asked him to stay for a longer period, he declined; ²¹ but on taking leave of them he said, "I will return to you if God wills," and he set sail from Ephesus.

---
[56] *Commentary*, p. 228.

22 When he had landed at Caesarea, he went up and greeted the
church, and then went down to Antioch. 23 After spending some
time there he departed and went from place to place through the
region of Galatia and Phrygia, strengthening all the disciples.

In six verses Luke disposed of a journey of about 1500 miles
stretching out over at least several months. Paul's purpose or
chief destination in Syria is not clear, and few clues are given to
Luke's own purpose in sketching these developments.

Destination.—Luke is explicit in saying that Syria was Paul's
destination upon leaving Corinth (v. 18), but Caesarea, Antioch,
or Jerusalem are possible main objectives. Caesarea is improbable, though its importance to early Christian work is less likely
to be exaggerated than overlooked. Its importance at this particular juncture is great if Dana is correct in his thesis that Ephesian
Christianity was pre-Pauline, as seems obvious from Acts, and
that the Fourth Gospel preserves "a tradition which arose in
Judea and Samaria, passed through Caesarea to Ephesus, and was
remolded and adapted to its developing needs by Ephesian Christianity." [57] Though from Corinth Paul "sailed for Syria," he
doubtless had Ephesus in mind as his next field of work, and a
close connection is likely between Ephesus and Caesarea in days
before Paul's Ephesian ministry. However, Jerusalem and not
Caesarea was his probable objective.

When Paul landed at Caesarea, "he went up and greeted the
church, and then went down to Antioch" (v. 22). "The church"
visited is not explicitly identified, so could refer to the one in
Caesarea or Jerusalem. Ordinarily "the church" would refer to
Jerusalem; but in a sentence where "Caesarea" has just been
mentioned, it would not necessarily imply Jerusalem as "the
church." Other considerations, however, favor Jerusalem. One
always went "up to" and "down from" Jerusalem, whatever the
direction of approach or departure; these were fixed expressions.[58] Certainly, Bruce is correct in observing that "went down"

---

[57] H. E. Dana, *The Ephesian Tradition* (Kansas City, Kansas: The Kansas City
Seminary Press, 1940), p. 141.
[58] In New Orleans, no one familiar with the local idiom would ever confuse "up
town" with "down town," though the expression may be meaningless to a stranger.

is an expression that "would not be used of going from Caesarea, a seaport, to Antioch, an inland town."[59] The vow (v. 18), if Paul's, would definitely favor Jerusalem, since there it would be consummated.

Purpose.—A visit to Jerusalem, then, seems to be indicated, but its purpose has been much debated. If the vow of verse 18 was Paul's, that would provide at least a part of the answer, unless the vow itself grew out of the decision to make a hazardous sea journey to a city where hostility to Paul was mounting. Though the statement is ambiguous, it must have been Paul who "cut his hair" in connection with a vow; Paul, not Aquila, is Luke's interest at this point. The vow would, it seems, call for a trip to Jerusalem for its completion; but, as indicated above, a contemplated trip could account for the vow. In the ancient Nazarite vow, one abstained for life from wine and cutting the hair; but in Paul's day a modified version of the vow obtained. This vow need not then be for life, but it was to be for a minimum of thirty days.[60] The head was shaved at the completion of the vow, and the hair was burned in the fire of a sacrifice offered at Jerusalem. If one were in a foreign land he could shave his head and save the hair until Jerusalem was reached. At the beginning of the vow, and in preparation for the "barberless days," one might "shear" or "cut" the hair. This reference, then, could refer to the beginning or the end of that period, though the word "shear," used here, favors the beginning; "shave" would refer to the end of the vow.

Assuming, then, that the haircutting and the vow were Paul's and that he journeyed to Jerusalem, we may come back to the question of Paul's purpose in making the trip, and Luke's in reporting it. The most plausible answer may be that Paul simply acted spontaneously and naturally as a Jew. If it was the season of one of the feasts, Pentecost or Passover, it would only be natural that Paul would want to revisit Jerusalem. The long and difficult campaign could easily give him reason for wanting the

---

[59] Bruce, *op. cit.,* p. 35.
[60] Cf. Bruce, *op. cit.* p. 349, who cites the Mishna tractate *Nazir.*

change that trip could provide. The desire to "prove" that he
was a good Jew or to offer a "sop" to the Hebrew party is a possible motive, but not as likely as a genuine desire to be present
for one of the great feasts.[61] This need imply no inconsistency
in Paul; conversely, it would suggest that in contending for a
universal kingdom, he did not think of himself as leaving
Judaism. Paul was still a Jew and saw no conflict between being
a loyal Jew (loyal to the true character and mission of Israel,
not to the particularism and narrow nationalism) and sharing
in a Christian brotherhood of Jew and Gentile. Most of the Jews
did see this as a necessary conflict and thus turned from Christianity. Luke's larger purpose would be served in so presenting
Paul.

At Antioch.—Paul spent "some time" at Antioch (v. 22f.), but
no clue is given in Acts as to the reason. It appears that it was a
delay, interrupting a purpose to hasten back to Ephesus (v. 21).
Paul evidently encountered something there which was sufficiently serious to interrupt careful plans. It is a plausible thesis,
the most convincing to this writer, that it was here that Paul
wrote the Galatian letter. Rumors may have reached him at
Corinth and influenced his decision to combine a visit to Syria
and Galatia, but it is more probable that it was upon arriving
at Antioch of Syria that the seriousness of the Galatian situation
was made known to him. Evidently Paul wrote this brutally
frank and sometimes caustic letter on the basis of a *report,* not
upon his personal observation (Gal. 4: 20). This informer was
certainly a man in whom Paul had full confidence; the letter
reflects Paul's acceptance of the report at face value.

It is at least a good guess that Timothy was the informer.
Though there is not a word to this effect, it is not unreasonable
to suspect that when Paul left Corinth for Syria, Timothy made
a visit to his home (Derbe?); and upon finding the Christians
there so acutely misled by the legalists (Jews or Judaizers), he
hastened on to inform Paul, actually meeting him at Antioch.
Timothy's report could be trusted for two reasons, Paul's long-

[61] Cf. Rackham, *op. cit.,* p. 332.

standing affection for and confidence in Timothy and Timothy's natural love for his own Galatian people. That Paul would write before visiting a troubled field is in keeping with his pattern in dealing with Corinth, and possibly with Thessalonica.

Disciples of John the Baptist and Pre-Pauline Christianity in Ephesus [18: 24 to 19: 7]

24 Now a Jew named Apollos, a native of Alexandria, came to Ephesus. He was an eloquent man, well versed in the scriptures. 25 He had been instructed in the way of the Lord; and being fervent in spirit, he spoke and taught accurately the things concerning Jesus, though he knew only the baptism of John. 26 He began to speak boldly in the synagogue; but when Priscilla and Aquila heard him, they took him and expounded to him the way of God more accurately. 27 And when he wished to cross to Achaia, the brethren encouraged him, and wrote to the disciples to receive him. When he arrived, he greatly helped those who through grace had believed, 28 for he powerfully confuted the Jews in public, showing by the scriptures that the Christ was Jesus. 1 While Apollos was at Corinth, Paul passed through the upper country and came to Ephesus. There he found some disciples. 2 And he said to them, "Did you receive the Holy Spirit when you believed?" And they said, "No, we have never even heard that there is a Holy Spirit." 3 And he said, "Into what then were you baptized?" They said, "Into John's baptism." 4 And Paul said, "John baptized with the baptism of repentance, telling the people to believe in the one who was to come after him, that is, Jesus." 5 On hearing this, they were baptized in the name of the Lord Jesus. 6 And when Paul had laid his hands upon them, the Holy Spirit came on them; and they spoke with tongues and prophesied. 7 There were about twelve of them in all.

It is probable that the same basic problem underlay the case of Apollos (18: 24-28) and that of the twelve disciples in Ephesus (19: 1-7). Both Apollos and the twelve knew only the baptism of John (18: 25, 19: 3). The twelve were "baptized in the name of the Lord Jesus" (19: 5) after further instruction from Paul; this is the earliest known case of rebaptism. It would seem that rebaptism would have been as much in order for Apollos as the twelve, but the record is silent at that point.

It seems from this incident in Ephesus and from other considerations that Christian baptism must be distinguished from that of John the Baptist. Christian baptism, in its fullest sense at least, was in the nature of the case possible only *after* the death and resurrection of Jesus, since it memorialized his burial and resurrection as well as symbolized the "death and resurrection" of the believer. Even the twelve apostles did not expect Jesus to die, much less arise, so how could they have understood a baptism which memorialized his burial and resurrection? Paul could write: "We were buried therefore with him by baptism into death, so that as Christ was raised from the dead by the glory of the Father, we too might walk in newness of life" (Rom. 6: 4), but this was *after* Golgotha.

Neither Apollos nor the twelve disciples of Ephesus had known Christian baptism, but only that of John. Furthermore, it seems that the twelve, at least, did not even understand John's baptism, for Paul had to explain it, pointing out that John's baptism was a baptism based on repentance and that John sought to turn his followers to Jesus (19: 4). Apollos was not merely a disciple of John; for "he had been instructed in the way of the Lord," and he "spoke and taught accurately the things concerning Jesus" (18: 25). The most plausible suggestion is that Apollos knew the life story of Jesus but did not know Christian Baptism.[62] Possibly the distinction assumed in this paragraph is the one given at the outset of Acts: "for John baptized with [in] water, but before many days you shall be baptized with the Holy Spirit" (1:5), but Apollos's basic limitation seems to have been in his failure to understand the death-resurrection experience as memorialized and symbolized in Christian baptism. In the case of the twelve, it is explicit that they had not been "baptized with the Holy Spirit" (see 19: 2).

The precise meaning of the statement of the twelve in 19: 2 is illusive, for the Greek is inconclusive at this point. The Revised Standard and other versions understand the twelve to mean that they had not even heard that there was a Holy Spirit. The American Standard version is probably correct in its rendering: "Nay, we did not so much as hear whether the Holy Spirit was *given*." The italics acknowledge that there is no Greek word

---

[62] Lake and Cadbury, *Commentary*, p. 231.

in the text for "given" but that it is an interpretation. It was not necessarily the Holy Spirit's existence, but his presence, that was unknown to them.

Surely Apollos and the twelve followers of John the Baptist had had prior experience with the Holy Spirit, else they would have had no such experience as had been theirs. It is possible for the Holy Spirit to bring one to conviction for sin and into other spiritual experience without that one's having an understanding that it is the Spirit who is so working in his life. The rationale, or understanding, of the experience may come only later. The Spirit certainly leads a child into genuine experience though the child may not understand that it is the Spirit so leading him. So with these at Ephesus, their experience had probably outrun their theology.

The laying on of hands according to 19: 6, as well as 8: 17, preceded the coming of the Holy Spirit. In Acts no fixed pattern is found with respect to baptism, the laying on of hands, and the coming of the Spirit. In the home of Cornelius the Spirit came upon the God-fearing Greeks while Peter was speaking (10: 44), and baptism *followed* the coming of the Spirit. In fact, the coming of the Spirit was cited as reason for not forbidding baptism (10: 47). No mention was made of laying on of hands. It would follow, then, that neither baptism nor the laying on of hands was necessary for the coming of the Spirit. Probably it was not the actual coming of the Spirit that followed the laying on of hands (8: 17; 19: 6) so much as the *recognition* that he had come. The special manifestations of the presence of the Spirit came at crucial points in early Christian development: at Pentecost for the Jews, at the conversion of the Samaritans, upon God-fearing Greeks at Caesarea, and now in the winning of these followers of John the Baptist.

Two intriguing questions emerge from these paragraphs: when did the gospel reach Alexandria and when did it reach Ephesus? Apollos had already been taught the life of Jesus when he came to Ephesus; but though he is identified as a native of Alexandria, it is not said *where* he was taught. The Western text has it that he had been instructed in the word of the Lord "in his own country," that is, Alexandria. That text is very ancient and must be reckoned with, whatever its accuracy. Though "in his own country" is seemingly a Western addition, it is probably a correct as well as an early interpretation of the text.

If Apollos received his Christian instruction in Alexandria, as the Western text has it, then there is evidence that Christianity reached that city by about A.D. 50. It would also be evidence that the tradition that reached Alexandria differed from the one known to Aquila and Priscilla. The twelve are called "disciples" (19: 1), and it does not follow that they were disciples only of John. At least followers of John preceded Paul to Ephesus, but it is likely that Christians did also. The "brethren" (18: 27) who wrote the Corinthians about Apollos were evidently Christians; they of course could have been won by Paul during his brief stop en route to Syria, but this is not necessarily so.

These two paragraphs, about Apollos and the twelve, possibly serve one of Luke's subsidiary purposes, namely, to show that there was as much concern to correct erroneous or incomplete expressions of Christianity as to challenge error from without.

Break with the Synagogue over Kingdom of God [19: 8-10]

8 And he entered the synagogue and for three months spoke boldly, arguing and pleading about the kingdom of God; 9 but when some were stubborn and disbelieved, speaking evil of the Way before the congregation, he withdrew from them, taking the disciples with him, and argued daily in the hall of Tyrannus. 10 This continued for two years, so that all the residents of Asia heard the word of the Lord, both Jews and Greeks.

This was not the first break with the synagogue, but it was a significant one. At Pisidian Antioch, Paul was seemingly forced out of the synagogue; at Corinth he may have departed before being actually forced out; but at Ephesus he clearly exercised a choice in the break with the synagogue. At Ephesus it appears that the synagogue itself was divided, and only some of them spoke evil of the "Way" before the congregation (v. 9). The stubbornness was willful rejection of the truth, and it seemed best to Paul to take his group to a place more suitable for preaching and teaching. Possibly he could have stayed on beyond the three months (v. 8), but he chose to separate his group from the synagogue. He did this not because of lessened concern for the Jews, but because that seemed the only way adequately to reach "both Jews and Greeks" (v. 10). The term "Greeks" here seems to be used for Gentiles at large, not simply for "God-fearing Greeks." This is another step toward the complete separation of synagogue and church before the end of the first century.

Another significant fact is the introduction of the term "kingdom of God," used only eight times in Acts: twice in the first six verses of Acts, twice in the last nine verses of the book, once of Philip, and the other three times involving Paul (cf. 1: 3, 6; 8: 12; 14: 22; 19: 8; 20: 25; 28: 23, 31). Christian groups had been in the synagogues of Ephesus for some time, but Paul's message had something in it which soon brought to an end the peace between unbelieving Jews and Paul. It is explicit that this disturbing issue had to do with Paul's preaching of the kingdom of God, not simply that the Messiah is Jesus. What he said about the kingdom of God is not stated here, but there can be little doubt about its substance. For one thing, when Paul drew out of the synagogue, he preached to Jews and Greeks; in all likelihood he preached a kingdom of God in which Jews and Greeks would share as brothers. Paul did not turn his back on the Jews; he withdrew from a synagogue which was opposed to the equality of Jews and Greeks.

The second factor which may make clear what Paul preached in connection with the kingdom of God is the Ephesian letter. This is not to ignore the fact that evidences are almost conclusive that Ephesians is a circular letter, nor does it overlook the overwhelming number of critical scholars who deny Pauline authorship of Ephesians. Though Ephesians is beyond reasonable doubt a general letter to several churches, only undue skepticism would exclude Ephesus from the churches involved. As to its authorship, for all the conclusiveness with which the majority write, the question is still an open one; many scholars are simply not convinced that the case is closed, and it is not on dogmatic grounds that they refuse to concede. Even if it be granted that

Ephesians is pseudonymous, the letter is germane to our problem; it was certainly written by a Paulinist, if not by Paul.

The thrilling theme of Ephesians is certainly true to Paul's message. Here the "plan of the ages" (3: 11) is set forth as God's purpose to unite humanity in Christ Jesus, breaking down the middle wall of partition between Jew and Greek (2: 14), and creating out of "the both" one new man (2: 15). In Ephesians the term for this new humanity is "church"; in Acts 19: 8 the same idea is probably in mind in the expression "kingdom of God." The primary idea in the "kingdom" is "kingship" or "sovereignty," but this reign of God in Christ is over humanity; God is not a national king. It was most likely this theme in Paul's preaching, a theme which found its classic expression later in the Ephesian letter, which caused the Jews to become "stubborn" and speak evil of the Way (Acts 19: 9).

The "hall of Tyrannus" served as the place of discussion for two years. The Greek word is literally "school," but that term probably gives the wrong impression; it was a hall, possibly connected with a gymnasium, used for lectures and other meetings. Lake and Cadbury aptly remark: "It is, of course, as uncertain as it is unimportant whether Tyrannus was a lecturer or a landlord." [63]

The Western text adds a statement which may be a trustworthy datum in saying that Paul taught "from the fifth to the tenth hour," roughly from 11:00 A.M. to 4:00 P.M. (There would be no exact correspondence to our time system, for the first hour began at sunup, which varied from day to day.) The period in the middle of the day was a period of leisure, serious work being suspended from the fifth to tenth hour. It is not clear why Paul chose this time for his teaching (assuming that the Western text is correct). It may be that it was then that the hall was available, or it may be that it was then that the *people* were available.

Luke makes a mere passing reference to the development of the work throughout the Roman province of Asia (19: 10), which we know from other sources to have included many vigorous

[63] *Commentary*, p. 239.

churches. Luke's interest is not in geographical expansion. Something more of this work will be reflected in chapter 20.

The Might of the Word [19:11-20]

11 And God did extraordinary miracles by the hands of Paul, 12 so that handkerchiefs or aprons were carried away from his body to the sick, and diseases left them and the evil spirits came out of them. 13 Then some of the itinerant Jewish exorcists undertook to pronounce the name of the Lord Jesus over those who had evil spirits, saying, "I adjure you by the Jesus whom Paul preaches." 14 Seven sons of a Jewish high priest named Sceva were doing this. 15 But the evil spirit answered them, "Jesus I know, and Paul I know; but who are you?" 16 And the man in whom the evil spirit was leaped on them, mastered all of them, and overpowered them, so that they fled out of that house naked and wounded. 17 And this became known to all residents of Ephesus, both Jews and Greeks; and fear fell upon them all; and the name of the Lord Jesus was extolled. 18 Many also of those who were now believers came, confessing and divulging their practices. 19 And a number of those who practiced magic arts brought their books together and burned them in the sight of all; and they counted the value of them and found it came to fifty thousand pieces of silver. 20 So the word of the Lord grew and prevailed mightily.

Luke's emphasis here is clearly on the power released through the Christians in Ephesus. Litotes (understatement) is employed in verse 11 as he speaks of "no ordinary powers." These powers were given to combat charms, amulets, and the mystic letters of Ephesus. Paul was but the instrument; the power was God's. It was one of the major necessities to dissociate Christianity from false spiritualism, as in the examples of Simon Magus in Samaria, Bar-Jesus in Cyprus, and these exorcists at Ephesus.

Two Latin words, transliterated into Greek, describe cloths, not clothes, used by Paul in this work. "Handkerchiefs" and "aprons" are probably the nearest English equivalents; Lake and Cadbury suggest that "towels" might better translate the second term.[64] The problem involved in the apparent accommodation to superstitious faith parallels that concerning Peter's shadow (Acts 5: 12-16) and has been discussed in that connection.

Exorcism and magic through pronouncing a sacred name

---

64 *Commentary*, p. 240.

were practiced all over the ancient world, so it is not strange that many tried to exploit the name of Jesus in the same way. Many such "charms'" could be cited similar to this one cited by Lake and Cadbury: [65] "Hail, God of Abraham, hail, God of Isaac, hail, God of Jacob, Jesus Chrestus, Holy Spirit, Son of the Father." One can hardly fail to think of the "Hail Mary" chants, repeated for as much as half an hour at the time, even over radio.

Sceva is possibly of Hebrew but probably of Latin origin. Though Luke does not say so, the sons of Sceva may only have claimed (falsely) to be sons of a high priest. Possibly "high priest" or "chief priest" means no more than "archpriest." [66] In verse 16 the Greek word is actually "both," but "all" is probably the correct idea. This Greek word has been found in the papyri as early as the second century of our era with the meaning of "all"; it is not improbable that it was so used earlier. "Naked" is probably a misleading translation for the word in verse 16. Though the Greek word does mean "naked," it also may simply mean without the outer garment.[67]

The impact upon Ephesus was terrific, and great numbers repudiated their false spiritualism by divulging the secret formulas and burning the parchments or papyri containing the magical words (vs. 19f.). The amount of silver at which they were appraised was great, though left obscure in Acts, for Luke does not specify the type of coin implied. Then, too, money values are subject to such rapid and radical change that it is absurd to give neat little lists of supposed equivalent values; a 1953 American dollar, for example, has little in common with a 1933 dollar.

ARRESTED IN JERUSALEM; UNHINDERED IN ROME—
A PEACE MISSION AND ITS RESULTS
[19: 21 to 28: 16]

THE FORMULA, "So the word of the Lord grew and prevailed mightily" (19: 20), clearly marks a major division in Acts. As

---

[65] Ibid., pp. 240f.
[66] Cf. Foakes Jackson, The Acts of the Apostles, p. 179.
[67] Lake and Cadbury, Commentary, p. 242.

we have seen, the author has used a similar device at several points in the book and does again in 28: 31. Though he had much more to tell about the work on the shores of the Aegean, the missions to Jerusalem and Rome overshadowed it all. The journey to Jerusalem with the great offering was a peace mission designed to draw Jew and Gentile together in the church. Rome, and frontiers beyond, serve as reminders of the world-embracing character of the Christian religion. The magnitude of Paul's spirit is amazing; he looked beyond immediate objectives to Rome (Acts 19: 21) and beyond Rome to Spain (Rom. 15: 24). He no longer had "room for work in these regions" (Rom. 15: 23), though his field stretched from Syria to Macedonia and Achaia! Luke, however, was concerned not so much with territory as with the issue of the Jew-Gentile relationship.

Lake and Cadbury, contrary to their many keen insights by which this writer has profited, naïvely write:

> One of the strongest arguments . . . that Luke intended to write a third book is the absence in Acts of any detailed account of what Paul actually did when he reached Rome. His relations with the Jews are described, but his missionary work is dismissed in a single verse.[68]

Thus the old theory, so blind, is continued and the main point is missed! The dramatic effect of a most carefully planned conclusion to a great book is lost while the exegetes speculate over a "third volume" which probably was never written—and likely never contemplated.

Projection of Plan [19: 21-22]

> 21 Now after these events Paul resolved in the Spirit to pass through Macedonia and Achaia and go to Jerusalem, saying, "After I have been there, I must also see Rome." 22 And having sent into Macedonia two of his helpers, Timothy and Erastus, he himself stayed in Asia for a while.

The twin goals, Jerusalem and Rome, towered above the remaining tasks in Asia, Macedonia, and Achaia. A great offering for the poor at Jerusalem was to be completed, and Luke was concerned with its results. Luke passes over the long and painful crisis in Corinth which resulted in at least two, and probably

---

[68] *Commentary*, p. 244.

204

four, letters from Paul and trips to Corinth by Paul, Timothy, and Titus. From the Corinthian letters much of this story can be reconstructed. Paul wrote at least one letter to the Corinthians, probably three, before leaving Ephesus, and he certainly wrote one from Macedonia. Possibly the Galatian letter, too, was written in this period (see pp. 194f. and 267ff. for argument to contrary). At Ephesus Paul went through one of his most trying periods and evidently came close to death. There was a probable imprisonment at Ephesus, and certainly from there Paul directed a great Asian campaign. Luke's concern, however, is with the greater problem of relationship of Jew and Gentile to each other and to the kingdom; consequently, he by-passes rich developments in Christian history.

To term this last section of Acts "The Passing of Paul" [69] is most unfortunate. Certainly Paul is featured throughout, but *Luke's interest is not primarily in Paul.* His interest is in the attitude and decisions of Jews and Gentiles and in the ultimate meaning of that for both groups and for the gospel. Certainly some materials were used simply because they were known and were interesting, and some were used because they concerned lesser but important problems, but Luke constantly returns in this section to his main purpose.

Rounding Out the Aegean Campaign [19: 23 to 20: 38]

Ephesus shaken by the Way [19: 23-41]

23 About that time there arose no little stir concerning the Way. 24 For a man named Demetrius, a silversmith, who made silver shrines of Artemis, brought no little business to the craftsmen. 25 These he gathered together, with the workmen of like occupation, and said, "Men, you know that from this business we have our wealth. 26 And you see and hear that not only at Ephesus but almost throughout all Asia this Paul has persuaded and turned away a considerable company of people, saying that gods made with hands are not gods. 27 And there is danger not only that this trade of ours may come into disrepute but also that the temple of the great goddess Artemis may count for nothing, and that she may even be deposed from her magnificence, she whom all Asia and the world worship."

---

[69] Cf. Rackham, *op. cit.,* p. 358.

28 When they heard this they were enraged, and cried out, "Great is Artemis of the Ephesians!" 29 So the city was filled with the confusion; and they rushed together into the theater, dragging with them Gaius and Aristarchus, Macedonians who were Paul's companions in travel. 30 Paul wished to go in among the crowd, but the disciples would not let him; 31 some of the Asiarchs also, who were friends of his, sent to him and begged him not to venture into the theatre. 32 Now some cried one thing, some another; for the assembly was in confusion, and most of them did not know why they had come together. 33 Some of the crowd prompted Alexander, whom the Jews had put forward. And Alexander motioned with his hand, wishing to make a defense to the people. 34 But when they recognized that he was a Jew, for about two hours they all with one voice cried out, "Great is Artemis of the Ephesians!" 35 And when the town clerk had quieted the crowd, he said, "Men of Ephesus, what man is there who does not know that the city of the Ephesians is temple keeper of the great Artemis, and of the sacred stone that fell from the sky? 36 Seeing then that these things cannot be contradicted, you ought to be quiet and do nothing rash. 37 For you have brought these men here who are neither sacrilegious nor blasphemers of our goddess. 38 If therefore Demetrius and the craftsmen with him have a complaint against any one, the courts are open, and there are proconsuls; let them bring charges against one another. 39 But if you seek anything further, it shall be settled in the regular assembly. 40 For we are in danger of being charged with rioting today, there being no cause that we can give to justify this commotion." 41 And when he had said this, he dismissed the assembly.

The most important thing about this long section is what it reveals about the magnitude of Paul's work in Ephesus and all Asia (v. 26). This amazing progress is vindication for Paul's yearning since his earliest Galatian mission to campaign in Ephesus and also for his decision to separate his work from the synagogue, where it was denied necessary freedom. Whatever the exaggeration of Demetrius in charging that Paul was upsetting the economic life of Ephesus and all Asia and even threatening the prestige of the goddess Artemis (vs. 26f.), it is clear that the "grain of mustard seed" had grown into a "tree" and that the "leaven" was at work in "the whole lump." When the epistles (and Revelation) are considered, it is apparent that the extent of Christian development in Asia is not exaggerated in Acts.

Paul's perils in Ephesus are certainly not overstated in Acts, but were seemingly even more critical than Luke indicates. It would be difficult to read too much into Paul's own words about his Ephesian experience: "For we do not want you to be ignorant, brethren, of the affliction we experienced in Asia; for we were so utterly, unbearably crushed that we despaired of life itself. Why, we felt that we had received the sentence of death . . . ." (2 Cor. 1: 8f.). That was written just after his departure from Ephesus. While yet in Ephesus he wrote, "Why am I in peril every hour? . . . I die every day! . . . I fought with beasts at Ephesus" (1 Cor. 15: 30f.). The fighting with beasts may have been literal; but if only figurative, as is likely, it yet reflects a terrible conflict.

This opposition, as at Philippi, was instigated by pagans and because of money. Naturally the real charge, that the evangelists were endangering their trade, was not the one used before the assembly, but appeal was made to religious prejudice and city pride. Demetrius rallied both the skilled craftsmen (v. 24) and the unskilled laborers (v. 25).

The description of the riot brings out many of the features of a free city and a Roman province. The Asiarchs (v. 31) were wealthy men who were responsible for the promotion of emperor worship, and they were the leading men of the cities of Asia. It is significant that Paul numbered these among his intimate associates. The "town clerk" (v. 35) was an Ephesian and was the most important native official in the city. His concern was that the riot not be construed by Rome as a revolution, which offense could easily result in the loss of the city's free status (v. 40). After the mob had somewhat worn itself out with two hours of shouting, he reminded them, with some sarcasm, that there were "court days" and there were such things as "proconsuls" (v. 38). These would be open to Demetrius and the craftsmen if they had a complaint against anyone. If the people themselves had a desire to press more fully into the case they could do so in the "regular assembly" (v. 39). The term used for this assembly is *ecclesia*, the New Testament term for church.[70] This *ecclesia*

---

[70] The English word "church" is of an entirely different origin, however, since it comes from the Greek word *kyriakon*, i.e., "pertaining to the Lord."

was democratic (the **meeting of the demos**), **and it** met three times each month.

Artemis seems to have been an Asiatic mother-goddess, a divinity of fertility,[71] and Ephesus was the keeper of the "sacred stone that fell from the sky" (v. 35). The object revered may have been a meteorite or possibly an image; legend had it that it had fallen from the sky. This would be the pagan's answer to the charge about "gods made by hand." The temple itself was one of the seven wonders of the ancient world. The exact nature of the original cult image is not certain, but evidently it developed from a very simple figure, resembling a block of wood or trunk of a tree, adornments being superimposed as the image was developed through the centuries. By the time of Acts the representation showed Artemis to be covered with breasts from the waist to neck, thus symbolizing fertility.

Paul, with characteristic indifference to personal safety, wanted to enter the theater (it could seat at least 24,000 people) to defend his friends, Gaius and Aristarchus, but the Asiarchs implored him not to do so. Alexander (v. 33) apparently spoke for the Jews to dissociate that group from the Christians, for the charge made against Paul was one frequently made against Jews. The wild howling for two hours reflected, among other things, the anti-Jewish feeling in the Roman world. The claim of the town clerk that Gaius and Aristarchus were "neither sacrilegious nor blasphemers" (v. 37) worried early Christian apologists, lest it reflect indifference to idolatry. The statement of the town clerk was true, no doubt, for both Jews and Christians were warned against desecrating a temple or blaspheming the gods (cf. Rom. 2: 22).

Events leading to rendezvous at Troas [20: 1-6]

> 1 After the uproar ceased, Paul sent for the disciples and having exhorted them took leave of them and departed for Macedonia. 2 When he had gone through these parts and had given them much encouragement, he came to Greece. 3 There he spent three months, and when a plot was made against him by the Jews as

---

[71] Cf. Lily Ross Taylor, "Artemis of Ephesus" (F. J. Foakes Jackson and Kirsopp Lake, editors, *The Beginnings of Christianity*, (London: Macmillan and Co., 1933), Part I, Vol. V, p. 252.

he was about to set sail for Syria, he determined to return through
Macedonia. 4 Sopater of Beroea, the son of Pyrrhus, accompanied
him; and of the Thessalonians, Aristarchus and Secundus; and
Gaius of Derbe, and Timothy; and the Asians, Tychicus and
Trophimus. 5 These went on and were waiting for us at Troas,
6 but we sailed away from Philippi after the days of Unleavened
Bread, and in five days we came to them at Troas, where we
stayed for seven days.

Probably a year is covered in this brief paragraph, and it was
one of the fullest and most critical for Paul. From Paul's letters
it is known that as he left Ephesus the situation at Corinth had
not cleared. Paul had planned to go directly to Corinth, but delayed his journey there, not wanting to have another painful
encounter (2 Cor. 1: 23-2: 1). Titus had been sent with a letter
to Corinth, and Paul awaited the outcome of that mission. He
had hoped to find Titus at Troas with news about Corinth, but
Titus was not there. Though Troas presented an open door, Paul
was so depressed over Corinth that he had no heart to preach,
choosing rather to hasten on to Macedonia, the next likely place
for news from Corinth (2 Cor. 2: 12f.). The weight lifted from
Paul by the good news of a change of attitude at Corinth can
be appreciated only by reading Second Corinthians itself (cf.
especially 2: 14ff. and 7: 5ff.).

In addition to strengthening the work in Macedonia (Acts
20: 1f.), Paul seems to have gone into Illyricum (Rom. 15: 19).
This was followed by three months (seemingly during the winter) in Greece (Acts 20: 2), doubtless at Corinth, whence according to all evidences he wrote the Roman letter. When Paul wrote
Romans he was soon to embark on a trip to Judea which he
considered most dangerous (Rom. 15: 31), and he purposed next
to visit Rome (Rom. 15: 32) and then Spain (Rom. 15: 22ff.).
During this time he gave major attention to the collections
promoted in Macedonia, Achaia, Asia, and Galatia (2 Cor. 8-9,
Rom. 15: 26ff.). This collection, to be given to the poor at
Jerusalem, was designed to relieve the physical need and the
tension between the Jewish and Gentile elements in the church
(Rom. 15: 27). Paul was careful to avoid charges of selfish interest
or dishonesty in the handling of the funds, so requested the

contributing provinces to appoint men to share the responsibility of delivering the money to Jerusalem (cf. 2 Cor. 9: 21). Because of another plot by the Jews, Paul's travel plans were again changed, and he returned through Macedonia (Acts 20: 3). Evidently Troas was agreed upon as the rendezvous for the party; Tychicus and Trophimus, those from Asia, would naturally be the ones to "await" the others at Troas. The return of the "we section" indicates that Luke joined the party in Macedonia, probably at Philippi.

It is understandable that Luke passed over the crisis at Corinth and the possible campaign in Illyricum. The divisions at Corinth and repudiation of Paul were not due primarily to the Jew-Gentile issue,[72] so were not vital to Luke's major purpose. To have traced out the causes and results of that crisis would have called for a lengthy treatment. Omission of reference to Illyricum is in keeping with Luke's pattern; he was not concerned with new territory for its own sake. But most difficult to understand is Luke's silence about the collection. It was of major importance to Paul and to the very issue with which Luke was most concerned. No satisfactory explanation is given for this silence concerning a project so germane to his purpose. However, the reader should have had some readiness for such an omission by the fact that in the Gospel, Luke sometimes departed from Mark at a point which seems most congenial to his own interests (cf. Mark 7: 1-23 and especially the omission of Mark's "for all nations," Mark 11: 17 = Luke 19: 46). Then too, it must be noted, Luke is not completely silent about the collection, for in Paul's speech before Felix there is a passing reference to "alms and offerings" as the occasion for the visit (24: 17). Luke knows about the collection, but does not feature it.[73]

Sunday in Troas [20: 7-12]

> 7 On the first day of the week, when we were gathered together to break bread, Paul talked with them, intending to depart on the morrow; and he prolonged his speech until midnight. 8 There were many lights in the upper chamber where we were gathered.

---

[72] Cf. Morton S. Enslin, *Christian Beginnings*, (New York: Harper and Brothers, 1938), pp. 245–261.
[73] Cf. pp. 216f. for further treatment of this problem.

9 And a young man named Eutychus was sitting in the window.
He sank into a deep sleep as Paul talked still longer; and being
overcome by sleep, he fell down from the third story and was
taken up dead. 10 But Paul went down and bent over him, and
embracing him said, "Do not be alarmed, for his life is in him."
11 And when Paul had gone up and had broken bread and eaten,
he conversed with them a long while, until daybreak, and so departed. 12 And they took the lad away alive, and were not a little
comforted.

The "first day of the week" would at least in part correspond to
our Sunday, but whether in part or in full depends on Luke's
method of reckoning time. If his method was Jewish, then the
first day of the week began Saturday evening at sunset and ended
at sunset on Sunday. Luke seems to distinguish "the first day of
the week" from "the morrow," so he probably was following the
Greco-Roman method of counting the beginning of the day to
be at dawn. The matter is inconclusive; the meeting could have
been on Saturday night or Sunday night. Lake and Cadbury are
probably correct in thinking that the meeting was on Sunday
evening.[74]

There is no explicit record of when or why Christians turned
to Sunday as their special day of worship, but the obvious inference is that they did so spontaneously because Jesus arose on
that day. The news of his resurrection naturally drew them together on that memorable "first day of the week," and they were
again assembled on the next Sunday (cf. John 20: 1, 26). The
earliest New Testament reflection of the custom is in 1 Corinthians 16: 1. Evidences are that the earliest Christians, being
Jewish, continued to worship in the synagogues. Thus they continued the sabbath observance, that being the outstanding day
for the synagogue services. After the separation from the synagogue, Gentile Christians would have no reason for observing
the Jewish sabbath. (Formerly, these Gentiles really had not been
observing the sabbath as such, but merely were sharing in synagogue services.) Full attention was then turned to the "first day
of the week." The Lord's Day was thus altogether separate from
the sabbath in origin and character. It was not until about a

century later that the unfortunate confusion of the Lord's Day
with the sabbath began.[75]

The breaking of bread (vs. 7 and 11) may refer to the *agape*,
that is, the supper meeting or love feast; or to the Lord's Supper;
or to both. These probably were observed together in earliest
days but later came to be observed separately. This change was
due in part to abuses of the *agape*, as at Corinth. The procedure
at Troas is not clear.

The "many lights" (v. 8) have suggested various theories to
the exegetes. Some have seen in this a reference to early Christian
symbolism, while others have understood Luke to be replying to
charges of immorality at these meals. The first cannot be established, and the other suggestion is highly improbable. The
charges of immoral practices belong to a later period of Gentile
Christianity and to the sects of a later date where immorality was
practiced and where the extinction of the lights was a part of the
ritual.[76] The most natural suggestion is that Luke mentions the
lights (with the heat given off) as contributions, along with Paul's
long sermon, to the deep sleep of Eutychus.

It is not clear that Luke intends to represent this as a miracle.
The issue of miracles as such is not at stake here, for Acts contains many incidents that are clearly represented as miracles.
In fairness to the problem, it should be acknowledged that the
text permits either interpretation. Verse 9 would seem to say explicitly that Eutychus was dead, but verse 10 may indicate the
opposite. Possibly Luke means only that he was taken up "as
dead."

Troas to Miletus [20: 13-16]

13 But going ahead to the ship, we set sail for Assos, intending to take
Paul aboard there; for so he had arranged, intending himself to go
by land. 14 And when he met us at Assos, we took him on board
and came to Mitylene. 15 And sailing from there we came the following day opposite Chios; the next day we touched at Samos;

---

[75] The earliest Christian view of the sabbath is that set forth in Hebrews, where
the proposition is developed that the old sabbath was a shadow, and its fulfillment
is the "sabbath rest" in Christ. The life in Christ, then, is the Christian's sabbath.
The Lord's Day is a separate day to which Christians spontaneously turn for worship and witnessing and to memorialize the resurrection of Jesus.
[76] Cf. Lake and Cadbury, *Commentary*, p. 256.

and the day after that we came to Miletus. [16] For Paul had decided
to sail past Ephesus, so that he might not have to spend time in
Asia; for he was hastening to be at Jerusalem, if possible, on the
day of Pentecost.

The reason for Paul's preference of the land journey from Troas
to Assos is not given, but possibly it was to avoid the rough voyage
which that particular run usually provided. There is no clue in
Acts to his means of land travel, whether literally "by foot" or by
some conveyance. What is apparent is that this part of the story
is narrated by an eyewitness who was intrigued by the details
of the journey.

It is altogether likely that the ship was chartered, and this
would account for the freedom Paul seemed to have in determining where and for how long the ship would stop.[77] In verse 13
the phrase, "for so he had arranged," could refer to the chartering of the ship. The size of the party and Paul's desire to hasten
on to Jerusalem by Pentecost would justify the chartering of a
ship. One must assume that the relief fund was large, considering
the size of the party and the probability of a chartered ship.

Paul's desire to reach Jerusalem for the day of Pentecost is
further evidence that he had no disposition to repudiate his
nation or the religion of his people. The Jewish feasts, the synagogue, and the temple were still objects of his affection. There
is no reason to believe that he wanted merely to prove to the
Jews that he was a good Jew—that idea belonged to James, not
to Paul (cf. Acts 21: 23ff.). Paul sincerely wanted to share in
the feast of Pentecost. His plan of avoiding a visit to Ephesus was
for the reason given, namely, that he might hasten on to Jerusalem. His concern for the Asian Christians was too great to
permit him to pass by with no conference, so he arranged a
meeting under circumstances which would provide for both concerns. Too, it should be noted, the course taken by the ship was
the shorter one. The refusal to linger in Ephesus and his deafness
to friendly warnings along the way attest to the importance to
Paul of this perilous Jerusalem visit.

---

[77] Cf. Rackham, *op. cit.*, p. 381; Lake and Cadbury, *Commentary*, p. 257.

Farewell message to elders of Ephesus [20: 17-38]

17 And from Miletus he sent to Ephesus and called to him the elders of the church. 18 And when they came to him, he said to them:

"You yourselves know how I lived among you all the time from the first day that I set foot in Asia, 19 serving the Lord with all humility and with tears and with trials which befell me through the plots of the Jews; 20 how I did not shrink from declaring to you anything that was profitable, and teaching you in public and from house to house; 21 testifying both to Jews and to Greeks of repentance to God and of faith in our Lord Jesus Christ. 22 And now, behold, I am going to Jerusalem, bound in the Spirit, not knowing what shall befall me there; 23 except that the Holy Spirit testifies to me in every city that imprisonment and afflictions await me. 24 But I do not account my life of any value nor as precious to myself, if only I may accomplish my course and the ministry which I received from the Lord Jesus, to testify to the gospel of the grace of God. 25 And now, behold, I know that all you among whom I have gone about preaching the kingdom will see my face no more. 26 Therefore I testify to you this day that I am innocent of the blood of all of you, 27 for I did not shrink from declaring to you the whole counsel of God. 28 Take heed to yourselves and to all the flock, in which the Holy Spirit has made you guardians, to feed the church of the Lord which he obtained with his own blood. 29 I know that after my departure fierce wolves will come in among you, not sparing the flock; 30 and from among your own selves will arise men speaking perverse things, to draw away the disciples after them. 31 Therefore be alert, remembering that for three years I did not cease night or day to admonish every one with tears. 32 And now I commend you to God and to the word of his grace, which is able to build you up and to give you the inheritance among all those who are sanctified. 33 I coveted no one's silver or gold or apparel. 34 You yourselves know that these hands ministered to my necessities, and to those who were with me. 35 In all things I have shown you that by so toiling one must help the weak, remembering the words of the Lord Jesus, how he said, 'It is more blessed to give than to receive.' "

36 And when he had spoken thus, he knelt down and prayed with them all. 37 And they all wept and embraced Paul and kissed him, 38 sorrowing most of all because of the word he had spoken, that they should see his face no more. And they brought him to the ship.

Its burden.—The burden of Paul's parting message [78] to the

---

[78] For an excellent summary of resemblances between this speech and Paul's epistles see Rackham, *op. cit.*, p. 384f. Also see Lake and Cadbury, *Additional Notes,* pp. 412f.

Ephesian elders is not apology but warning. It is true that Paul
does defend his own character and conduct, but it is so done
as to alert them more fully to their responsibility. In brief, Paul
is pressing upon them the fact that *they know* that his ministry
to them had been the very best of which he was capable—it would
follow then that they had access to a full gospel. He then tells
them frankly that he feels that his own personal ministry to
them is ended—it would follow, then, that they were on their
own, and that these leaders would have to bear the full responsibility for the church. He warned that "fierce wolves" from without and false brethren from within would greatly imperil them.
He returned to an apology for his ministry, but did so in order
to submit a contrast to the destructive exploitation of those above
mentioned destroyers and perverters. From beginning to end,
then, though Paul makes repeated reference to himself, his concern is for the church which he must bid farewell, possibly for
the last time.

If it is remembered that Paul had just gone through the bitter
experience of repudiation and misrepresentation at the hands
of a strong element in the Corinthian church (and possibly of
the Galatian churches), it is understandable that he would appeal
to their own knowledge of the character of his ministry in Asia
(v. 18); they could verify any claim he made for himself.
"Humility" does not adequately convey Paul's statement about
his service (v. 19); this translation might mislead one into believing that Paul was "proud of his humility." The Greek word
seems to be of Christian coinage[79] and carries the idea of one's
recognition that before God he is sinful and helpless.[80] It must
be remembered, too, that until the Christian era "humility" was
a vice rather than a virtue. The "plots of the Jews" in Asia
receive passing reference but they are nowhere in Acts described;
this is another evidence that Luke knew more than he wrote
(v. 19).

---

[79] R. C. Trench, *Synonyms of the New Testament* (London: Kegan Paul, Trench,
Trubner and Co., Ltd., 1906), p. 139.
[80] *Ibid.*, p. 141.

The full gospel.—Paul affirms that he did not suppress, "shrink from declaring," any part of the message which they needed to hear (v. 20) or any part of the purpose of God (v. 27). What part of it would he have been tempted to suppress? It will be remembered that the Christians lived peacefully in the synagogue (or synagogues) at Ephesus until Paul's preaching entered the scene; it was then that the cleavage came between church and synagogue (cf. Acts 19: 8f.). Apparently there was something in Paul's preaching that was absent from the earlier preaching in Ephesus. It will be remembered that there was something in Stephen's preaching that was absent from that of the twelve in Jerusalem. Was the divisive issue the purpose of God (v. 27) to unite Jew and Gentile by creating out of the two one new man, thus destroying the middle wall of partition (cf. Ephesians 2: 14ff.)? Were Christians *divided* over God's purpose to *unite?* The importance of this refusal to suppress the gospel is made clear by the fact that Paul states (v. 20) and then restates it (v. 27). It is not necessarily to the credit of the minister that his message is inoffensive. There is unfortunately some basis for the caustic remark: "Today we do not kill the prophets, instead we ask them to dinner." [81] When the *full* gospel impinges upon the historical situation, there is always crisis.

Verse 21, with its reference to both Jews and Greeks, would seem to bear out the suggestion that that which Paul did not suppress (vs. 20 and 27) concerned the Jew-Gentile issue. Each had the same basic need: "repentance to God" and "faith in our Lord Jesus Christ." The term "repentance" translates a Greek word which literally meant "change of mind." This idea was basic in the word as used by Paul, but it also included the idea of "turn," and possibly the latter idea was more prominent. Jews as well as Greeks were urged to change their minds about God and to *turn to God.* Inseparable from this would be commitment in faith to the Lord Jesus Christ in whom alone one fully encounters God.

---

[81] Cf. Raymond Calkins, *The Modern Message of the Minor Prophets* (New York: Harper and Brothers, 1947), p. 58.

The collection.—It has already been noted that Acts is strangely silent about the collection for the saints at Jerusalem—a silence which seriously challenges this writer's thesis as to Luke's purpose, because the collection was very important to the problem of the Jew-Gentile relationship and hence would be germane to Luke's purpose as this writer understands it.[82] Throughout the journey to Jerusalem, and emphatically here to the Ephesian elders, it was anticipated that "imprisonment and afflictions" awaited Paul (20: 22ff.). Though Acts makes constant reference to Paul's insistence upon going to Jerusalem in the face of repeated warning of the danger, it does not give explicit answer to either of two obvious and important questions: why was it so important for Paul to go to Jerusalem, and why was it so dangerous? Surely it was not worth the risk of life merely to be present for the day of Pentecost.

From the comparative study of Acts and the epistles we know that it was the growing tension over the basis for Jewish and Gentile fellowship that made Paul's presence so dangerous in Jerusalem, and it was the collection as a peace maneuver that made Paul so determined to go to Jerusalem. Luke stranglely enough did not explicitly mention the collection, although he described the trip of the "collection committee" and stressed the tenseness of the situation at Jerusalem. In his speech before Felix, Paul made an incidental reference to "alms and offerings" (24: 17) which he had just brought to his nation. Luke, then, certainly knew of the offering, but for some reason did not give it any prominence.

Verse 24 seems to reflect a particular "ministry"—such as the collection—as well as Paul's general "course." The Greek word for ministry (*diakonia*) often describes a particular assignment; it is the word used in Colossians 4: 17 for an assignment which the Colossians were to urge Archippus to accomplish.[83] Paul used this very word to describe the collection as he asked the Romans

[82] See above, pp. 208f.
[83] Cf. John Knox, *Philemon Among the Letters of Paul* (Chicago: University of Chicago Press, 1935) for an excellent study of not only this word but of the letter to Philemon.

to join him in the prayer that his service (*diakonia*) might be acceptable to the Jerusalem saints (Rom. 15: 30-31). There is in this a possible veiled reference to the collection. Whether that is true or not, this verse stresses the "grace of God" as central in the gospel, the proclaiming of which was vital to his "course" and "ministry." The first part of the verse is difficult to translate, but the idea is clear—Paul counted himself expendable! [84] He is willing to be "used up" in the attempt to complete his "course" and "ministry."

It is significant that several ideas are closely related in Paul's impassioned speech: "I know that all you . . . will see my face no more . . . I am innocent of the blood of all of you, for I did not shrink from declaring to you the whole counsel of God" (vs. 25-27). That which he did not suppress seemed to be connected with the danger at Jerusalem. The endangering "counsel" he had preached, and consequently he was "cleansed from the blood of all." Whatever his particular reference here, it was his courage in clearly defining the relationship of Jew and Gentile under God that brought upon him most of his dangers.

The leaders.—In view of his feeling that his personal ministry to Asia was ending, Paul urged upon the elders their fuller responsibility. There was a free interchange of terms for these leaders: they were called "elders" (v. 17), "guardians" (v. 28), and, by implication, "shepherds" (v. 28). "Elder," or "presbyter," is a good rendering of the term used in verse 17. This term was familiar in Jewish circles and was retained by the disciples. "Guardians" in verse 28 translates the Greek word which literally means "overseers" and which is usually translated "bishops." The terms "bishop" and "elder" were used interchangeably here as well as elsewhere in the New Testament (cf. Titus 1: 5, 7). In verse 28 "to feed" is literally "to shepherd." It is interesting to note that, though he had just spoken of "the flock," here he urged them to "shepherd *the church*." The three titles, then, (elder, bishop, and pastor) were used interchangeably for the same men.

---

[84] This term need not be explained to those who remember World War II.

218 THE BOOK OF ACTS

Saved alive by life given.—In verse 28 "obtained" is a better translation than the usual "purchased." The Greek word sometimes means "to obtain," but the obtaining is not necessarily by purchase. Not only is the "purchase" idea read into the Greek term, but theologians in times past have built upon the idea with mechanical logic, even to the point of suggesting ones to whom the price may have been paid. Though a word like "obtain" or "acquire" is better than "purchase," it is more likely that the idea is "save alive" or "rescue from destruction."[85] In Luke 17: 33 this Greek term is used in apparent parallelism to the word for "preserve alive."

"With his own blood" (v. 28) seems harsh to many, because the antecedent is "God"; hence, "with God's own blood" is implied. The Greek literally reads "through the blood, that of his own." The Greek would naturally imply "his own self," but some suggest that the implication is "his own Son." Probably the point is more disturbing to the commentators than to Luke, who could pass easily from one to the other. "Blood" in Biblical thought stands for the life; and, whatever the immediate reference here, the "rescue" or "saving alive" of the church has come only by God's willingness to give his life (or that of his Son).

The "fierce wolves" seem to have been distinguished from the men arising "from among your own selves" (vs. 29-30). The wolves, then, were evidently outsiders who would persecute, and the others were members who would pervert. Possibly the perverters are to be identified with the incipient gnosticism which was just then arising, but it is more likely that the reference is to the Judaizers; this conclusion is buttressed by the fact that Jews from Asia were the ones who brought about Paul's arrest in Jerusalem.

Only here are the beautiful words of Jesus preserved: "It is more blessed to give than to receive" (v. 35). Before the Gospels were written the sayings of Jesus were repeated orally, and this is one of the sayings preserved apart from the Gospels.

That Paul felt that they would "see his face no more" (vs. 25,

---

[85] Cf. Lake and Cadbury, *Commentary*, p. 261f.; Rackham, *op. cit.*, p. 392.

38) does not preclude a subsequent visit to Ephesus as many hold, contrary to the implication of the Pastoral Epistles. Many hold that when Luke wrote these words he *knew* that Paul's death had already taken place. It must be pointed out that according to Acts 27: 10 Paul said, "Sirs, I perceive that the voyage will be with injury and much loss, not only of cargo and the ship, *but also of our lives.*" Later he was able to report the message of the angel of God: "God has granted you all those who sail with you" (27: 24); and he said to the men, "not a hair is to perish from the head of any of you" (v. 34). Luke concludes that chapter with the statement: "And so it was that *all escaped to land*" (27: 44). This does not mean that God changed his mind, but it does follow that Paul was changed in his understanding of what was to take place. If Paul could have been mistaken in his belief that there would be loss of life (27: 10), why could he not have been mistaken about the Asians not seeing his face again? God is infallible, but Paul was not. This does not "prove" that Paul had a further ministry after his Roman imprisonment, but it does discredit the so-called "proof" that he did not survive the first Roman imprisonment.

On to Jerusalem [21: 1-16]

1 And when we had parted from them and set sail, we came by a straight course to Cos, and the next day to Rhodes, and from there to Patara. 2 And having found a ship crossing to Phoenicia, we went aboard, and set sail. 3 When we had come in sight of Cyprus, leaving it on the left we sailed to Syria, and landed at Tyre; for there the ship was to unload its cargo. 4 And having sought out the disciples, we stayed there for seven days. Through the Spirit they told Paul not to go on to Jerusalem. 5 And when our days there were ended we departed and went on our journey; and they all, with wives and children, brought us on our way till we were outside the city, and kneeling down on the beach we prayed and bade one another farewell. 6 Then we went on board the ship, and they returned home.

7 When we had finished the voyage from Tyre, we arrived at Ptolemais; and we greeted the brethren and stayed with them for one day. 8 On the morrow we departed and came to Caesarea; and we entered the house of Philip the evangelist, who was one of the seven, and stayed with him. 9 And he had four unmarried daughters, who prophesied. 10 While we were staying for some days, a

prophet named Agabus came down from Judea. ¹¹ And coming
to us he took Paul's girdle and bound his own feet and hands,
and said, "Thus says the Holy Spirit, 'So shall the Jews at Jerusalem bind the man who owns this girdle and deliver him into the
hands of the Gentiles.' " ¹² When we heard this, we and the people
there begged him not to go up to Jerusalem. ¹³ Then Paul answered, "What are you doing, weeping and breaking my heart?
For I am ready not only to be imprisoned but even to die at
Jerusalem for the name of the Lord Jesus." ¹⁴ And when he would
not be persuaded, we ceased and said, "The will of the Lord be
done."

15 After these days we made ready and went up to Jerusalem. ¹⁶ And
some of the disciples from Caesarea went with us, bringing us to
the house of Mnason of Cyprus, an early disciple, with whom we
should lodge.

The main purpose of this section seems to be impressionistic;
Luke is dramatically portraying the tense situation at Jerusalem
and the awareness of that tension throughout the Christian
world. Paul and those who attempted to dissuade him alike
realized that the Jerusalem situation was explosive. These were
the days when the Jewish Zealots were becoming ever more
restless, and though the actual revolt against Rome was some
years away, a stampede could be precipitated by any charge of
disloyalty to Jewish traditions. The ever-growing Gentile mission, in which Paul was now the dominant influence, would add
to the tension. These were decisive days for the Jews and for
Christianity.

One can easily become absorbed by the intriguing narrative,
which in its many details reflects the account of an eyewitness.
The change of ships at Patara was probably necessary because
the rest of the voyage would be in the open sea, rather than near
the coast. This would follow whether the first ship was chartered
or not. From this point on Paul seemed to be subject to the ship's
schedule. At Tyre he evidently knew of disciples, but had to hunt
them up, as the Greek implies (v. 4). Here, as at Miletus, the
unashamed affection of these disciples stood in sharp contrast
with the bitter hatred of those who rejected the proposition that
in Christ all are brothers, including Jew and Gentile. Brethren
were found at Ptolemais, but about that work Acts is otherwise
silent. Philip seems to have settled in Caesarea after his earlier

missions. His daughters are presented as prophetesses and virgins, but Acts does not exalt celibacy. The prophecy of Agabus was not necessarily typical of the warnings Paul received but did climax them. The concerted effort of all, including Paul's companions in travel, crushed his heart but did not turn him from his purpose to go on to Jerusalem (v. 13).

It is futile to debate what Paul ought to have done. Agabus and all the rest understood the Spirit to be guiding against the mission; Paul felt that the Spirit was leading him to Jerusalem. Paul was not seeking to die at Jerusalem—he was seeking to heal the breach between Jews and Gentiles—but he was *willing* to die there.

Verse 15 in the obscure word "made ready" (a participle in Greek) may contain a veiled reference to the collection. The idea may be "having packed up," and the reference could be to the regular baggage or to the fund of money. Mnason, the Cypriote, is described as either an "early" or an "original" disciple. Whether his home was between Caesarea and Jerusalem, as seems indicated, or actually in Jerusalem, he provided lodging for the party and probably was one of the eyewitnesses of Christian beginnings from whom Luke received information. Philip and his daughters, too, doubtless supplied valuable information.

Jerusalem Christianity: Myriads Zealous for the Law [21: 17-26]

17 When we had come to Jerusalem, the brethren received us gladly. 18 On the following day Paul went in with us to James; and all the elders were present. 19 After greeting them, he related one by one the things that God had done among the Gentiles through his ministry. 20 And when they heard it, they glorified God. And they said to him, "You see, brother, how many thousands there are among the Jews of those who have believed; they are all zealous for the law, 21 and they have been told about you that you teach all the Jews who are among the Gentiles to forsake Moses, telling them not to circumcise their children or observe the customs. 22 What then is to be done? They will certainly hear that you have come. 23 Do therefore what we tell you. We have four men who are under a vow; 24 take these men and purify yourself along with them and pay their expenses so that they may shave their heads. Thus all will know that there is nothing in what they have been told about you but that you yourself live in observance of the law. 25 But as for the Gentiles who have believed, we have

sent a letter with our judgment that they should abstain from what
has been sacrificed to idols and from blood and from what is
strangled and from unchastity." 26 Then Paul took the men and
the next day he purified himself with them and went into the
temple, to give notice when the days of purification would be fulfilled and the offering presented for every one of them.

Here is a picture of Jewish Christianity—or Christian Judaism—
in the middle fifties of the first century. There had been a phe-
nomenal growth numerically, but no evidence of growth in that
for which Stephen died. "Myriads" is the word used to describe
the multitude of Jewish believers in Jerusalem (v. 20). A myriad
is ten thousand; there is no reason for reducing "myriads" to
"thousands" as is usually done. These myriads of believers among
the Jews were "all *zealous for the law.*" The substantive, zealots,
is used, but it is not to be understood in the technical sense of the
political party known by that name. Their zeal for the law gave
them "security" in Jerusalem; we hear nothing more of their
being persecuted. Jewish Christianity had identified itself with
the state *and it died with the state.* It was inoffensive, not disturbing the "customs," the *status quo.*

Jerusalem Christians were disturbed because they had been
told (literally, "instructed") that Paul taught "apostasy" (this
is the Greek word used) from Moses, telling Jews not to circumcise their children or walk according to the customs (v. 21). Who
gave them this instruction? Why were Jewish Christians so much
concerned about circumcision? What had James and the elders
done about correcting these attitudes? These leaders seemed to
be as nervous as anyone. Though non-Christian Jews may have
been the ones to mob Paul in the temple, James' fear was that
Christian Jews would hear of Paul's presence in Jerusalem and
give trouble (vs. 20-22)! It seems that James had assembled the
elders for the meeting with Paul but had not assembled the
church at Jerusalem. Was Paul's life in danger among Jerusalem
"Christians" too?

James has been upheld for his advice to Paul, and probably his
motive was good. He is placed in extremely bad light, however,
by apparently doing nothing to defend Paul after Paul's arrest.

It is unwise to argue from silence; but if James did attempt to help Paul, it was an injustice to him for Luke to omit that fact. The testimony of Josephus and Hegessipus to the effect that James lived on in Jerusalem until about A.D. 62 and was held in high esteem by the Jews is evidence that Luke did not misrepresent James.

It is understandable that Paul would share in the purification with the four Jews and bear the expense for the completion of their vows (v. 24). From Paul's own pen it is known that he was willing to be "unto the Jews . . . a Jew" (1 Cor. 9: 20). He was willing to bear the heavy expense involved which included two lambs, a ram, bread, cakes, and meat and drink offerings for each person (Num. 6: 14f.). Judging from this expense, the cost of the trials, the attempts to bribe him, and two years in Rome at his own expense, Paul evidently had come into possession of some money, possibly through inheritance.

Non-Christian Jews and Paul: Arrest and Defense [21: 27 to 26: 32]

Shut doors and Paul's arrest [21: 27 to 22: 2]

27 When the seven days were almost completed, the Jews from Asia, who had seen him in the temple, stirred up all the crowd, and laid hands on him, 28 crying out, "Men of Israel, help! This is the man who is teaching men everywhere against the people and the law and this place; moreover he also brought Greeks into the temple, and he has defiled this holy place." 29 For they had previously seen Trophimus the Ephesian with him in the city, and they supposed that Paul had brought him into the temple. 30 Then all the city was aroused, and the people ran together; they seized Paul and dragged him out of the temple, and at once the gates were shut. 31 And as they were trying to kill him, word came to the tribune of the cohort that all Jerusalem was in confusion. 32 He at once took soldiers and centurions, and ran down to them; and when they saw the tribune and the soldiers, they stopped beating Paul. 33 Then the tribune came up and arrested him, and ordered him to be bound with two chains. He inquired who he was and what he had done. 34 Some in the crowd shouted one thing, some another; and as he could not learn the facts because of the uproar, he ordered him to be brought into the barracks. 35 And when he came to the steps, he was actually carried by the soldiers because of the violence of the crowd; 36 for the mob of the people followed, crying, "Away with him!"

37 As Paul was about to be brought into the barracks, he said to the tribune, "May I say something to you?" And he said, "Do you know Greek? 38 Are you not the Egyptian, then, who recently stirred up a revolt and led the four thousand men of the Assassins out into the wilderness?" 39 Paul replied, "I am a Jew, from Tarsus in Cilicia, a citizen of no mean city; I beg you, let me speak to the people." 40 And when he had given him leave, Paul, standing on the steps motioned with his hands to the people; and when there was a great hush, he spoke to them in the Hebrew language, saying:

22: 1 "Brethren and fathers, hear the defense which I now make before you."

2 And when they heard that he addressed them in the Hebrew language, they were the more quiet.

Temple doors are slammed shut to Gentiles or "Gentile lovers." This is the sad counterpart to the open doors into the kingdom. In Acts two developments are parallel: as it becomes increasingly apparent that Christianity must open its doors to Jews and Gentiles on an equal basis, the doors to synagogues and temple gradually close to Christianity. Christian Jews of the outlook of Stephen, Philip, and Paul would open the doors to all, "unhindered." The particularists would set up the sign: "road closed."

Jews from Asia (v. 27) touched off the riot in the temple. It has already been observed, in connection with the stoning of Stephen, that the dispersion produced both the most liberal and most narrowly fanatical Jews. These Jews, not Christians, had probably shared in the fight against Paul in Ephesus and were looking for an excuse to fight him in Jerusalem. They jumped to a wrong conclusion without the effort—and doubtless without the disposition—to verify that conclusion (v. 29). The charge that Paul had taken Greeks into the temple was sufficient to stampede a crowd already tense over the Roman rule.

The charges against Paul are almost those against Stephen and have much in common with the charges against Jesus; the temple was featured in the charges against each of the three. Paul was accused of teaching everywhere "against the people and the law and this place" and with defiling the temple by bringing Greeks into it (v. 28). Archaeological discoveries have established conclusively the fact that there were stone blocks in the temple warning aliens of the death penalty should they enter the enclosure around the sanctuary. A limestone block was found in 1871 in the temple area having the inscription in Greek to this effect: "Let no foreigner enter within the screen and enclosure surrounding the sanctuary. Whosoever is taken so doing will be the cause that death overtaketh him." [86] The studied bigotry behind the inscription, posted in Latin and Greek, was worse than the murderous hate of the mob which it encouraged. Anti-Jewish feeling and action is to be deplored in any age, but it is precisely this sanctified bigotry which encourages the same disposition in the "foreigners." "Jim Crow" laws may have their defenders, but they have no defense.

The rescue by the Romans is easily understood. The fortress of Antonia was joined by two flights of stairs to the court of the Gentiles, and in it was stationed a Roman cohort (1000 men). Because of frequent riots in the temple area, especially during the feasts, Roman sentries were stationed around the court. These quickly detected the riot and soldiers rushed down to get it under control. Since centurions (plural) were dispatched, it may be assumed that at least two hundred soldiers were called out to quell the mob. (A centurion, as the term suggests, was in charge of a hundred men.)

The tribune (the Greek has chiliarch, i.e., ruler of a thousand) had reason to be elated in the thought that he had captured the notorious Egyptian who had recently stirred up a revolt and led four thousand men of the Sicarii (from Latin word sica, a dagger) into the desert (v. 38). This is probably the Egyptian described by Josephus (Jewish Wars, ii. 13. 4f. and Ant. xx. 8. 6). He led several thousand men (Josephus says 30,000) in revolt, assuring them that the walls of Jerusalem would fall before them, as had the walls of Jericho before Joshua. Instead the Roman soldiers of Felix fell on them. They were dispersed; some were killed, others captured, but the Egyptian escaped. The tribune was no doubt disappointed when Paul proved not to be the Egyptian.

Paul's Greek (v. 30) surprised the tribune. Paul's pride in

[86] Cf. Adolf Deissman, *Light from the Ancient East* (L. R. M. Strachan, translator, newly revised edition; New York: Harper and Brothers, 1927), pp. 80f., for translation and facsimile of inscription.

Tarsian citizenship is obvious, but the tribune was more impressed by the later disclosure of the Roman citizenship (22: 27f.). Paul's Hebrew (which in the New Testament seems to mean Aramaic) impressed the Jews. The courage of Paul in facing an angry mob was characteristic, but more important was his desire to convert them to a better attitude toward the gospel and the Gentiles.

Paul's defense to the Jews [22:3-21]

3 "I am a Jew, born at Tarsus in Cilicia, but brought up in this city at the feet of Gamaliel, educated according to the strict manner of the law of our fathers, being zealous for God as you all are this day. 4 I persecuted this Way to the death, binding and delivering to prison both men and women, 5 as the high priest and the whole council of elders bear me witness. From them I received letters to the brethren, and I journeyed to Damascus to take those also who were there and bring them in bonds to Jerusalem to be punished.

6 "As I made my journey and drew near to Damascus, about noon a great light from heaven suddenly shone about me. 7 And I fell to the ground and heard a voice saying to me, 'Saul, Saul, why do you persecute me?' 8 And I answered, 'Who are you, Lord?' And he said to me, 'I am Jesus of Nazareth whom you are persecuting.' 9 Now those who were with me saw the light but did not hear the voice of the one who was speaking to me. 10 And I said, 'What shall I do, Lord?' And the Lord said to me, 'Rise, and go into Damascus, and there you will be told all that is appointed for you to do.' 11 And when I could not see because of the brightness of that light, I was led by the hand by those who were with me, and came into Damascus.

12 "And one Ananias, a devout man according to the law, well spoken of by all the Jews who lived there, 13 came to me, and standing by me said to me, 'Brother Saul, receive your sight.' And in that very hour I received my sight and saw him. 14 And he said, 'The God of our fathers appointed you to know his will, to see the Just One and to hear a voice from his mouth; 15 for you will be a witness for him to all men of what you have seen and heard. 16 And now why do you wait? Rise and be baptized, and wash away your sins, calling on his name.'

17 "When I had returned to Jerusalem and was praying in the temple, I fell into a trance 18 and saw him saying to me, 'Make haste and get quickly out of Jerusalem, because they will not accept your testimony about me.' 19 And I said, 'Lord, they themselves know that in every synagogue I imprisoned and beat those who believed

in thee. [20] And when the blood of Stephen thy witness was shed, I also was standing by and approving, and keeping the garments of those who killed him.' [21] And he said to me, 'Depart; for I will send you far way to the Gentiles.' "

Paul's defense rests on two major propositions: (1) he has always been a loyal Jew and (2) his ministry has been in obedience to God's command. His life is contrary to his own former plans for it, and he has no other accounting for it except divine intervention.

Paul addressed these Jews as "brethren and fathers" (22: 1) and identified himself as a Jew (v. 3). Though born outside Palestine, he (with his family) was loyal enough as a Jew to seek the best training in Jerusalem, "at the feet of Gamaliel," and was disciplined according to the strictest manner of the ancestral law (v. 3). His zeal for God was evidenced by his persecutions of the Way at Jerusalem and as far as Damascus. To that point none could question his devotion to his nation; his subsequent course he will show to be the direct result of divine intervention.

In telling of his conversion, Paul is submitting evidence that this whole course now under their judgment had its beginning in an experience which was not of his planning. His orders were from "the God of our fathers" and it was "*his* will," not Paul's which Paul was to know (v. 14). It was by God's appointment that he should see and hear the "Just One," that is, Jesus, and witness "for him to all men" of what he had seen and heard (v. 14f.). The conversion, commission, and message were all, then, of divine origin; they were not Paul's ideas. Moreover, this divine initiative at every point was recognized at the time by "one Ananias, a devout man according to the law, well spoken of by all the Jews who lived there" (v. 12).

Further evidence of God's initiative and Paul's loyalty to his nation is submitted in connection with a trance (ecstasy) which he experienced sometime after his conversion in this very temple (vs. 17-21). God had then warned him of Jewish rejection of his testimony and told him to leave Jerusalem. Paul had asked for the privilege of remaining in Jerusalem, pleading that the Jews

would surely know that his conversion was genuine, for they had
seen how fervently he had opposed the believers.[87] It may be
that he was excusing the Jews on the grounds that they could
be expected to be suspicious of one so vacillating. Whichever
is meant, Paul is saying that he was reluctant to leave Jerusalem
because of his countrymen. God overruled, however, and not
only insisted that he depart from Jerusalem, but that he go to
the Gentiles (v. 21). Each step, then, was at God's command, and
in each step Paul had been concerned for his own people.

Luke's first account of Paul's conversion appears in chapter
9 (see pp. 109ff. for discussion). The experience is so narrated
here as to bring out the best evidences for the refutation of the
charges. This purpose accounts for some of the differences between the account here and in chapter nine. (Some of the differences were discussed earlier; see p. 109.)

Verse 16 does not teach baptismal regeneration, even though
it might serve as a proof text for one ignoring the plain opposition of Acts and Paul's epistles to legalism and ritualism. The
verse should be translated: "Arising, get yourself baptized and
get your sins washed away, calling (or, having called) upon his
name."

Frenzy over one word [22: 22-24]

> 22 Up to this word they listened to him; then they lifted up their
> voices and said, "Away with such a fellow from the earth! For he
> ought not to live." 23 And as they cried out and waved their gar-
> ments and threw dust into the air, 25 the tribune commanded him
> to be brought into the barracks, and ordered him to be examined
> by scourging, to find out why they shouted thus against him.

One word—then mad frenzy! The mob listened quietly, as Paul
spoke in Aramaic, until he mentioned the Gentiles. This confirmed for these people the reports that he was a traitor to the
nation. Then they yelled that such a fellow was not fit to live.
Contempt for Paul was accompanied by a wild demonstration,
the waving of garments and throwing of dust into the air. Were
they as sure of Paul's guilt as they pretended? Such frenzy sug-

---

[87] Cf. F. F. Bruce, *op. cit.*, p. 404.

gests misgivings about their own position which they were unwilling to acknowledge. Judaism in these times had an uneasy
conscience on the Gentile issue—with one hand reaching out for
proselytes and with the other pushing them off.[88]

This paragraph is closely paralleled by the next-to-the-last one
of the book, where it is said that the Roman Jews listened to
Paul until he made *one statement* (28: 25), and that statement
concerned God's purpose to save the Gentiles (28: 26-28).
Clearly, it is this that Luke was concerned to demonstrate: the
gradual victory for an unhindered gospel, providing for the
equality of the Gentile with the Jew, and the consequent Jewish
rejection of the gospel so defined. As one door was opened, another was shut.

Paul the Jew forced to become Paul the Roman [22: 25-30]

25 But when they had tied him up with the thongs, Paul said to
the centurion who was standing by, "Is it lawful for you to scourge
a man who is a Roman citizen, and uncondemned?" 26 When the
centurion heard that, he went to the tribune and said to him,
"What are you about to do? For this man is a Roman citizen."
27 So the tribune came and said to him, "Tell me, are you a Roman
citizen?" And he said, "Yes." 28 The tribune answered, "I bought
this citizenship for a large sum." Paul said, "But I was born a
citizen." 29 So those who were about to examine him withdrew
from him instantly; and the tribune also was afraid, for he realized
that Paul was a Roman citizen and that he had bound him.

30 But on the morrow, desiring to know the real reason why the Jews
accused him, he unbound him, and commanded the chief priests
and all the council to meet, and he brought Paul down and set
him before them.

Since Aramaic was spoken by Paul and the Jews, the Romans
probably understood little of what was said. Paul had been given
an opportunity to clear things up with the Jews, but only renewed
tumult followed, so the tribune decided to proceed in his way.
Scourging would be the natural way for a Roman soldier to "get
the truth." The Greek is ambiguous in verse 25, and it is not
clear whether Paul was stretched out "with the thongs" or "for

---

[88] Cf. W. D. Davies, *Paul and Rabbinic Judaism* (London: S.P.C.K., 1948), p. 63;
Geo. Foote Moore, *Judaism* (Cambridge, Mass.: Harvard University Press, 1927),
I, 341ff.

the lashes." The point is of little importance, for what is clear is that the soldiers were prepared to give him a cruel scourging. The Roman scourging was far more brutal than the Jewish one, and it could easily cripple or kill. It is not known why Paul delayed giving the information about his Roman citizenship, just as was true at Philippi, but a most plausible suggestion is that he was reluctant to appeal to that citizenship. His great purpose in making the hazardous trip to Jerusalem was to win his Jewish people to what was to him the right understanding of the gospel and attitude toward the Gentiles. It was most important that he stand among them *as a Jew,* true at the same time to the history of Israel and the hope of Israel. Only when repudiated by the Jews and faced with possible loss of life, did the Jew become a Roman.

It is idle to speculate about how Paul's family had gained Roman citizenship. None of the theories can be established. There are isolated cases where Roman citizens were scourged, and these cases may have been simply irregular, but certainly no uncondemned Roman citizen was to be so treated. The fact that Paul had been "stretched out" (v. 25) for scourging was enough to give anxiety to the soldiers; consequently Paul was immediately "unbound" from the torture instrument (v. 29). On the next day he was released (not the same word as in the previous verse) in some other sense, either from the chains or from the cell.

The hope of Israel and the resurrection [23: 1-10]

> 1 And Paul, looking intently at the council, said, "Brethren, I have lived before God in all good conscience up to this day." 2 And the high priest Ananias commanded those who stood by him to strike him on the mouth. 3 Then Paul said to him, "God shall strike you, you whitewashed wall! Are you sitting to judge me according to the law, and yet contrary to the law you order me to be struck?" 4 Those who stood by said, "Would you revile God's high priest?" 5 And Paul said, "I did not know, brethren, that he was the high priest; for it is written, 'You shall not speak evil of a ruler of your people.' "
> 6 But when Paul perceived that one part were Sadducees and the other Pharisees; he cried out in the council, "Brethren, I am a

Pharisee, a son of Pharisees; with respect to the hope and the resurrection of the dead I am on trial." 7 And when he had said this, a dissension arose between the Pharisees and the Sadducees; and the assembly was divided. 8 For the Sadducees say that there is no resurrection, nor angel, nor spirit; but the Pharisees acknowledge them all. 9 Then a great clamor arose; and some of the scribes of the Pharisees' party stood up and contended, "We find nothing wrong in this man. What if a spirit or an angel spoke to him?" 10 And when the dissension became violent, the tribune, afraid that Paul would be torn in pieces by them, commanded the soldiers to go down and take him by force from among them and bring him into the barracks.

Paul apparently faced the members of the Sanhedrin as his equals. By birth, training, ability, and experience he felt himself to be on their level. Paul seems to have adjusted easily to the weak and lowly (cf. 1 Cor. 1: 26ff.); but he mingled freely and normally with proconsuls, Asiarchs, and the leaders in both Jewish and Gentile circles, meeting them as his social equals. Paul's family was not newly rich, newly free, or newly prominent, and that may have had something to do with his personal poise and indifference to the superficialities by which many measure men. Only little men kowtow to others or want others to kowtow to them. To Paul the members of the Sanhedrin were "brothers." Whether or not he had once been a member of the Sanhedrin is not known, but it is clear that he moved freely in such circles.

Paul's defense began with the claim that his manner of life (literally "citizenship") before God had been in sincerity; he actually believed that for which he stood, and in so doing he felt that he was true to God (v. 1). Exactly why Ananias ordered Paul to be struck is not made clear. Paul's failure to acknowledge the members of the Sanhedrin as superiors or his blunt claim to innocency may account for the action. The conduct of Ananias here is in keeping with his character as otherwise known, for he was cruel and selfish. His own life was stormy; in the year 52 he had been summoned to Rome for a reckoning about his management of affairs, but he had been acquited and thus was at his greatest power. Later he was deposed, A.D. 58 or 59, and was assassinated in 66. With understandable quick temper, Paul

voiced his contempt for one who stooped to such low conduct
of so high an office (the charge would apply to any member of
the Sanhedrin, not just to its high priest).

Paul's plea, "I did not know, brethren, that he was high priest"
(v. 5), is difficult. Poor eyesight, ignorance of who currently held
the office, and irony have been among the suggestions. None of
these is very convincing, and it is inconceivable that Paul would
not know who was high priest, however frequent the changes.
Would any exegete acknowledge that he himself could be ignorant of who held the highest office among his own people?
Possibly in the confusion Paul actually failed to detect the one
from whom came the command, knowing only that someone had
spoken out of the group. The solution however, is probably to
be found in the wide range of meanings possible in the word
"know"; this is true in both Greek and English. Paul probably
meant, "I spoke without taking note of the fact that he is high
priest." That would be psychologically normal for Paul who was
not intimidated by rank or office. Paul was facing Ananias "man
to man." When someone appealed to the technicality, Paul
conceded the point; he was in the wrong for failure to respect
"the office."

The next problem, as Paul pits the Pharisees against the
Sadducees, is yet more difficult. It is said that Paul would not
pose as a Pharisee and that to raise the question of the resurrection was to evade the charge. It may be conceded that Paul's
motive *could* have been less than the best; he was not infallible.
The New Testament does not spare James, John, Peter, and
others in its disclosure of their weaknesses; so it is not inconceivable that Paul could start a partisan fight as a stratagem for
escaping the condemnation of the council. It is not on dogmatic
grounds, then, but simply because the arguments are not convincing that they are rejected.

Paul no doubt felt that he was a true Pharisee; he had followed
through on basic tenets and interests of Pharisaism. He had
already appealed to the fact of divine guidance as the explanation
for his Christian life. To Paul the truth or fallacy of his whole
position did depend upon the reality of the resurrection. He

dated his Christian life and commission by his encounter with the risen Jesus. About a year earlier he had written to the Corinthians that everything stood or fell with the resurrection (cf. 1 Cor. 15: 12ff.). His mission to the Gentiles he traced to the risen Christ; this assumed the reality of resurrection. So Paul was not evading the issue; he was getting to the heart of it. The resurrection was vital to Pharisaic faith, and apart from it Paul would never have entered the life which brought him to this trial. It is understandable that the Pharisees would, for the moment at least, rally to Paul; their battle with the Sadducees was as serious as that with Christians. Some Pharisees did become Christians and remain Pharisees; no Sadducee could be Sadducee and Christian at the same time.

Comfort and direction [23: 11]

> 11 The following night the Lord stood by him and said, "Take courage, for as you have testified about me at Jerusalem, so you must bear witness also at Rome."

Paul's position was precarious, with Christians and non-Christian Jews in bitter opposition and with his loyalty to his nation exposed to further charge in that he had fallen back on his Roman citizenship. As at Corinth when his work was separated from the synagogue, he needed comfort and guidance. The appearance of the Lord himself would serve to reassure him about past choices and point the way through the trying years ahead.

Jewish plot to kill Paul [23: 12-22]

> 12 When it was day, the Jews made a plot and bound themselves by an oath neither to eat nor drink till they had killed Paul. 13 There were more than forty who made this conspiracy. 14 And they went to the chief priests and elders, and said, "We have strictly bound ourselves by an oath to taste no food till we have killed Paul. 15 You therefore, along with the council, give notice now to the tribune to bring him down to you, as though you were going to determine his case more exactly. And we are ready to kill him before he comes near."
> 16 Now the son of Paul's sister heard of their ambush; so he went and entered the barracks and told Paul. 17 And Paul called one of the centurions and said, "Bring this young man to the tribune; for

he has something to tell him." 18 So he took him and brought
him to the tribune and said, "Paul the prisoner called me and
asked me to bring this young man to you, as he has something
to say to you." 19 The tribune took him by the hand, and going
aside asked him privately, "What is it that you have to tell me?"
20 And he said, "The Jews have agreed to ask you to bring Paul
down to the council tomorrow, as though they were going to inquire somewhat more closely about him. 21 But do not yield to
them; for more than forty of their men lie in ambush for him,
having bound themselves by an oath neither to eat nor drink till
they have killed him; and now they are ready, waiting for the
promise from you." 22 So the tribune dismissed the young man,
charging him, "Tell no one that you have informed me of this."

Luke does not identify the conspirators beyond calling them "the
Jews." Possibly they belonged to the group known later as the
Zealots. These encouraged rebellion against Rome and sought
to destroy those in Judaism who favored peace. These made
themselves "anathema," or devoted to God for destruction,
should they not kill Paul (vs. 12 and 14). Since Paul escaped
them, their oath would have brought about their deaths by
starvation, had it been kept. Luke does not give us the sequel,
but probably the priests found some technical "loophole" by
which they could escape the penalty.

How Paul's nephew learned of the plot is not revealed. Bruce
has a plausible suggestion:

If he was present at the conspiracy, either his relation to Paul was
unknown, or Paul's bitterest enemies may have been those of his own
household, in which case the presence of one of Paul's relatives would
have occasioned no misgivings.[89]

This part of Paul's family at least was now sympathetic. Since
Paul is silent about his family and Luke gives nothing beyond
this, speculation is of little worth. The details of the narrative
reflect the report of an eyewitness.

Paul delivered to Felix [23: 23-35]

23 Then he called two of the centurions and said, "At the third hour
of the night get ready two hundred soldiers with seventy horsemen and two hundred spearmen to go as far as Caesarea. 24 Also

---
[89] Bruce, op. cit., p. 415.

provide mounts for Paul to ride, and bring him safely to Felix the governor." 25 And he wrote a letter to this effect:
26 "Claudius Lysias to his Excellency the governor Felix, greeting. 27 This man was seized by the Jews, and was about to be killed by them, when I came upon them with the soldiers and rescued him, having learned that he was a Roman citizen. 28 And desiring to know the charge on which they accused him, I brought him down to their council. 29 I found that he was accused about questions of their law, but charged with nothing deserving death or imprisonment. 30 And when it was disclosed to me that there would be a plot against the man, I sent him to you at once, ordering his accusers also to state before you what they have against him."
31 So the soldiers, according to their instructions, took Paul and brought him by night to Antipatris. 32 And on the morrow they returned to the barracks, leaving the horsemen to go on with him. 33 When they came to Caesarea and delivered the letter to the governor, they presented Paul also before him. 34 On reading the letter, he asked to what province he belonged. When he learned that he was from Cilicia 35 he said, "I will hear you when your accusers arrive." And he commanded him to be guarded in Herod's praetorium.

The extreme precautions taken by Claudius Lysias, for such is his name now shown to be, are understandable. He had learned little about the charges against Paul, but he had seen evidence that Paul was a very important person and that his enemies were strong and determined. In addition to this, Paul was a Roman citizen and Lysias had already been negligent in dealing with his prisoner. Moreover, restless bands had already engaged in violence, and Lysias knew that this situation was explosive. Consequently, he was anxious to be relieved of this grave responsibility. The size of the escort reflects his conception of the potential of the fanatical group bent on Paul's assassination.

"Spearmen" is simply a guess for the word in verse 23 which it translates. The Greek word literally means "to take with the right (hand)," and from this is the suggestion of "spearmen." The word could refer to "led horses," but that again is a guess.[90] Certainty is impossible with present evidence; fortunately, the problem is of little importance. The foot soldiers traveled no farther than Antipatris (vs. 31f.); beyond that there would be little danger from the Jerusalem Jews. If Antipatris was as far

[90] Cf. Lake and Cadbury, *Commentary*, pp. 292f.

from Jerusalem as usually thought, from thirty-five to forty miles, it would seem impossible for them to travel that far by the next day. There are some uncertainties, and any one of them could clear up the problem. To begin with, the exact location of Antipatris is unknown, so the mileage involved is uncertain. Again, although the Greek seems to indicate that the full trip to Antipatris was by night, Luke's meaning may be only that it was a "night journey" in that it got under way early in the night (about 9:00 p.m.) and continued through the night. The foot soldiers may have traveled on into the day, or they may not have traveled all the way to Antipatris.

The letter of Claudius Lysias is about what would be expected. Luke does not claim to give it verbatim, but only its substance (v. 25). The tribune naturally presented the case to best advantage for himself. Thus he omitted any reference to the attempted scourging of Paul. At one point he probably misrepresented the case, depending on what relative time (antecedent or coincident) is seen in the Greek participle in the clause, "having learned that he was a Roman citizen" (v. 27). This translation is probably correct; and, if so, it indicates that Lysias implied that he rescued Paul *because* he was a Roman citizen. In fairness to Lysias, however, it should be acknowledged that the passage could be translated: "I . . . rescued him, learning that he is a Roman."

Felix was appointed procurator of Judea A.D. 51 or 52. He and his brother Pallas were Greeks and were once slaves of Antonia, mother of the Emperor Claudius. Tacitus (*Hist.* V. 9) said of him that "he reveled in cruelty and lust, and wielded the power of a king with the mind of a slave." His third wife was Drusilla (24: 24), sister of Agrippa II and Bernice (25: 23) and former wife of Azizus, King of Emesa, whom she left for Felix.

Several of Luke's major interests are served in this section dealing with Paul's arrest and trials. Luke wanted to leave no doubt about the circumstances under which Paul ultimately appealed to Caesar. Paul took no initiative in bringing charges against his nation. On the other hand, it was the persistence of Jewish opposition that finally issued in his Roman imprisonment. Even some of the Pharisees of the Sanhedrin had rec-

ognized that he was not untrue to his nation (23: 9), and Lysias
wrote Felix (v. 29) that he found Paul charged with nothing
deserving of death or imprisonment (from the standpoint of a
Roman).

Tertullus: the case against Paul [24: 1-9]

1 And after five days the high priest Ananias came down with some
elders and a spokesman, one Tertullus. They laid before the governor their case against Paul; 2 And when he was called, Tertullus
began to accuse him, saying:
"Since through you we enjoy much peace, and since by your
provision, most excellent Felix, reforms are introduced on behalf
of this nation, 3 in every way and everywhere we accept this with
all gratitude. 4 But, to detain you no further, I beg you in your
kindness to hear us briefly. 5 For we have found this man a pesti-
lent fellow, an agitator among all the Jews throughout the world,
and a ringleader of the sect of the Nazarenes. 6 He even tried to
profane the temple, but we seized him. 8 By examining him yourself you will be able to learn from him about everything of which
we accuse him."
9 The Jews also joined in the charge, affirming that all this was so.

Though Jews did employ heathen lawyers, it is not clear whether
Tertullus was Roman, Greek, or Jew; the name is the diminutive
of Tertius.[91] Verse 6 would suggest that he was a Jew, though
as a lawyer he may simply be identifying himself with his clients.
The smooth, flattering speech is about what would be expected
of a Roman lawyer. Though Felix was a despicable character and
was finally recalled from office by Rome, there were acts on his
part which could serve as the basis for these praises. Tertullus
merely made the most of the work of Felix in suppressing in-
surrections and passed over the evil in the man and his administration of office.

The charges against Paul were political and religious: Paul
was a "pest," a creator of dissensions among the Jews throughout
the world, and a ringleader of the sect of the Nazarenes (v. 5).
It was further charged that he had attempted to profane the
temple—the former charge that he actually took Greeks into the
temple was modified for lack of evidence. The charge implying

---

[91] Cf. Lake and Cadbury, *Commentary*, p. 297.

sedition was the most serious that could be submitted to a Roman court, and the hope for getting Paul condemned made it necessary to stress the political rather than the theological aspect of the charges. "Sect" is a good rendering of the word in verse 5. Though the Greek word originally meant "party," it is no doubt used here to describe those discredited. Christianity had not been given independent status in the Roman Empire, so Judaism could claim the right to judge it as a disloyal sect within its own ranks.

A textual problem is involved in verses 6-8. All of verse 7 and and parts of verses 6 and 8 are omitted in most Greek Testaments of today. The Western text has a longer reading: "And we would have judged him according to our law. But the chief captain Lysias came and with great violence took him out of our hands, commanding his accusers to come before you." This longer reading may well be the original, but the case is not so conclusive as A. C. Clark would indicate.[92] This longer reading would make Lysias rather than Paul the one whom Felix might examine for verification of the charges (see v. 8). If this is original to the text, then Tertullus was charging Lysias with interference with the Jewish prerogative at the temple—a serious charge, indeed. But he would also be distorting the facts in the case in such way as to incriminate Lysias. Could Lysias be appealed to to verify *this charge?*

On the other hand, the shorter reading would mean that an examination of Paul would bring out the truth of the charges. Clark thinks this ". . . produces nonsense, since the evidence of Paul in his own case could be of no value, while that of Lysias, who made the arrest, would be of great importance."[93] This "logic" is not so conclusive as Clark supposes, and it certainly does not justify the condescending attitude which he seems to hold toward J. H. Ropes.[94] Tertullus did not say that Paul would admit the charges; he suggested (if the shorter reading is

---

[92] Cf. A. C. Clark, *The Acts of the Apostles* (Oxford, at the Clarendon Press, 1933) p. xlvii. for a strong, but unduly dogmatic, argument.
[93] *Ibid.*, p. 380.
[94] J. H. Ropes in *The Text of Acts* (F. J. Foakes Jackson and Kirsopp Lake, editors, *The Beginnings of Christianity;* London: Macmillan and Co., 1926), p. 225, prefers the shorter reading and is Clark's "pet peeve" throughout his book. Clark's work is brilliant, but his patronizing attitude is to be regretted.

original) that an examination of Paul would verify "all of the things" of which he was charged. Tertullus could easily have assumed that Paul would betray his dangerous attitudes any time he was given an opportunity to speak. "Give him enough rope and he will hang himself" would be a modern paraphrase.

The best manuscripts have the shorter reading, and internal evidence is simply not decisive for either. Neither Tertullus nor Lysias would want too much inquiry into the "arrest." The Jews had been attempting to lynch Paul, not try him; and Lysias had attempted to scourge him. The shorter reading would be congenial to the willingness of Tertullus to say simply, "We arrested him"; and Lysias would be content to surpress the matter saying, "I rescued him." On the basis of the longer reading, Paul could have placed both in extremely bad light.

Paul's defense before Felix: true Judaism survives in the Way [24: 10-21]

> 10 And when the governor had motioned to him to speak, Paul replied:
> "Realizing that for many years you have been judge over this nation, I cheerfully make my defense. 11 As you may ascertain, it is not more than twelve days since I went up to worship at Jerusalem; 12 and they did not find me disputing with any one or stirring up a crowd, either in the temple or in the synagogues, or in the city. 13 Neither can they prove to you what they now bring up against me. 14 But this I admit to you, that according to the Way, which they call a sect, I worship the God of our fathers, believing everything laid down by the law or written in the prophets, 15 having a hope in God which these themselves accept, that there will be a resurrection of both the just and the unjust. 16 So I always take pains to have a clear conscience toward God and toward men. 17 Now after some years I came to bring to my nation alms and offerings. 18 As I was doing this, they found me purified in the temple, without any crowd or tumult. But some Jews from Asia— 19 they ought to be here before you and to make an accusation, if they have anything against me. 20 Or else let these men themselves say what wrongdoing they found when I stood before the council, 21 except this one thing which I cried out while standing among them, 'With respect to the resurrection of the dead I am on trial before you this day.' "

Paul answered each of the three charges: that he was a disturbing agitator, a ringleader of a sect, and one who attempted to profane

the temple (24: 5-6). He denied the charge that he was disturbing
the peace in Jerusalem. He had come to Jerusalem to worship
(v. 11) and to bring to his nation alms and offerings (v. 17).
"Alms" is presumably a reference to the fund collected for
Jerusalem; if so, this is the nearest Luke has come to mentioning
it. "Offerings" may refer to the ones in which Paul joined with
the four (21: 23). Of course Paul had not come to Jerusalem for
that purpose; Luke has probably condensed Paul's speech, omit-
ting the explanatory detail. Paul insists that he was not found
arguing or *collecting a crowd* (such the difficult phrase seems to
mean) in the temple, synagogue, or about the city (v. 12).

Paul acknowledged in part the second charge, but corrected
it at important points. He confessed that he shared in the "Way"
which the Jews called a "sect," but this Way was true Judaism.
In fact, as a follower of the Way he was a more loyal Jew than
his accusers. He worshipped the ancestral God—so the Way was
not a new religion—and he fully believed the Jewish scriptures
(v. 14). He shared in the hope of Israel and actually realized it
in terms of the resurrection. Of course the Sadducees would
reject this, and the Pharisees might not follow all the way about
the resurrection of "the just and the unjust."

The third charge, that he attempted to profane the temple,
was absurd. Paul pointed out that contrary to this he was found
"purified in the temple, without any crowd or tumult" (v. 18).
The tumult came from his opponents, Jews from Asia. Paul
perhaps started to say this; but because the charge was so false
and the "star witnesses" were absent, he broke off the sentence
and did not complete it. A close translation of verse 19 brings
out the emotion: "But certain ones from Asia, Jews—who ought
to be present before you and to accuse if anything they might
have against me." Even the Sanhedrin was unable to establish
a charge against him, except one that was theological, concerning
the resurrection (vs. 20f.).

Felix delays decision [24: 22-23]

> 22 But Felix, having a rather accurate knowledge of the Way, put
> them off, saying, "When Lysias the tribune comes down, I will
> decide your case." 23 Then he gave orders to the centurion that

he should be kept in custody but should have some liberty, and
that none of his friends should be prevented from attending to
his needs.

Felix reserved judgment on the grounds that more consideration or evidence was necessary.[95] His motives were doubtless
mixed, being both good and bad. Since Paul and his accusers
contradicted each other, there was some reason for awaiting the
arrival of Lysias. On the other hand, Felix was evidently convinced that Paul was not guilty of any crime with which his
court was concerned, but there were two reasons for continuing
to keep Paul in custody: he feared the Jews and he hoped for a
bribe from Paul. His confidence in Paul's innocency is reflected
in the liberty granted; Paul was probably chained to a soldier,
but otherwise free. His friends were to be unhindered in attending to his needs. Felix had some knowledge of the Way (v. 22).
This is often explained by the fact that his wife, Drusilla, was
a Jewess, but Felix had lived in Palestine long enough to have
learned about the movement first hand.

Two years of waiting [24: 24-27]

24 After some days Felix came with his wife Drusilla, who was a
Jewess; and he sent for Paul and heard him speak upon faith in
Christ Jesus. 25 And as he argued about justice and self-control
and future judgment, Felix was alarmed and said, "Go away for
the present; when I have an opportunity I will summon you."
26 At the same time he hoped that money would be given him by
Paul. So he sent for him often and conversed with him. 27 But
when two years had elapsed, Felix was succeeded by Porcius
Festus; and desiring to do the Jews a favor, Felix left Paul in
prison.

As already indicated, Drusilla was the third wife of Felix, and
he was her second husband. She was the daughter of Herod
Agrippa I, hence sister to Agrippa II and Bernice (see 25: 23).
According to Josephus, she was six years old at her father's death,
A.D. 44, so was born A.D. 38. In 53 she married Azizus, king of
Emesa, but soon left him for Felix. The two sisters were jealous
of each other's beauty and took advantage of each opportunity to
climb the social ladder. Paul's appearance before Felix and

---

[95] Cf. Lake and Cadbury, *Commentary*, p. 304.

Drusilla is fixed as *not earlier* than late 53, but how much later is not clear.

Paul's words about "justice, self-control, and future judgment" (v. 25) would have special point before this royal pair. "Self-control" is a better word than the familiar "temperance"; and the reference probably was to money as well as the flesh, considering the willingness of Felix to accept a bribe (v. 26). In the case of Drusilla, Paul's word about "self-control" could equally contemplate her vanity, jealousy, and social climbing. Made uncomfortable by Paul's preaching, Felix broke off the interview "for the present" and until he would have "spare time" (so the idioms seem to mean). His double concern for a bribe and to appease the Jews has already been observed. Since the Roman law against bribery was so widely violated, it does not necessarily follow that Felix thought Paul had access to a large amount of money, though the suggestion is plausible.

Josephus tells of growing tension in Caesarea between the Jews and Syrians, resulting in a serious riot. Felix sent his soldiers against the Jews. After his recall to Rome to answer for the riots, they pressed charges of misgovernment against him. This would account for his desire "to do the Jews a favor" at the time of his recall (v. 27).

Festus succeeded Felix possibly in 55 or 56, or even as late as 57 or 59. It is to be regretted that the data are confusing and at points (between Suetonius and Tacitus) contradictory. To begin with, Luke's statement that "two years had elapsed" is ambiguous (v. 27). It could mean two years after Paul was arrested or two years after Felix had taken office as procurator. According to Josephus (*Ant.* xx. 8. 9), when Felix was summoned to Rome, he was saved from complete ruin by the influence of his brother Pallas. Though Tacitus and Suetonius are in some disagreement, it seems that Pallas was repudiated by Nero in 55. (Nero owed his adoption into the family of Claudius, and hence his throne, to Pallas and could not endure a man to whom he was indebted.) It would follow that Felix was tried by Nero *before* Pallas lost power, hence the recall of Felix seems to have been early in 55. If Festus arrived in Caesarea immediately afterward, it would have been in the summer of 55. This would mean that Paul left Caesarea in the fall of 55 and arrived in Rome in the spring of 56. If the arrival of Festus was delayed, which is not improbable, these dates would be at least a year later, fixing Paul's arrival in Rome in the spring of 57 or 58.[96] Uncertainty follows at every point, however, for in 55, Pallas was cleared of the charges made against him (Tacitus, *Annals*, xiii, 13 and 23) and, because of his wealth, he probably continued to exercise considerable influence for some years. It is possible that he could have saved Felix after 55.[97] Then, too, the more certain dating of Gallio's proconsulship in Corinth, probably begun in July, 51, is to be reckoned with. To assume Paul's arrival in Rome in 57 barely leaves room for the intervening events; arrival in 58 would leave ample room.

Appeal to Caesar [25: 1-12]

1 Now when Festus had come into his province, after three days he went up to Jerusalem from Caesarea. 2 And the chief priests and the principal men of the Jews informed him against Paul; and they urged him, 3 asking as a favor to have the man sent to Jerusalem, planning an ambush to kill him on the way. 4 Festus replied that Paul was being kept at Caesarea, and that he himself intended to go there shortly. 5 "So," said he, "let the men of authority among you go down with me, and if there is anything wrong about the man, let them accuse him."

6 When he had stayed among them not more than eight or ten days, he went down to Caesarea; and the next day he took his seat on the tribunal and ordered Paul to be brought. 7 And when he had come, the Jews who had gone down from Jerusalem stood about him, bringing against him many serious charges which they could not prove. 8 Paul said in his defense, "Neither against the law of the Jews, nor against the temple, nor against Caesar have I offended at all." 9 But Festus, wishing to do the Jews a favor, said to Paul, "Do you wish to go up to Jerusalem, and there

---

[96] For discussion of this important but difficult problem of chronology, see Lake and Cadbury, *Additional Notes*, pp. 464ff.; John Knox, *Chapters in a Life of Paul*, pp. 47–88; and Emil Schürer, *A History of the Jewish People in the Time of Jesus Christ* (Eng. tr. New York: Charles Scribner's Sons, n.d.), I, ii, 174–184.

[97] Though this is not the place to debate the date and authorship of the Pastoral Epistles, and though the problem of the Pastorals should certainly not prejudice the dating of Paul's Roman imprisonment, the early dating would open up new possibilities for that problem. If Paul reached Rome by A.D. 57 or 58, there would be ample time for the events implied in the Pastorals *before* A.D. 64–65, the most likely date for Paul's death.

THE BOOK OF ACTS

be tried on these charges before me?" 10 But Paul said, "I am standing before Caesar's tribunal, where I ought to be tried; to the Jews I have done no wrong, as you know very well. 11 If then I am a wrongdoer, and have committed anything for which I deserve to die, I do not seek to escape death; but if there is nothing in their charges against me, no one can give me up to them. I appeal to Caesar." 12 Then Festus, when he had conferred with his council, answered, "You have appealed to Caesar; to Caesar you shall go."

Luke's main concern here is to show historically how Paul came to the decision to appeal to Rome. It was important from Luke's standpoint to establish the fact that the break between synagogue and church came from the side of the synagogue and that Paul in turning to the Gentiles did not purpose to turn from the Jews. Just as the Gospels and early apostolic preaching were forced to explain the Roman cross, so Luke feels compelled to explain Paul's Roman chain, and especially his appeal to Rome. Paul's innocency and his freedom from any disposition to turn against his own nation are brought out in the trials in Jerusalem and Caesarea, and in his interview with Jewish leaders in Rome. Luke is not interested in the trial of Paul as such, but in making it clear that the charges were pressed from the Jewish side rather than the Christian side. If this is recognized, it makes unnecessary all the debate about why Luke did not tell of the outcome of Paul's trial.

Festus is probably to be credited with an attempt at fairness to all. He was at a disadvantage as a Roman, puzzled by the strange interests and laws of the Jews. He was convinced that Paul was not guilty of criminal offense, yet Jewish rulers could hardly be ignored by a new procurator. But he cannot be cleared of the inference that he lacked courage to act decisively. Festus probably purposed to appease the Jews by conducting a trial in Jerusalem, as per their request, but at the same time to protect Paul by keeping the Jerusalem trial under his own control (v. 9). It is important to observe that Festus did not propose to turn Paul over to the Sanhedrin, but only to move the trial to Jerusalem. "Before me" is emphatic in the proposal of Festus (v. 9). Festus, as tension mounted, was doubtless happy to turn Paul over to a higher court in Rome and thus avoid the dilemma of either sacrificing an innocent man or offending the Jewish rulers. Paul's appeal to Caesar involves many problems for the exegete. Evidently the appeal in Paul's day was a blending of two ancient appeals, *provocatio* and *appellatio*. Under the Roman Republic, appeal could be made to the assembly of the people themselves against the decision of a magistrate of the people. This right of *provocatio* was provided for in a law of 509 B.C. The right was limited to Rome and a mile beyond its walls, but evidently was later extended throughout the Empire, though this cannot be conclusively demonstrated. *Appellatio* was another ancient Roman provision for justice. Under the constitution of the Roman Republic each magistrate had a colleague who could veto his decision. The tribune of the people also had the right to appeal the decision for a citizen. These two procedures, *provocatio* and *appellatio,* seem to have been combined when the republic gave way to the emperors.[98]

A further problem concerns Paul's intention in his appeal to Caesar. Did he actually ask to be sent to Rome or merely that his case continue as a Roman trial? It is possible that he was asking only for the latter, and that Festus, to escape his dilemma, gladly interpreted it as an appeal to the emperor at Rome. Luke, however, seems to represent this as an appeal to the emperor at Rome. His point is that, though Paul did appeal to Caesar, it was only as a last resort to which he was driven by the Jewish rulers and that he did not do so in order to accuse his nation.

Agrippa II and Bernice [25: 13-27]

13 Now when some days had passed, Agrippa the king and Bernice arrived at Caesarea to welcome Festus. 14 And as they stayed there many days, Festus laid Paul's case before the king, saying, "There is a man left prisoner by Felix; 15 and when I was at Jerusalem, the chief priests and the elders of the Jews gave information about him, asking for sentence against him. 16 I answered them that it was not the custom of the Romans to give up any one before the accused met the accusers face to face, and had opportunity to make his defense concerning the charge laid against him. 17 When there-

---

[98] For full discussion see Schürer, *op. cit.,* I, ii, 59f.; Lake and Cadbury, *Additional Notes,* pp. 312–319.

fore they came together here, I made no delay, but on the next day took my seat on the tribunal and ordered the man to be brought in. 18 When the accusers stood up, they brought no charge in his case of such evils as I supposed; 19 but they had certain points of dispute with him about their own superstition and about one Jesus, who was dead, but whom Paul asserted to be alive. 20 Being at a loss how to investigate these questions, I asked whether he wished to go to Jerusalem and be tried there regarding them. 21 But when Paul had appealed to be kept in custody for the decision of the emperor, I commanded him to be held until I could send him to Caesar." 22 And Agrippa said to Festus, "I should like to hear the man myself." "Tomorrow," said he, "you shall hear him."

23 So on the morrow Agrippa and Bernice came with great pomp, and they entered the audience hall with the military tribunes and the prominent men of the city. Then by command of Festus Paul was brought in. 24 And Festus said, "King Agrippa and all who are present with us, you see this man about whom the whole Jewish people petitioned me, both at Jerusalem and here, shouting that he ought not to live any longer. 25 But I found that he had done nothing deserving death; and as he himself appealed to the emperor, I decided to send him. 26 But I have nothing definite to write to my lord about him. Therefore I have brought him before you, and especially before you, King Agrippa, that, after we have examined him, I may have something to write. 27 For it seems to me unreasonable, in sending a prisoner, not to indicate the charges against him."

Agrippa II, Bernice, and Drusilla were the children of Agrippa I, and great grandchildren of Herod the Great. They were pro-Roman and maintained a close relationship with the imperial family. Agrippa II was born A.D. 27 and spent much of his youth in Rome. He was seventeen when his father died (A.D. 44), and the Emperor Claudius was persuaded not to give him his father's throne. When Herod, King of Chalcis, died, his kingdom was given to Agrippa II; and with it the latter received the authority for appointing the high priests and controlling the temple. In 53 he was given the title of king along with Batanea, Gaulonitis, Trachonitis, and Abila, in exchange for Chalcis. At this time he moved his residence from Rome to Palestine.

Bernice (formerly spelled Berenice) was married to her uncle, Herod, King of Chalcis. When he died (A.D. 48) she joined her brother at Rome, and it was believed that they lived in incest.

She then married Polemon, King of Cilicia, but soon left him to return to her brother. They were probably living in incest when Paul appeared before them, but Luke had no disposition to exploit their scandals. Later she lived with Titus as his mistress until he became Emperor; public opinion was then too strong to permit the scandal to continue.

Though Agrippa II and Bernice were pro-Roman, they did have an interest in the Jews and often served their interests. They often played the difficult role of trying to reconcile the Jews and Romans. They sought to turn the Jews from war with Rome, and through the war they remained faithful to the Romans.

Agrippa II was just the man Festus needed, for Agrippa had a good understanding of Jewish affairs (cf. v. 26). Festus briefed him on the case, confessing that he was "at a loss" to understand the point of the quarrel between Paul and his accusers (v. 20). Festus did not call the religion of the Jews a "superstition" as the translation suggests (v. 19). The term corresponds to the one used by Paul at Athens (17: 22), and it is probably best translated "religion." Further evidence is given that Paul continued to make the issue primarily that of the resurrection (v. 19).

Verse 22 poses a problem in translation, but possibly should read: "I myself was wishing to hear the man." Probably it is best to recognize a polite idiom here and translate it: "I was just wishing to hear the man myself." [99] It is not improbable that Agrippa had already heard of Paul. This is further evidence of the extent to which Jews and Romans were feeling the impact of the Christian movement.

In addition to an honest desire for help in formulating the statement which must accompany the prisoner to Rome, Festus welcomed the opportunity to improve relations with Agrippa. The puppet king had only such powers as were granted by the Romans, so he made much of "pomp" or brilliant display. Festus even went so far as to yield the "bench" to Agrippa for this audience with Paul. This was not a real trial; it was an audience given for the dual purpose of honoring Agrippa (and Bernice)

---

[99] Cf. A. T. Robertson, *A Grammar of the Greek New Testament in the Light of Historical Research* (fourth edition; New York: George H. Doran Co., 1923) pp. 918f.

and securing information for the letter to Rome. Agrippa and Bernice entered with royal apparel and an escort of the notables of Caesarea. There they were with all their "pomp"—and their incest; and before them Paul stood with his chains (26: 29)! Fortunately, heaven reverses many of earth's evaluations.

Luke's chief interest is probably served by the statement of Festus: "But I found that he had done nothing deserving death ... I have nothing definite to write my lord about him" (vs. 25f.).

Paul's defense before Agrippa [26: 1-23]

1 Agrippa said to Paul, "You have permission to speak for yourself." Then Paul stretched out his hand and made his defense:

2 "I think myself fortunate that it is before you, King Agrippa, I am to make my defense today against all the accusations of the Jews, 3 because you are especially familiar with all customs and controversies of the Jews; therefore I beg you to listen to me patiently.

4 "My manner of life from my youth, spent from the beginning among my own nation and at Jerusalem, is known by all the Jews. 5 They have known for a long time, if they are willing to testify, that according to the strictest party of our religion I have lived as a Pharisee. 6 And now I stand here on trial for hope in the promise made by God to our fathers, 7 to which our twelve tribes hope to attain, as they earnestly worship night and day. And for this hope I am accused by Jews, O king! 8 Why is it thought incredible by any of you that God raises the dead?

9 "I myself was convinced that I ought to do many things in opposing the name of Jesus of Nazareth. 10 And I did so in Jerusalem; I not only shut up many of the saints in prison, by authority from the chief priests, but when they were put to death I cast my vote against them. 11 And I punished them often in all the synagogues and tried to make them blaspheme; and in raging fury against them, I persecuted them even to foreign cities.

12 "Thus I journeyed to Damascus with the authority and commission of the chief priests. 13 At midday, O king, I saw on the way a light from heaven, brighter than the sun, shining round me and those who journeyed with me. 14 And when we had all fallen to the ground, I heard a voice saying to me in the Hebrew language, 'Saul, Saul, why do you persecute me? It hurts you to kick against the goads.' 15 And I said, 'Who are you, Lord?' And the Lord said, 'I am Jesus whom you are persecuting. 16 But rise and stand upon your feet; for I have appeared to you for this purpose, to appoint you to serve and bear witness to the things in which you have seen me and to those in which I will appear to you, 17 delivering you from the people and from the Gentiles—to whom I send you

18 to open their eyes, that they may turn from darkness to light and from the power of Satan to God, that they may receive forgiveness of sins and a place among those who are sanctified by faith in me.'

19 "Wherefore, O King Agrippa, I was not disobedient to the heavenly vision, 20 but declared first to those at Damascus, then at Jerusalem and throughout all the country of Judea, and also to the Gentiles, that they should repent and turn to God and perform deeds worthy of their repentance. 21 For this reason the Jews seized me in the temple and tried to kill me. 22 To this day I have had the help that comes from God, and so I stand here testifying both to small and great, saying nothing but what the prophets and Moses said would come to pass: 23 that the Christ must suffer, and that, by being the first to rise from the dead, he would proclaim light both to the people and to the Gentiles."

Paul was not compelled to speak, having appealed to Caesar, but he welcomed the opportunity to testify before this most influential group. It was not a trial; Festus was not asking for advice about the merit of the charges against Paul or Paul's appeal to Caesar. He had already declared Paul's innocency and his purpose to send him to Rome (25:25ff.). As already stated, he combined two objectives in honoring Agrippa and seeking his help in formulating a statement to Caesar. Paul's address was a defense for his own life and ministry but more so a defense for *the gospel of a suffering and risen Christ proclaimed as light for Jews and Gentiles* (26:23).

Paul did not falsify or indulge in mere flattery in addressing Agrippa. He had reason to rejoice in the opportunity of stating the case for himself and Christianity before the highest official among the Jews. This was especially important in view of the fact that Agrippa did understand Jewish customs and controversies. The Herods may have been depraved but they were not asleep. For all their cruelty and lust, their power exerted among Jews and Romans is amazing.

After the acknowledgment of Agrippa, Paul's address developed the following points: (1) his thorough Judaism (vs. 4-11); (2) his conversion, which could be accounted for only in terms of divine intervention (vs. 12-15); (3) his commission to Jews and Gentiles (vs. 16-18); (4) his life in obedience to God,

leading to his arrest (vs. 19-21); and (5) his climactic statement
of the gospel of the suffering-risen Christ, true to Moses and the
prophets and proclaimed as light to "the people" and the
Gentiles (vs. 22-23).

His thorough Judaism, he affirmed, could be recognized by
all who were willing to see it (vs. 4ff.). None could deny that he
had lived according to the strictest party of their religion, as a
Pharisee (v. 5). His present hope was no innovation but the
very hope of Israel. This hope was not a mere sectarian hope, but
was the "twelve-tribe" hope, the hope of all Israel (v. 7). With
suppressed irony he stated the almost unbelievable turn of events:
"And *for this hope* I am accused *by Jews,* O King!" Emotion
mastered Paul for the moment as he faced again this almost incredible fact that Jews, of all people, could be so blind to the
realization of their historic hope. Again, Paul based the whole
issue on the fact of the resurrection (v. 8).

It has been said that Paul evaded the real charge, which concerned the temple. But Paul is simply getting back to that which
underlies his conflict with his people. Nothing short of his conviction that he saw the risen Christ caused him to break with the
very position of his opponents. Could they but share with him
in that experience, all their conflicts would be resolved. The
mission to the Gentiles, so offensive to them, would never have
been endorsed by Paul except for his encounter with the risen
Christ. The exchange of roles, from persecutor to persecuted, was
not otherwise to be explained.

Paul gave further evidence of his thorough Judaism in terms
of his zeal, sincere though misguided, when he persecuted the
followers of Jesus (vs. 9-11). His words here indicate a more
serious persecution than is elsewhere indicated. His statement
that he "cast his vote" does not settle the question as to whether
or not he was a member of the Sanhedrin. The expression could
be used for official or unofficial action.

"Conversion" is not too strong a term for Paul's Damascus
experience (vs. 12-15). What happened there reversed his whole
life and is not to be explained except in the light of an encounter
with the risen Christ. Full allowance should be made for the

"goads" against which he kicked (v. 14). Certainly Paul's conversion did not take place in a vacuum; many forces and factors helped condition him for the conversion experience (see above, p. 110).[100] Tensions were doubtless set up within him even as a boy in Tarsus, where the exclusiveness and advantages of his family were likely to elicit taunts of "Jew boy" from others of the city. Further tensions were probably experienced at Jerusalem as his sensitive nature may have unconsciously resisted the superficialities and artificialities in the tradition in which he was schooled. Possible tension could result from Jewish and Roman conflicts; young Saul took pride in both his citizenships, but they sometimes were opposed to each other. Then there were in all likelihood unacknowledged misgivings as he dealt with Stephen and his kind. The mad zeal with which he sought to destroy the Way was itself a symptom of an uneasy conscience. To recognize in Saul both sincerity and "goads" against which he kicked is possible and can be verified by anyone who looks back on a liberation which he himself has experienced. A maturing Christian of the white race may recall with pain the days he sincerely believed what he had been taught, that the Negro should be "kept in his place," and at the same time struggled with principles which contradicted his narrow prejudices. Chapter seven of Romans probably reflects some of Paul's pre-conversion struggle.

In his commission (vs. 16-18) Paul was told to witness to what he had seen and would see. He was also informed that the mission would throw him into such relationship with "the people" (Jews) and with Gentiles that there would be occasions for "rescue" from each (v. 17). His commission was "to open their eyes, that they may turn from darkness to light and from the power of Satan to God, that they may receive forgiveness of sins and a place

---

[100] There are many excellent studies of Paul, including his conversion experience. Cf. Elias Andrews, *The Meaning of Christ for Paul* (New York: Abingdon-Cokesbury Press, 1949); Adolf Deissmann, *Paul, A Study in Social and Religious History* (London: Hodder and Stoughton, 1926); W. D. Davies, *Paul and Rabbinic Judaism* (London: S.P.C.K., 1948); E. J. Goodspeed, *Paul* (Philadelphia: J. C. Winston Co., 1947); W. L. Knox, *St. Paul and the Church of the Gentiles* (Cambridge: Cambridge U. Press, 1939); J. G. Machen, *The Origin of Paul's Religion* (London: Hodder & Stoughton, 1921); D. W. Riddle, *Paul, Man of Conflict* (Nashville: Abingdon-Cokesbury Press, 1940); James A. Stewart, *A Man in Christ*, (New York: Harper & Bros., 1935); and Hugh J. Schonfield, *The Jew of Tarsus* (N. Y.: The Macmillan Co., 1947).

among those who are consecrated by faith" in Jesus (v. 18). This
verse is usually understood to refer to the Gentiles, but there is
no reason why all of it cannot refer equally to Jews and Gentiles.
This interpretation would better suit the viewpoint of Acts and
Paul's own interpretation of his ministry.

It was precisely in obeying this commission that Paul came to
his arrest (vs. 19-21). It is important from Luke's standpoint, as
well as Paul's, to register this fact. True Judaism survived in this
mission, not in that of its opponents.

A minor problem arises from Paul's statement that he preached
"throughout all the country of Judea" (v. 20). Taken literally,
this verse cannot be harmonized with Galatians 1 : 22. There is a
possible textual disturbance, or some datum may be lacking to
the exegete.

Paul's summary statement is his climax as he reaffirms that
he is preaching nothing at all but what was anticipated by Moses
and the prophets, that the Messiah must suffer and arise and
thus provide light for both Jews and Gentiles (vs. 22f.). There
is no evidence that first century Jews expected or wanted a
suffering Messiah, but the role of suffering was not overlooked
by the prophets. The inclusion of the Gentiles in God's purpose
to save was also seen by his prophets. Paul insists that his emphasis
upon a suffering Saviour, the resurrection, and the Gentile mission is in the tradition of ancient and true prophetic Judaism.

Paul presses Agrippa for commitment [26: 24-29]

> 24 And as he thus made his defense, Festus said with a loud voice,
> "Paul, you are mad; your great learning is turning you mad."
> 25 But Paul said, "I am not mad, most excellent Festus, but I am
> speaking the sober truth. 26 For the king knows about these things,
> and to him I speak freely; for I am persuaded that none of these
> things has escaped his notice, for this was not done in a corner.
> 27 King Agrippa, do you believe the prophets? I know that you
> believe." 28 And Agrippa said to Paul, "In a short time you think
> to make me a Christian!" 29 And Paul said, "Whether short or
> long, I would to God that not only you but also all who hear
> me this day might become such as I am—except for these chains."

Festus found the whole controversy and discussion confusing,
and especially was he puzzled by Paul's reference to Jews' and

Gentiles' being enlightened by a suffering Christ who arose from the dead (v. 23). This was too much for him and he, "with the voice loud," said, "Paul, you are mad; your great learning is turning you mad" (v. 24). Because the Greek word for "mania" or "madness' is related to the Greek word for "prophet" or "inspired person," some suggest that Festus' remark was not offensive, but may have represented Paul's speech as being inspired.[101] Certainly, the word could suggest either madness or inspiration, and for Festus the two ideas would be closely related.

Paul's reply, however, makes it clear that Festus did not mean simply that Paul was inspired; he meant that Paul was not fully rational. Paul protested that what he had to say about the resurrection was sober truth. He then turned back to Agrippa, with whom he was naturally more concerned than with Festus, and pressed him for a commitment. He directed his question to Agrippa in such a manner that it was difficult to evade. Agrippa dared not say that he did not believe the prophets (v. 27), and he did not want to be drawn into a personal endorsement of Paul, who at the very time was pressing the claims of the gospel. Agrippa showed typical Herodian shrewdness by evading a most difficult question; and in so doing, he left a puzzle which the exegetes to this day have not solved.

We do not know exactly what Agrippa said or meant in his reply to Paul (v. 28). The Authorized Version's familiar translation, "Almost thou persuadest me to be a Christian," is indefensible; but to say exactly what Agrippa meant is beyond our knowledge. To begin with, the manuscripts do not agree at two points. The strongest evidence by far favors "to make" rather than "to become." It may be almost positively assumed that the phrase was "to make a Christian," but this is capable of two ideas. Does it mean "to act the part of a Christian" or "to convert another (Festus) into a Christian"?

The mood of the verb for "persuade" differs in the manuscripts, and that has bearing on the translation. Then, too, the phrase which literally reads "in a little" (the erroneous "almost" of the AV) may actually mean any one of several things: "briefly,"

---

[101] Cf. Foakes-Jackson, *The Acts of the Apostles*, p. 226; Bruce, *op. cit.*, p. 448.

"in a little while," "with a little effort." Agrippa's statement, then, could be: "In brief, you are persuading me to play the Christian." Again, it could mean: "In brief, you are persuading me to make a Christian," that is, to help convert Festus. Whatever the meaning of Agrippa, Paul considered it an evasion; and he became yet bolder in affirming his yearning that all might become as he—except for the chains.

Festus and Agrippa agree as to Paul's innocence [26 : 30-32]

> 30 Then the king rose, and the governor and Bernice and those who were sitting with them; 31 and when they had withdrawn, they said to one another, "This man is doing nothing to deserve death or imprisonment." 32 And Agrippa said to Festus, "This man could have been set free if he had not appealed to Caesar."

Paul had turned so completely preacher and evangelist that the dignitaries were glad to terminate the audience. In their conference, however, they agreed that Paul was not guilty and deserved to be released. Their only reason for keeping him in custody was that he had appealed to Caesar. Either Roman law was such that once the appeal was made the trial had to proceed, or Festus simply took refuge in that conclusion to avoid alienating the Jews by the release of Paul. More important than those considerations to Luke was the fact that now Festus, Agrippa, and Lysias had all affirmed Paul's innocence.

Journey to Rome: Pre-eminence of a Prisoner [27: 1 to 28: 16]

The fascinating story of the journey to Rome is primarily the story of Paul. The exciting and intriguing account of the storm and shipwreck can easily become an end in itself, and Luke was certainly absorbed in the interesting narrative of experiences in which he shared; but the center of interest is never there, even for Luke.[102] Though Luke's obvious fascination for the sea and his interest in nautical details must not be minimized, one should see that the constant interest is in Paul.

---

[102] It is generally agreed that the outstanding work in English on this chapter is *The Voyage and Shipwreck of St. Paul,* by James Smith (4th edition, 1880). Also see Lake and Cadbury, *Commentary, in loc.* No attempt will be made by this writer to deal with all of the numerous nautical terms and factors in the chapter.

Even as a prisoner, Paul was pre-eminent. With his chain he towered above the centurion, shipowner, crew, and natives of an island, even as he had towered above Festus and Agrippa. Rejected by his own nation, he was received by Romans and simple island natives, as well as by his many Christian friends along the way. When the storm made artificial distinctions in rank and office of no importance, the sheer force of Paul's personality made him the central figure. Though by status a prisoner, he was by his deep faith, strong courage, and experienced wisdom, the one to whom all were compelled to look for their very lives.

Though it is not to be suggested as a part of Luke's purpose, one can hardly resist the thought that this whole section provides a good picture of Paul's life and ministry. His entire ministry was a stormy one; he was often repudiated; he was often in a mood of depression; but his far-reaching decisions were amply vindicated by subsequent history.

Caesarea to Fair Havens [27: 1-8]

1 And when it was decided that we should sail for Italy, they delivered Paul and some other prisoners to a centurion of the Augustan Cohort, named Julius. 2 And embarking in a ship of Adramyttium, which was about to sail to the ports along the coast of Asia, we put to sea, accompanied by Aristarchus, a Macedonian from Thessalonica. 3 The next day we put in at Sidon; and Julius treated Paul kindly, and gave him leave to go to his friends and be cared for. 4 And putting to sea from there we sailed under the lee of Cyprus, because the winds were against us. 5 And when we had sailed across the sea which is off Cilicia and Pamphylia, we came to Myra in Lycia. 6 There the centurion found a ship of Alexandria sailing for Italy, and put us on board. 7 We sailed slowly for a number of days, and arrived with difficulty off Cnidus, and as the wind did not allow us to go on, we sailed under the lee of Crete off Salmone. 8 Coasting along it with difficulty, we came to a place called Fair Havens, near which was the city of Lasea.

The first person reappears in the narrative, indicating the presence of Luke. The capacity in which he was included is not disclosed. He may have been a prisoner or may have been an attendant upon Paul, possibly as his physician. It is unlikely that he would have been given passage except for some special reason.

There is evidence that Aristarchus was a prisoner. An Aristarchus was Paul's "fellow prisoner" when he wrote to the Colossians (4: 10), but he was called "fellow worker" in Philemon 24 and was seemingly distinguished from the prisoner Epaphras (Philemon 23). Julius secured passage for the group on a coasting vessel as far as Myra and then on a grain ship going from Alexandria to Italy. The kindness with which he treated Paul is further evidence that in the eyes of the Romans he was not guilty.

Paul's advice rejected [27: 9-12]

9 As much time had been lost, and the voyage was already dangerous because the fast had already gone by, Paul advised them, 10 saying, "Sirs, I perceive that the voyage will be with injury and much loss, not only of the cargo and the ship, but also of our lives." 11 But the centurion paid more attention to the captain and to the owner of the ship than to what Paul said. 12 And because the harbor was not suitable to winter in, the majority advised to put to sea from there, on the chance that somehow they could reach Phoenix, a harbor of Crete, looking northeast and southeast, and winter there.

Sailing was unsafe from September 14 until November 11, at which time it was suspended until the end of winter. The "fast" (v. 9) was the Jewish day of Atonement, which fell near the end of September or the beginning of October, varying from year to year. The mention of this fast in a setting so un–Jewish suggests that Paul must have observed it at Fair Havens. If so, this is another evidence that Paul had no disposition to break with Judaism as he now conceived of it.

The voyage to this point had consumed much more time than anticipated, because of unfavorable winds. The men in charge of the ship agreed to give up the idea of reaching Italy before winter but were divided over the harbor in which to winter. Paul was overruled by the centurion, who seemed to have the final word. Fair Havens was merely a small bay, almost open to the sea; and the nearest town, Lasea, was apparently an insignificant place. The majority, including the ship captain and owner, perferred to risk reaching Phoenix with its harbor "looking down the southwest and northwest winds."

The Euraquilo: all hope abandoned [27: 13-20]

13 And when the south wind blew gently, supposing that they had obtained their purpose, they weighed anchor and sailed along Crete, close inshore. 14 But soon a tempestuous wind, called the northeaster, struck down from the land; 15 and when the ship was caught and could not face the wind, we gave way to it and were driven. 16 And running under the lee of a small island called Cauda, we managed with difficulty to secure the boat; 17 after hoisting it up, they took measures to undergird the ship; then, fearing that they should run on the Syrtis, they lowered the gear, and so were driven. 18 As we were violently storm-tossed, they began next day to throw the cargo overboard; 19 and the third day they cast out with their own hands the tackle of the ship. 20 And when neither sun nor stars appeared for many a day, and no small tempest lay on us, all hope of our being saved was at last abandoned.

The gentle south wind seemed to confirm the judgment of those in charge, so they tried to coast along, close to shore. Though the name is found here only, Euraquilo evidently was the name of the northeast wind. This storm suddenly swept down upon them and they were at its mercy until driven under the lee of Cauda. This small island afforded some protection, and while drifting by it they hoisted the small boat (which was usually towed) and reinforced the hull of the ship by "frapping" it, that is, by undergirding it with cables (or canvass?). The Syrtis, or quicksands off the coast of Africa near Cyrene, presented a great danger, so they "lowered the gear" and "were driven" (v. 17). This could mean that they used a minimum of sail so as to head as near the wind as possible. Cargo and tackle (evidently extra sails and other equipment) were thrown overboard during the next two days (vs. 18f.). As serious as the wind, was their inability to know where they were. Having no compass or other mechanical device, ancient seamen were dependent upon the sun and stars for navigation. Hope for their lives was abandoned.

Paul in command: shipwreck and deliverance [27: 21-44]

21 As they had been long without food, Paul then came forward among them and said, "Men, you should have listened to me, and should not have set sail from Crete and incurred this injury and

loss. 22 I now bid you take heart; for there will be no loss of life among you, but only of the ship. 23 For this very night there stood by me an angel of the God to whom I belong and whom I worship, 24 and he said, 'Do not be afraid, Paul; you must stand before Caesar; and lo, God has granted you all those who sail with you.' 25 So take heart, men, for I have faith in God that it will be exactly as I have been told. 26 But we shall have to run on some island."

27 When the fourteenth night had come, as we were drifting across the sea of Adria, about midnight the sailors suspected that they were nearing land. 28 So they sounded and found twenty fathoms; a little farther on they sounded again and found fifteen fathoms. 29 And fearing that we might run on the rocks, they let out four anchors from the stern, and prayed for day to come. 30 And as the sailors were seeking to escape from the ship, and had lowered the boat into the sea, under pretense of laying out anchors from the bow, 31 Paul said to the centurion and the soldiers, "Unless these men stay in the ship, you cannot be saved." 32 Then the soldiers cut away the ropes of the boat, and let it go.

33 As day was about to dawn, Paul urged them all to take some food, saying, "Today is the fourteenth day that you have continued in suspense and without food, having taken nothing. 34 Therefore I urge you to take some food; it will give you strength, since not a hair is to perish from the head of any of you." 35 And when he had said this, he took bread, and giving thanks to God in the presence of all he broke it and began to eat. 36 Then they all were encouraged and ate some food themselves. 37 (We were in all two hundred and seventy-six persons in the ship.) 38 And when they had eaten enough, they lightened the ship, throwing out the wheat into the sea.

39 Now when it was day, they did not recognize the land, but they noticed a bay with a beach, on which they planned if possible to bring the ship ashore. 40 So they cast off the anchors and left them in the sea, at the same time loosening the ropes that tied the rudders; then hoisting the foresail to the wind they made for the beach. 41 But striking a shoal they ran the vessel aground; the bow struck and remained immovable, and the stern was broken up by the surf. 42 The soldiers' plan was to kill the prisoners, lest any should swim away and escape; 43 but the centurion wishing to save Paul, kept them from carrying out their purpose. He ordered those who could swim to throw themselves overboard first and make for the land, 44 and the rest on planks or on pieces of the ship. And so it was that all escaped to land.

Precisely when all hope was abandoned did Paul rise most fully to the occasion. From this point on he dominated the scene, not by deliberate choice of himself or of the others, but simply because he was the biggest man among them. For all Paul's greatness, he was also frail; he could not resist saying, "I told you so." Because of a special revelation Paul was able to modify his earlier statement in which he had predicted the loss of lives as well as cargo and ship (cf. v. 10). He now gave repeated assurance that if they would all stick together, none would perish (vs. 22, 24, 34, 44). With his assurance that all could be saved, he had the conviction that he must stand before Caesar (v. 24).

During the fourteenth night the seamen detected that "land was nearing them" (so they stated it). It is generally accepted that it was what is now called St. Paul's Bay that they were entering, and the breakers from the point of Koura could be heard. They were in the Adriatic Sea, which was distinguished from the Adriatic Gulf. The sailors selfishly sought to escape in the small boat, but Paul detected their scheme and warned the centurion and soldiers. These sailors would be needed in handling the ship, so the lives of all would be endangered by their desertion. The soldiers acted hastily by cutting loose the boat and permitting it to fall off into the sea. In so doing they prevented the escape of the sailors, but also deprived the men of a much-needed boat. It does not follow that Paul intended for the soldiers to cut loose the boat; he may have intended only that their desertion be frustrated. Had the boat not been lost, it may have been possible for them to have gotten to shore by relays in it, and hence to have saved the ship (at least until another storm struck).

Paul's courage and open faith was good for their morale, and he finally succeeded in getting them to eat (vs. 33-36). After eating, they threw out the wheat that remained in the ship; some had been jettisoned earlier (v. 18). The manuscripts differ as to the number on the ship, but probably the larger number, two hundred seventy-six, is to be preferred over seventy-six as given by the Vatican manuscript and the Sahidic version. There is nothing improbable about this large number. Josephus (*Life*, 3) tells of a voyage to Rome in which his ship "was drowned," and along with only eighty out of about six hundred, he survived.

After the ship had been grounded on a shoal, the soldiers matched the earlier selfishness of the sailors. Since they were responsible for the prisoners, they planned to kill them rather

than risk the forfeit of their own lives, should they escape. Whatever his reason, Julius was willing to risk the escape of the
prisoners in order to save Paul. Gratitude or a sense of dependence could account for his action. Some swam to shore and some
reached there by planks (made into rafts?). It has been suggested
that the planks had been used to hold the cargo in place. The
Greek is ambiguous in saying: "and some upon certain of the
(things or people) from the boat" (v. 44). It is impossible (and
inconsequential) to know whether Luke meant that some reached
shore by floating on "things" from the ship or by the help of
some who could swim.

Kindness on Malta [28: 1-10]

1 After we had escaped, we then learned that the island was called
Malta. 2 And the natives showed us unusual kindness, for they
kindled a fire and welcomed us all, because it had begun to rain
and was cold. 3 Paul had gathered a bundle of sticks and put them
on the fire, when a viper came out because of the heat and fastened
on his hand. 4 When the natives saw the creature hanging from his
hand, they said to one another, "No doubt this man is a murderer.
Though he has escaped from the sea, justice has not allowed him
to live." 5 He, however, shook off the creature into the fire and
suffered no harm. 6 They waited, expecting him to swell up or
suddenly fall down dead; but when they had waited a long time
and saw no misfortune come to him, they changed their minds
and said that he was a god.
7 Now in the neighborhood of that place were lands belonging to
the chief man of the island, named Publius, who received us and
entertained us hospitably for three days. 8 It happened that the
father of Publius lay sick with fever and dysentery; and Paul
visited him and prayed, and putting his hands on him healed him.
9 And when this had taken place, the rest of the people on the
island who had diseases also came and were cured. 10 They presented many gifts to us; and when we sailed, they put on board
whatever we needed.

Kindness was mutual on Malta (Melita) as the refugees were
received with more than ordinary hospitality and as they im-
parted such benefits as were at their command. The natives are
termed "barbarians" in the Greek, but with no disparagement;
it was simply a designation for those who did not speak Greek.
These natives gave immediate relief (v. 2), temporary accom-

modations (v. 7), and parting gifts (v. 10). Extraordinary kindness (the Greek word is "philanthropy") from these natives stands in sharp contrast with the "chosen people" who tried to murder Paul as they assumed the role of protectors of God and the temple. Their kindness stands in just as sharp contrast with the madness of the earlier Saul of Tarsus. It is an embarrassment to many that kindness is often found in the "unchurched" and strangely lacking in the religiously zealous.

Luke's story about the viper (v. 3) has been doubted on the grounds that there are no poisonous snakes on Malta. This is true now, but it does not follow that there were none in Paul's time. Moreover, the Greek word leaves open the question of whether or not this snake was poisonous, though obviously the natives thought it was. (Mark 16: 18 is recognized by all textual critics to be a late addition to Mark's Gospel, and it was probably influenced by this verse.) If the snake was poisonous, then obviously Luke treated this as a miracle. The natives probably saw Paul's chains, and they concluded that he was a murderer. They possibly had deified "Justice" as a goddess whom they expected to bring about Paul's death. When Paul showed no signs of harm they reversed their opinion, concluding that he was a god.

Publius may have been the the representative of the Roman government or a native. Inscriptions have been found bearing the very title, "the chief man," but with no indication as to whether this was a public office or simply a complimentary title. That is of no importance, but his generous hospitality is of major importance. The healings correspond to those in more primitive days in Palestine. As a physician Luke may have rendered medical service, but there is no hint of this in the text; the healings were miraculous.

Rome at last [28: 11-16]

11 After three months we set sail in a ship which had wintered in the island, a ship of Alexandria, with the Twin Brothers as figurehead. 12 Putting in at Syracuse, we stayed there for three days. 13 And from there we made a circuit and arrived at Rhegium; and after one day a south wind sprang up, and on the second day we came to Puteoli. 14 There we found brethren, and were invited to

stay with them for seven days. And so we came to Rome. 15 And
the brethren there, when they heard of us, came as far as the
Forum of Appius and Three Taverns to meet us. On seeing them
Paul thanked God and took courage. 16 And when we came into
Rome, Paul was allowed to stay by himself, with the soldier that
guarded him.

The "Twin Brothers" were Castor and Pollux, patron gods of
sailors. The ship bearing this figurehead had wintered in Malta.
All would be eager to set sail as soon as the season permitted, but
Paul probably had both hopes and fears as he realized that at
last he was nearing Rome. His fears would not be in terms of
the Roman courts but of Jewish and Christian reaction to his
presence. Christians were found at Puteoli, the port of Rome and
about 140 miles from Rome. How long the Christian community
had been there or how many Christian congregations there were
in Italy or in Rome itself is not known. Paul's letter to the
Romans, some years earlier, leaves the impression that there were
several congregations in Rome and that Christianity was so well
established there that Paul took great care to avoid any appearance of being missionary to them.

Two Christian parties met Paul, one at the Forum of Appius,
about forty miles from Rome, and one at the Three Taverns,
about thirty miles from Rome. These probably represented
different congregations. They were perhaps notified of Paul's
approach by messengers from Puteoli. This gesture of fellowship
did much for Paul, giving him new courage.

Paul was probably delivered over by Julius to the praetorian
prefect. At this time the prefect was Afranius Burrus (A.D. 51-62),
one of the nobler Romans. Nero was emperor, but for his first
five years his depravity was chiefly expressed in his private life,
the affairs of state being left for the most part to Burrus and
Seneca. The honesty of Burrus, along with the favorable communication from Festus, and possibly with some local Christian influence, made it possible for Paul to live in private quarters. He
was, of course, in custody of a soldier at all times, to whom he was
seemingly bound with a chain (28: 20). The Western text indicates that Paul stayed outside the barracks.

CONCLUSION: JEWISH SELF-EXCLUSION AND
THE GOSPEL UNHINDERED [28: 17-31]

No PART OF Luke's two volumes is more carefully or effectively
planned than the conclusion. Most of the commentaries, Rackham's being the outstanding exception, are miserably weak at
this point. Typical final paragraphs on a negative note are to be
deplored. Endless debates about Luke's "unsatisfactory conclusion" reflect a strange blindness to his studied purpose. How
could one improve on this dramatic and climactic summary of
the issues with which he—and Christianity—was most concerned:
the self-exclusion of the Jews because of the Gentile inclusion and
the Gospel boldly preached—unhindered!

Paul's Defense Before Roman Jews [28: 17-22]

17 After three days he called together the local leaders of the Jews;
and when they had gathered, he said to them, "Brethren, though
I had done nothing against the people or the customs of our fathers, yet I was delivered prisoner from Jerusalem into the hands
of the Romans. 18 When they had examined me, they wished to
set me at liberty, because there was no reason for the death penalty
in my case. 19 But when the Jews objected, I was compelled to
appeal to Caesar—though I had no charge to bring against my
nation. 20 For this reason therefore I have asked to see you and
speak with you, since it is because of the hope of Israel that I am
bound with this chain." 21 And they said to him, "We have received no letters from Judea about you, and none of the brethren
coming here has reported or spoken any evil about you. 22 But we
desire to hear from you what your views are; for with regard to this
sect we know that everywhere it is spoken against."

Paul's anxiety about Roman Christians was relieved by the two
groups which came out to meet him on the way (v. 15). His other
anxiety was over the Roman Jews, and he lost little time in
establishing contact with their leaders. His first concern was to
make it clear that he had not been untrue to his nation, that the
Romans had found him innocent, and that he himself had no
charges to make against his nation (vs. 17-19). Paul at no time
desired to be alienated from his people. He repeated his insistence that his Christianity was thorough Judaism; the hope of

Israel, its regeneration, could be realized only in the risen Christ (v. 20).

The Roman Jews viewed Christianity as a sect, and they professed to have little certain knowledge about it, as is implied by their desire to hear Paul's version of it. Evidently the synagogue and the church were already separate in Rome; the expulsion edict of Claudius may have precipitated the separation. It is understandable that no direct charges had reached them from the Jerusalem Jews. There was not only the problem of distance, but that of delicate relationship with the Romans. One who was unsuccessful in prosecuting a case in a Roman court jeopardized himself. (Strange it is that in legal as well as in theological controversies the accusers who are proved to be wrong in their charges are in most circles simply permitted to drop the charges. If one falsely accuses another of being criminal or heretical, why does it not follow that the accuser is criminal or heretical?) To her credit, Rome did not tolerate the disposition to make unfounded charges. Having failed before Felix and Festus, the Jerusalem Jews may have feared to press the case in Rome.

Had Peter been in Rome, it is strange that the Roman Jews would need to turn to Paul for an authentic word about this "sect" that was everywhere spoken against (v. 22). A strong case can be made for the martyrdom of Peter at Rome after the fire which destroyed the city (July 19, 64), but all of the evidences are against the theory that he had been in Rome prior to Paul's arrival. Roman Christianity evidently started without any apostolic leadership. Peter may have rallied Roman Christians after the initial persecution under Nero, and thus have won the name of "founder." [103]

One Statement and Self-Exclusion [28: 23-28]

23 When they had appointed a day for him, they came to him at his lodging in great numbers. And he expounded the matter to them from morning till evening, testifying to the kingdom of God and trying to convince them about Jesus both from the law of Moses and from the prophets. 24 And some were convinced by what he said, while others disbelieved. 25 So, as they disagreed among them-

---

[103] Cf. Rackham, *op. cit.*, p. 511.

selves, they departed, after Paul had made one statement: "The
Holy Spirit was right in saying to your fathers through Isaiah the
prophet:
> 26 'Go to this people, and say,
> You shall indeed hear but never understand,
> and you shall indeed see but never perceive.
> 27 For this people's heart has grown dull,
> and their ears are heavy of hearing,
> and their eyes they have closed;
> lest they should perceive with their eyes,
> and hear with their ears,
> and understand with their heart,
> and turn for me to heal them.'
> 28 Let it be known to you then that this salvation of God has been
> sent to the Gentiles; they will listen."

As Paul presented the claims for Jesus as the anointed King,
reasoning from Moses and the Prophets, he won respectful attention and some converts. One word, however, as at Jerusalem
(22: 22) and elsewhere, was too much. When he contrasted
Jewish willful blindness with Gentile responsiveness, that broke
up the interview. Moffatt not only misses the point but destroys
it in his unfortunate translation which represents Paul's last word
as a parting thrust *after* or as the Jews were turning away. Though
the Greek does not forbid this, it is not the natural translation,
and it distorts the whole of Luke's closing scene. Paul did not
make this statement *because* they were turning away; they turned
away *when* Paul made the statement. The whole book leads to
that point.

In quoting Isaiah, Paul is not saying that God predetermined
it that Israel could not see. The point is that Israel would not
see: "their eyes *they* have closed" (v. 27). The blindness was
not the cause of the rejection of Jesus, but the result of that rejection. Wrath is never more terrible than in the inevitable price
of light willfully rejected—the blindness that follows (cf. John
9: 38ff.).

The Revised Standard Version is excellent in its translation of
verse 28. Paul did not say of the Gentiles, "They will also hear,"
but "it is they who will hear." [104] The far-reaching results of
choices then being made were clearly seen.

---

[104] Cf. Lake and Cadbury, *Commentary*, p. 348.

Unhindered [28: 30-31]

30 And he lived there two whole years at his own expense, and welcomed all who came to him, 31 preaching the kingdom of God and teaching about the Lord Jesus Christ quite openly and unhindered.

Paul lived two whole years "at his own expense" or "on his own earnings"; either idea is possible.[105] Whatever happened beyond the two years, Luke is not concerned to tell. It is beside the point to suggest that he wrote no more because he knew no more, that he contemplated a third volume, that he died with the work unfinished, that at this point his sources stopped, or that he simply assumed that his readers knew the sequel. In letting the curtain fall on Paul with no information as to the outcome of the trial, he writes in keeping with his pattern throughout the book. He earlier permitted the curtain to fall on Philip, the Ethiopian eunuch, Barnabas and Mark, Peter, and others. Luke is writing about the gospel, not about Paul.

Openly and unhinderedly Paul preached the kingdom of God and taught about the Lord Jesus Christ. Luke no doubt includes the idea that Roman authorities did not interfere with this freedom in preaching, but beyond that is a larger message. The gospel had fought off numerous efforts to limit it. At first, all, including the twelve, expected the kingdom to expand within Judaism (1: 6). These unwittingly would have made Christianity's cradle its grave. Stephen, then others, began to catch a vision of what was inherent in the gospel—inherent because it was first in the heart and mind of God. The painful fight was made for an unshackled gospel. The saddest cost of the victory was the self-exclusion of the Jews; the glorious victory was a gospel preached "unhinderedly!"

---

[105] Cf. Lake and Cadbury, *Commentary*, p. 348.

Appendix

Duncan's Argument That Galatians 2 : 1–10
Parallels Acts 11 : 30

ONE OF THE stronger arguments for identifying the conference of Galatians 2 : 1–10 with the visit of Acts 11 is that of Duncan in his commentary on Galatians.[1] He holds to the integrity of Acts 15, but distinguishes that as a formal conference from the earlier private conference referred to in Galatians 2 (= Acts 11). This theory, contrary to that of Lake, does not challenge the integrity of Acts, but it does to some extent affect interpretation. There are important considerations involved, and Duncan's theory must be appraised.

In brief Duncan would reconstruct the historical situation with which we are concerned as in the following outline: [2]
1. The famine visit to Jerusalem (Acts 11 : 30; 12 : 25 = Gal. 2: 1–10).
    (1) Relief sent to Jerusalem from Antioch.
    (2) Paul privately seeks recognition for his gospel.
    (3) Titus probably circumcised, Paul voluntarily yielding.
2. Paul and Barnabas back in Antioch: Paul rebukes Peter for withdrawing from table of Gentiles; Barnabas, too, withdraws (Gal. 2 : 11ff.).
3. Missionary journey by Paul and Barnabas (Acts 13 : 1–14 : 28).
4. Paul and Barnabas return to Antioch; Paul learns that Judaizers have been at work at Antioch and in Galatia; Paul writes Galatian letter.
5. Jerusalem Conference (Acts 15).
6. Return to Antioch; separation from Barnabas; second campaign.

---

[1] Cf. George S. Duncan, *The Epistle of Paul to the Galatians* ("The Moffatt New Testament Commentary" [New York and London: Harper and Brothers, 1934]), pp. xxi–xxxiv. This argument is selected as a strong and full treatment of a position held by many excellent scholars.

[2] This outline is not in Duncan's own words or arrangement but is gleaned from his discussion.

267

Along with its strength, there are numerous weaknesses in Duncan's argument. Much is made of Paul's oath to the effect that he is telling the truth (Gal. 1 : 20). This is understood to be Paul's plea that he is more careful than usual to tell the truth. In fact, his earnest plea is not because he is now more trustworthy than usual, but because the Galatians are less willing to trust than they should be. Duncan laments that:

... what is the *second* visit to Jerusalem in the narrative of Galatians, where every sentence is carefully weighed, is to be identified (say the critics) with a visit which in Acts is the *third* visit.[3]

But Paul does not use the term "second"; it is important to acknowledge that he merely says "again" (Gal. 2 : 1) in describing his conference at Jerusalem. Paul may *imply* that this was the second visit, but he does not say that it was; Duncan's comment is misleading, however correct he may be in his theory. Furthermore, when he calls it "a mere evasion of the difficulty" (p. xxiv) for one to suggest that Paul omitted reference to the visit of Acts 11 : 30 because he saw only the presbyters, not the apostles, Duncan is ignoring Paul's point of departure. If Paul is accounting for his meetings with the apostles, why should he describe a visit in which he did not meet with them? The theory that Paul saw no apostles in Jerusalem during his visit of Acts 11 : 30 may be incorrect, but the theory is not a "mere evasion." Can Duncan prove that Paul *did* meet with apostles on this visit? He can do so only by begging the major question by assuming that Galatians 2 : 1–10 is equivalent to Acts 11 : 30, and that is not a *mere* but a *major* evasion of a difficult problem.

In order to date Galatians *before* the conference of Acts 15, it is necessary to reckon with Galatians 4 : 13, "You know it was because of a bodily ailment that I preached the gospel to you at first," which, according to Duncan and most readers, seems to refer to two visits to Galatia; the Greek says "formerly." But the so-called "second missionary journey" of Paul, with Silas, clearly came *after* the conference of Acts 15. Duncan, therefore, concludes that the second visit was "the return visit on the first mis-

---
[3] *Op. cit.,* p. xxiv. Italics are Duncan's.

sionary journey" (p. xxii, cf. Acts 14:21). But Paul surely does not mean to say that only the outgoing part of the journey was due to "a bodily ailment"; he is not thus distinguishing between the outgoing trip and the return through Galatia. This bodily ailment was responsible for the whole campaign with Barnabas in Galatia. Evidently Paul had planned to go to another territory, but because of illness campaigned in Galatia. Should one tour a foreign country today, he would not upon returning write his friends there of his *two* visits to their country. On the other hand, if Paul wrote Galatians after his journey with Silas he would naturally refer to the campaign there with Barnabas as the "former visit"; it would be the visit because of an ailment, while the one with Silas would be by deliberate choice. Duncan ridicules the "critics" for the liberty they take in counting visits to Jerusalem; but he takes quite some liberty in counting visits to Galatia. The method is or is not "evasion," depending on what visits are being counted.

Duncan recognizes that a major purpose of Paul in his letter is to refute the charge that in going to Jerusalem (Acts 11) he was judged by the apostles there (pp. 47ff., *et passim*). If, then, this letter was written before the Jerusalem council (Acts 15), it is strange that Paul is willing so soon after the letter to go back to these same apostles. Duncan even suggests (though it is not his conclusion) the possibility that Paul may have been on his way to Jerusalem for the conference when he wrote Galatians (cf. pp. xxix and 10). Strange, indeed, if on his way to a conference with the Jerusalem apostles, he would write a letter vehemently protesting that when he did the same thing two years before it was not a submission to them! If in writing Galatians Paul was trying to clear up the misunderstanding about his earlier visit to Jerusalem (Acts 11), why would he invite more trouble by rushing right back to Jerusalem and the same apostles? If Paul knew that he was going to the Jerusalem council (Acts 15) when he wrote Galatians, why did he not explain the purpose of the proposed trip? By Duncan's theory, Paul wrote a letter to clear up a problem and then intensified the problem by repeating the occasion for the problem.

If the theory is correct that Galatians 2:1–10 equals Acts 11 and that Galatians was written before the conference of Acts 15, then as Paul wrote Galatians he had *one* private conference with the apostles to explain, but immediately after the letter he had a new formal conference to explain. Are we to believe that even as the saints in Galatia were reading Paul's bold statement, "to them we did not yield submission even for a moment" (Gal. 2:5), Paul was again in conference with them!

If Galatians was written after the conference of Acts 15, none of the above problems obtains; and the obvious reference would be to the visit of Acts 15, and not of Acts 11.

Duncan holds that Paul, with Barnabas, went to Jerusalem on Paul's second visit to carry the relief money for the famine victims, but also to present his gospel to the twelve; while there the private debate developed. At the close of the debate the apostles spoke approvingly of Paul's position, and James pleaded for *one thing*—that they not forget the poor (Gal. 2:10). If this visit of Galatians 2:1–10 is to be identified with the one of Acts 11, why did James need to plead that they not forget the very thing that brought them to Jerusalem?

Arguing that Galatians 2 cannot equal Acts 15, Duncan says, "In Acts there is a formal conference; in Galatians Paul has a private interview with the Jerusalem leaders" (p. xxv). This is true, but it does not rule out a private conference also in Acts 15. It is not impossible to see an implication of a private conference in Acts 15:6.

Duncan submits as further evidence that Galatians is earlier than Acts 15 the fact that at the council in Acts decrees were passed, but in Galatians Paul makes no reference to them; in Galatians he boasts that the "authorities" made no addition to his gospel (p. xxv). Acts does tell of decrees passed (or suggested), but these were not additions to Paul's gospel; they did not relate to salvation, but to fellowship. Duncan asks, "Why, if a formal ruling on the situation was arrived at, is there no reference to it in the Epistle?" (p. xxv). If Galatians was written *after* the council (Acts 15), then at least those at Derbe and Lystra had received the apostolic letter from the council and knew the formal ruling. Possibly all the churches of Galatia received the letter from Jerusalem; Acts 16:14 certainly does not rule out that possibility.

It would be fatal to Duncan's theory should it be established that the Judaizers were not at work in Galatia before the council of Acts 15. That cannot be established and need not be; the burden of proof is upon Duncan's theory. The apostolic letter was addressed only to Syria-Cilicia, and this seems to imply that the trouble *had not* yet started in Galatia. Paul seems to have delivered the letter beyond Derbe and Lystra; but he did it on his own initiative, not because it was addressed to them.

It is important for Duncan's theory to hold that Titus was circumcised, though not by compulsion (Gal. 2:3). The statement, "if I still preach circumcision" (5:11), presumably reflects the charge that Paul had consented to some Christian's circumcision. If Galatians was written *before* the "second missionary journey," then it was before Timothy's circumcision (Acts 16:3), and the reference could not be to him. To understand with Duncan that Titus was circumcised (voluntarily) is wholly subjective, depending on where the emphasis falls in a Greek sentence. Titus may have been circumcised, but no exegete knows that he was; many think otherwise. If on the other hand, Galatians was written *after* the "second journey," the reference is obviously to Timothy.

Duncan, in a footnote, says, "No safe argument [about the agreement of Barnabas with Paul] may be deduced from the fact that Barnabas is not associated with Paul in the writing of Galatians" (p. xxx). But the argument as it has bearing on the relation of Galatians to Acts 11 and 15 has more weight than the footnote allows. From Galatians one gets the impression that the attack is on Paul and not on Paul and Barnabas jointly. This is understandable if Galatians was written some time after the separation of Paul and Barnabas and if it deals with a situation that developed in Galatia *after* Paul and Barnabas were separated. Barnabas is not only not associated with Paul in the writing of Galatians, but the letter leaves the impression that neither was he associated with the problem there.

If Galatians was written immediately after the campaign of Barnabas and Paul, this is without explanation. Even if it be true that Barnabas was not fully sympathetic with Paul's position on fellowship between Jew and Gentile, he certainly stood with Paul on the proposition that circumcision was not essential to salvation, and that was the problem in Galatia. How could Paul be singled out and Barnabas be considered of no importance to that situation in Galatia? Duncan says, "Paul writes in his own name because it is he and he alone whom the Judaizers have attacked; it is his own personal position (his apostleship and his gospel) that must be vindicated" (p. 10). But was Paul's position on salvation different from that of Barnabas?

If we assume that Galatians was written some time *after* the separation of Barnabas and Paul, there is nothing to explain about the fact that Barnabas is associated with neither letter nor situation. If the letter was written immediately after their joint mission, no satisfactory explanation is apparent.

In discussing chronology, Duncan is forced to date the conversion of Paul A.D. 31; this is necessary because he identifies Galatians 2:1–10 with Acts 11:30. Only by placing the famine visit as late as possible (A.D. 46) and by making the Arabian period as short as possible (viewing the "three years" as just over two years) is he able to avoid dating Paul's conversion earlier than A.D. 31 (p. xxxii). To place the famine visit (Acts 11:30) as late as A.D. 46 is to be in conflict with Luke's apparent dating of that visit *before* the death of Herod Agrippa (A.D. 44). At best the date of the visit of 11:30 (which Duncan identifies with the visit of Gal. 2:1–10) is uncertain. If any one of Duncan's conjectures is wrong, he could end up by dating Paul's conversion before the death of Jesus! Even the year 31 is probably too early. The problem is eased if Paul's "after fourteen years" visit is identified with Acts 15 rather than with Acts 11.

There is some evidence for a party of "spiritual perfectionists" in Galatia. These, in contrast to the Judaizers, had a tendency toward antinomianism (cf. Gal. 5:13 and 6:1f.). In any case, the complexity of the Galatian situation calls for a longer period than the duration of the campaign by Paul and Barnabas.

In conclusion, it may be said that the strongest argument for identifying Galatians 2:1-10 with Acts 11 is the inconclusive statement in Galatians 2:1: "Then after fourteen years I went up again to Jerusalem . . . ." Acts 15 may validly be studied in the light of the Galatian letter. Though, admittedly, there are many problems involved, the similarities are many, and the two accounts supplement each other. Even Duncan, in describing the Judaizers of Galatians, turns repeatedly to Acts 15, not to Acts 11!

Bibliography

ANDERSON, PARK H., *John Mark, Servant of Christ*. Boston: The Christopher Publishing House, 1949. 139 pp.

ANDREWS, ELIAS, *The Meaning of Christ for Paul*. New York: Abingdon-Cokesbury Press, 1949. 266 pp.

BARRETT, C. K., *The Holy Spirit and the Gospel Tradition*. New York: The Macmillan Co., 1947. 176 pp.

BARTH, KARL, *The Epistle to the Romans*. Translated by Edwyn C. Hoskyns. Oxford: University Press, 1933. 547 pp.

BLACK, MATTHEW, *An Aramaic Approach to the Gospels and Acts*. Oxford: At the Clarendon Press, second edition, 1954. 304 pp.

BRUCE, F. F., *The Acts of the Apostles*. London: The Tyndale Press, 1951. 491 pp.

CADBURY, HENRY J., *The Making of Luke-Acts*. New York: Macmillan and Co., 1927. 385 pp.

CALKINS, RAYMOND, *The Modern Message of the Minor Prophets*. New York: Harper and Brothers, 1947. 205 pp.

CARVER, W. O., *The Glory of God in the Christian Calling*. Nashville: Broadman Press, 1949. 239 pp.

CLARK, A. C., *The Acts of the Apostles*. Oxford: Clarendon Press, 1933. 427 pp.

CULLMANN, OSCAR, *Die Tauflehre des Neuen Testaments, Erwachsenen- und Kindertaufe*. Zürich: Zwingli-Verlag, 1948. 76 pp.

———, *Baptism in the New Testament*. Translated by J. K. S. Reid. London: SCM Press Ltd., 1950. 84 pp.

———, *Peter: Disciple, Apostle, Martyr*. Translated by Floyd V. Filson. London: SCM Press Ltd., 1953. 252 pp.

———, *Die Tradition als exegetisches, historisches und theologisches Problem*. Translated from the French by Pierre Schönenberger. Zürich: Zwingli-Verlag, 1954. 56 pp.

———, *Urchristentum und Gottesdienst*. Zürich: Zwingli-Verlag, 1950. 120 pp.

DANA, H. E., *The Ephesian Tradition*. Kansas City, Kansas: Kansas City Seminary Press, 1940. 175 pp.

DAVIES, W. D., *Paul and Rabbinic Judaism*. London: Society for the Promotion of Christian Knowledge, 1948. 376 pp.

DEISSMANN, ADOLF, *Light from the Ancient East*. Translated by

L. R. M. Strachan. Revised ed. New York: Harper and Brothers, n.d. 535 pp.

——, *Paul, a Study in Social and Religious History*. Translated by William E. Wilson. Second ed. London: Hodder and Stoughton, 1926. 323 pp.

DIBELIUS, MARTIN, *Aufsätze zur Apostelgeschichte*. Göttingen: Vandenhoeck & Ruprecht, 1953. 192 pp.

DODD, C. H., *The Apostolic Preaching and its Developments*. New York: Harper and Brothers, 1936. 167 pp.

DUNCAN, GEORGE S., *The Epistle of Paul to the Galatians*. ("The Moffatt New Testament Commentary.") New York: Harper and Brothers, 1934. 199 pp.

ENSLIN, MORTON S., *Christian Beginnings*. New York: Harper and Brothers, 1938. 533 pp.

FINKELSTEIN, LOUIS, *The Pharisees, the Sociological Background of Their Faith*. Philadelphia: The Jewish Publication Society of America, 1946. 2 vols.

FOAKES-JACKSON, F. J., *Peter Prince of Apostles*. New York: George H. Doran Co., 1927. 320 pp.

——, *The Acts of the Apostles* ("The Moffatt New Testament Commentary.") New York: Harper and Brothers, 1931. 236 pp.

——, and KIRSOPP LAKE, editors, *Prolegomena II, Criticism*. Vol. II, *The Beginnings of Christianity*. London: Macmillan and Co., 1922. 539 pp.

GOODSPEED, EDGAR J., *Paul*. Philadelphia: J. C. Winston Co., 1947. 246 pp.

HARNACK, ADOLF, *The Acts of the Apostles*. Translated by J. R. Wilkinson. New York: G. P. Putnam's Sons, 1909. 303 pp.

JOSEPHUS, FLAVIUS, *The Life and Works of Flavius Josephus*. Translated by William Whiston. Philadelphia: The John C. Winston Co., n.d. 1055 pp.

KLAUSNER, JOSEPH, *From Jesus to Paul*. Translated by William F. Stinespring. New York: Macmillan Co., 1944. 624 pp.

KNOX, JOHN, *Philemon Among the Letters of Paul*. Chicago: University of Chicago Press, 1935. 57 pp.

——, *Marcion and the New Testament*. Chicago: University of Chicago Press, 1942. 195 pp.

——, *Chapters in a Life of Paul*. New York: Abingdon-Cokesbury Press, 1950. 168 pp.

KNOX, W. L., *St. Paul and the Church of the Gentiles*. Cambridge: Cambridge University Press, 1939. 261 pp.

KNOWLING, R. J., "The Acts of the Apostles." (Vol. II, *The Expositor's Greek Testament*, edited by W. Robertson Nicoll.) Grand

Rapids, Michigan: Wm. B. Eerdmans Publishing Co., n.d. 953 pp.

KÜMMEL, WERNER GEORG, *Das Bild des Menschen im Neuen Testament*. Zürich: Zwingli-Verlag, 1948. 59 pp.

LAKE, KIRSOPP, and HENRY J. CADBURY, editors, *English Translation and Commentary*. (Vol. IV, *The Beginnings of Christianity*, edited by F. J. Foakes-Jackson and Kirsopp Lake.) London: Macmillan and Co., 1933. 420 pp.

———, editors, *Additional Notes to the Commentary*. Vol. V, *The Beginnings of Christianity*, edited by F. J. Foakes-Jackson and Kirsopp Lake. London: Macmillan and Co., 1933. 548 pp.

LAMONT, CORLISS, *The Illusion of Immortality*. Second edition. New York: Philosophical Library, 1950. 316 pp.

LENSKI, R. C. H., *Interpretation of the Acts of the Apostles*. Columbus, Ohio: The Wartburg Press, 1944. 1134 pp.

LIDDELL, HENRY GEORGE, and ROBERT SCOTT, *A Greek-English Lexicon*. New edition by Henry Stewart Jones. Oxford: Clarendon Press, 1939. 2 vols.

MACHEN, J. G., *The Origin of Paul's Religion*. New York: Macmillan Co., 1921. 329 pp.

MACMURRAY, JOHN, *Conditions of Freedom*. London: Faber and Faber Ltd., 1950. 106 pp.

MANSON, T. W., *The Church's Ministry*. London: Hodder and Stoughton Ltd., 1948. 112 pp.

MANSON, WILLIAM, *The Gospel of Luke*. ("The Moffatt New Testament Commentary.") New York: Harper and Brothers, 1930. 282 pp.

MOORE, GEORGE FOOTE, *Judaism*. Cambridge: Harvard University Press, 1927. 2 vols.

MOULTON, JAMES HOPE, and GEORGE MILLIGAN, *The Vocabulary of the Greek New Testament*. London: Hodder and Stoughton, Ltd., 1949. 835 pp.

MORGENSTERN, JULIAN, "Universalism and Particularism," *The Universal Jewish Encyclopedia*, Vol. X.

NESTLE, D. EBERHARD, *Novum Testamentum Graece*. Twentieth ed. New York: American Bible Society, 1950. 671 pp.

RACKHAM, R. B., *The Acts of the Apostles*. ("Westminster Commentaries.") Twelfth edition. London: Metheun and Co., Ltd., 1939. 524 pp.

RAMSAY, W. M., *The Church in the Roman Empire Before A.D. 170*. London: Hodder and Stoughton, 1893. 494 pp.

———, *St. Paul the Traveller and the Roman Citizen*. New York: G. P. Putnam's Sons, 1896. 394 pp.

RIDDLE, D. W., "The Occasion of Luke-Acts," *Journal of Religion,* October, 1930.

——, *Paul, Man of Conflict.* Nashville: Abingdon-Cokesbury Press, 1940. 244 pp.

ROBERTSON, A. T., *A Harmony of the Gospels.* New York: Harper and Brothers, 1922. 305 pp.

——, *A Grammar of the Greek New Testament in the Light of Historical Research.* Fourth edition. New York: George H. Doran Co., 1923. 1454 pp.

ROBINSON, JOHN A. T., *The Body, A Study in Pauline Theology.* Chicago: Henry Regnery Co., 1952. 93 pp.

ROPES, J. H., *The Text of Acts.* (Vol. III, *The Beginnings of Christianity,* edited by F. J. Foakes-Jackson and Kirsopp Lake.) London: Macmillan and Co., 1926. 464 pp.

SCHONFIELD, HUGH J., *The Jew of Tarsus.* New York: Macmillan Co., 1947. 254 pp.

SCHWEITZER, ALBERT, *The Mysticism of Paul the Apostle.* Translated by William Montgomery. London: A. and C. Black, Ltd., 1931. 411 pp.

SHÜRER, EMIL, *A History of the Jewish People in the Time of Jesus Christ.* Authorized English translation. New York: Charles Scribner's Sons, n.d. 5 vols.

STEWART, JAMES S., *A Man in Christ.* London: Hodder and Stoughton, 1935. 327 pp.

SUETONIUS, C., TRANQUILLUS, *The Lives of the Twelve Caesars.* Translated by Alexander Thompson. London: G. Bell and Sons, Ltd., 1926. 557 pp.

TACITUS, *Complete Works.* Translated by Alfred John Church and William Jackson Brodribb. New York: The Modern Library, 1942. 773 pp.

TAYLOR, R. O. P., *The Groundwork of the Gospels.* Oxford: Basil Blackwell, 1946. 161 pp.

TRENCH, R. C., *Synonyms of the New Testament.* London: Kegan Paul, Trench, Trubner and Co., Ltd., 1906. 384 pp.

WEISS, JOHANNES, *Der erste Korintherbrief.* Göttingen: Vandenhoeck & Ruprecht, 1910.

WILLIAMS, C. S. C., *Alterations to the Text of the Synoptic Gospels and Acts.* Oxford: Basil Blackwell, 1951. 93 pp.

WILLIAMS, R. R., *The Acts of the Apostles.* London: SCM Press Ltd., 1953. 173 pp.

Index